Manchuria

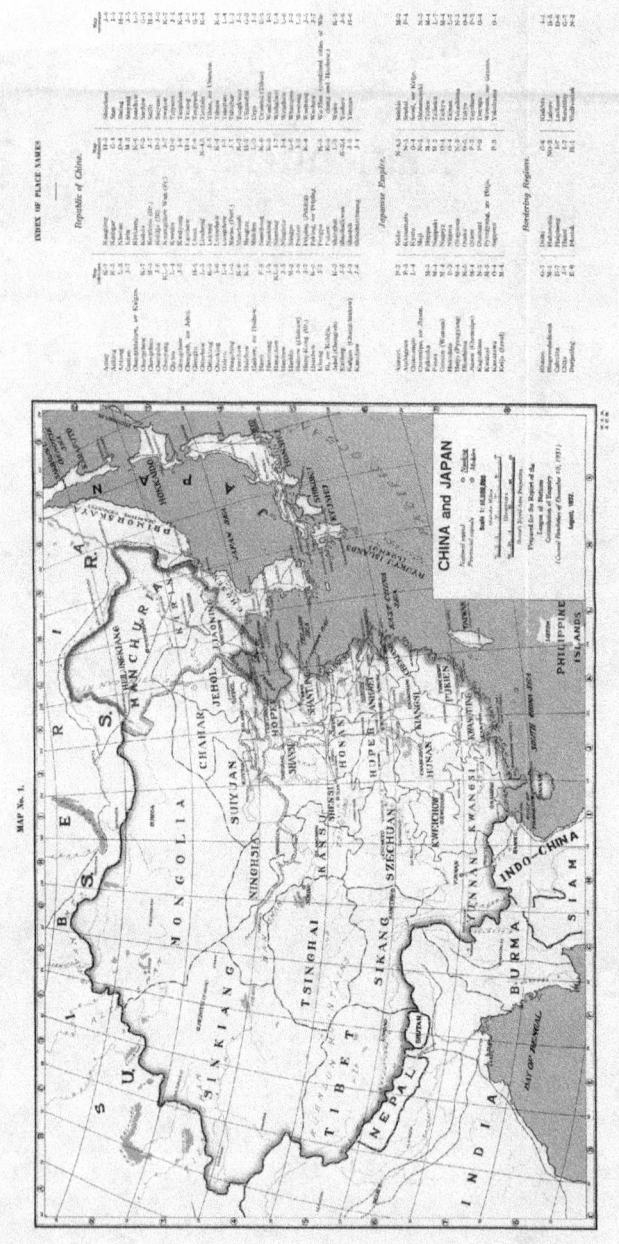

Frontispiece: 'China and Japan'. Map by the League of Nations, showing Manchuria, 1932.

Manchuria

A Concise History

Mark Gamsa

I.B. TAURIS
LONDON • NEW YORK • OXFORD • NEW DELHI • SYDNEY

I.B. TAURIS
Bloomsbury Publishing Plc
50 Bedford Square, London, WC1B 3DP, UK
1385 Broadway, New York, NY 10018, USA
29 Earlsfort Terrace, Dublin 2, Ireland

BLOOMSBURY, I.B. TAURIS and the I.B. Tauris logo are
trademarks of Bloomsbury Publishing Plc

First published in Great Britain 2020
Paperback edition first published 2021

Copyright © Mark Gamsa, 2020

Mark Gamsa has asserted hisright under the Copyright,
Designs and Patents Act, 1988, to be identified as Author of this work.

For legal purposes the Acknowledgements on p. viii constitute
an extension of this copyright page.

Cover design by Adriana Brioso
Cover image: Windblown snow. Postcard, South Manchuria Railway.
Lafayette College, East Asia Image Collection.

All rights reserved. No part of this publication may be reproduced or
transmitted in any form or by any means, electronic or mechanical,
including photocopying, recording, or any information storage or retrieval
system, without prior permission in writing from the publishers.

Bloomsbury Publishing Plc does not have any control over, or responsibility for,
any third-party websites referred to or in this book. All internet addresses given
in this book were correct at the time of going to press. The author and publisher
regret any inconvenience caused if addresses have changed or sites have
ceased to exist, but can accept no responsibility for any such changes.

A catalogue record for this book is available from the British Library.

A catalogue record for this book is available from the Library of Congress.

ISBN: HB: 978-1-7883-1427-5
PB: 978-0-7556-3711-9
ePDF: 978-1-7883-1789-4
eBook: 978-1-7883-1790-0

Typeset by RefineCatch Limited, Bungay, Suffolk

To find out more about our authors and books visit
www.bloomsbury.com and sign up for our newsletters.

Contents

List of Illustrations — vii

Part One

Introduction: Manchuria and a Regional Approach to Chinese History — 3

1. The Ethnic Mosaic of the Northeast — 11
2. The 'Rise of the Manchus' and Their Later Fortunes — 17
3. Russian Expansion into Asia and the Way to the Treaty of Nerchinsk — 25
4. Qing–Russian Relations in the Eighteenth Century — 33
5. The Treaties of Aigun and Peking (1858–60) — 41
6. From the First Sino-Japanese War to the Russo-Japanese War in Manchuria — 45
7. The Chinese Eastern Railway — 55
8. The Japanese Sphere of Influence and the South Manchuria Railway — 63
9. Chinese Migrant Society in the Northeast — 69
10. Manchuria in the 1920s, Banditry and Warlord Rule — 75
11. The Manchukuo State: Resistance and Collaboration, 1932–45 — 87
12. Soviet Occupation, Civil War and Communist Victory, 1945–9 — 107
13. The Northeast through Literature — 115
14. The Northeast under Mao — 121
15. The Northeast after Mao — 127

Part Two

16 History and Geography: Heilongjiang   135

17 History and Geography: Jilin   143

18 History and Geography: Liaoning   153

19 The Mongol Component in Manchuria   161

20 Jehol / Rehe / Chengde: The Perspective of 'New Qing History'   173

Select Bibliography   181
Index   199

List of Illustrations

Frontispiece	'China and Japan'. Map by the League of Nations, showing Manchuria, 1932.	ii
1	A Gol'd village on the Amur, north of Khabarovsk. Photograph by William Henry Jackson (1843–1942), 1895. Library of Congress.	14
2	A 'Manchurian' (Manchu) archer. In the distance houses razed by Boxers in search of Christians. Photograph by C. H. Graves (1867–1943), 1902. Library of Congress.	20
3	Coat of arms of the Princes Gantimurov. Obshchii gerbovnik dvorianskikh rodov Vserossiiskoi imperii (General Armorial of the Noble Families of the All-Russian Empire), part 17. St Petersburg, 1904.	26
4	The tea trade in Kiakhta. Photograph by Jules Legras (1866–1939), 1890s.	36
5	'Manchuria–USSR Boundary'. Map showing Russian territorial gains by the treaties of Aigun and Peking.	43
6	'Chinese Camp Peddlers', stereoview card, from 'Stereoviews of the Siege of Port Arthur', 1905, by T. W. Ingersoll (1862–1922). Lafayette College, East Asia Image Collection.	51
7	The Trans-Siberian Railway. Russian map (by Al'dona Zabello), showing the journey from Moscow to Harbin and Dal'nii. 1903.	55
7a	Kitaiskaia ulitsa (Chinese Street; now Zhongyang dajie), Harbin's main avenue. Hotel Moderne can be seen on the right. Undated postcard. Courtesy of Olga Bakich.	58
8	South Manchuria Railway: Most Important Link between the Far East and Europe. Japanese lithographic print, dated between 1907 and 1919. University of Southern California Digital Library.	64
8a	A small transport of soybeans, Manchuria. Undated Japanese postcard. Lafayette College, East Asia Image Collection.	66
9	Chinese workers on the CER. Undated Russian postcard. Author's collection.	70
10	Zhang Zuolin's former residence in Shenyang, 2017. Photograph by H. Sinica.	80
11	'A Political Map of Manchuria'. League of Nations, 1932.	89
11a	Emperor of Manchuria, Puyi, visits Yasukuni shrine. Japanese postcard, 1935. Lafayette College, East Asia Image Collection.	99
12	Soviet soldiers in process of removing industrial equipment from Manchurian factories. Photograph by US Army Signal Corps, 1946. Library of Congress.	110

13	Xiao Hong Museum ('old residence of Xiao Hong'), Hulan. Public domain.	116
14	Soldiers reassigned to agricultural work in Beidahuang. Public domain.	122
15	Anshan Steelworks, 2000. Photograph by Frühtau.	128
15a	Harbin Grand Theatre, 2016. Photograph by Katushang.	129
16	Heilongjiang. From Hsieh. *China Provincial Atlas*. © 1995 Gale, a part of Cengage, Inc. Reproduced by permission.www.cengage.com/permissions.	135
16a	View of Heihe from the Amur River, 2006. Photograph by Viktor Bakhmutov.	137
17	Jilin. From Hsieh, *China Provincial Atlas*. © 1995 Gale, a part of Cengage, Inc. Reproduced by permission.www.cengage.com/permissions.	143
17a	Tianchi, The Heavenly Pond in the Changbaishan. Photograph by Shaani Applebaum.	145
18	Liaoning. From Hsieh, *China Provincial Atlas*. © 1995 Gale, a part of Cengage, Inc. Reproduced by permission.www.cengage.com/permissions.	153
18a	Dalian city hall in the Russian Period, subsequently a Yamato Hotel and the Dalian Natural History Museum (abandoned since 1998). Photograph by Qu Changliang, July 2016.	156
19	Inner Mongolia. From Hsieh, *China Provincial Atlas*. © 1995 Gale, a part of Cengage, Inc. Reproduced by permission.www.cengage.com/permissions.	161
19a	Matryoshka Square in Manzhouli, 2009. Photograph by Niklaus Berger.	167
20	Northeast China, including Jehol (Rehe) province. Atlas for China, ed. G. S. Foster Kemp (London: Macmillan & Co., 1934).	174
20a	Panoramic view of the Rehe Imperial Palace, late nineteenth century. Library of Congress.	176

The image used for the book cover, and images 6, 8a and 11a, are published courtesy of Special Collections and College Archives, Skillman Library, Lafayette College, and the East Asia Image Collection (https://dss.lafayette.edu/collections/east-asia-image-collection/).

Images 10, 12, 15, 15a, 16a and 19a are used by the generous permission of the wonderful photographers, who exhibit their work on flickr.com.

Part One

INTRODUCTION

Manchuria and a Regional Approach to Chinese History

On today's maps, you will not see Manchuria. The common historical definition of this region comprises the three north-eastern provinces of China, which were known under the Qing dynasty as Dongbei san sheng 東北三省, the north-eastern edge of Inner Mongolia and the northernmost part of Hebei province around Chengde 承德. At present, the term Dongbei is more often used in a narrow sense, to indicate the three provinces of the Northeast: Heilongjiang, Jilin and Liaoning. In this book, I will refer to 'Manchuria' and 'the Northeast' interchangeably when discussing the region's history before the establishment of the People's Republic of China (PRC), but will only use 'the Northeast' for the period thereafter.[1] Some scholars, like the linguist and anthropologist Juha Janhunen, speak of a greater or 'outer' Manchuria, which extends the scope of this historical term further to the north and east so as to include the territories ceded by the Qing to Russia by 1860, from the Amur and the Ussuri to the Stanovoy mountain range between Yakutia and the Pacific Ocean, and even encompassing Sakhalin Island beyond the Strait of Tartary.[2] A broad transnational perspective on this region has been proposed recently in a monograph by historian Evelyn S. Rawski.[3]

Historical research on Manchuria as contained within the borders of present-day China can be situated within the regional approach to the study of Chinese history as opposed to discussing China as a whole, or focusing on particular provinces. One rationale for this is the often arbitrary nature of provincial borders (indeed, those of the three north-eastern provinces have changed repeatedly, as have their names). There are clusters of culturally and economically homogenous areas in China,[4] and the Dongbei is among the most important of these. The second part of this book surveys the three provinces and the Mongol element in Manchuria, combining historical and geographical perspectives. Another discipline relevant to research on Manchuria is border studies: the Northeast is one of the border regions where China has experienced the reciprocal influence of other cultures.[5] Lastly, since the later 1990s, research on the two port cities in Manchuria, Harbin 哈爾濱 and Dalian 大連, has emerged as something of an alternative to the customary focus on Shanghai as the urban centre where contact between China and the West was a catalyst for modernization.

To find a comprehensive history of Manchuria in a Western language one has to go very far back indeed, perhaps as far back as *Manchuria: Its People, Resources and Recent History*, by the British diplomat in China, explorer and botanist Sir Alexander Hosie (1853–1925). This book first came out in London in 1901, saw two editions and was republished in the handsomely illustrated 'Oriental series' in Boston in 1910.[6] Immediately after the Russo-Japanese War and, once again, when Manchuria attracted worldwide interest because of the Japanese invasion in 1931, several books about this region were published in English. The work of Owen Lattimore (1900–89) stands out within this literature and will be mentioned again here. Most recently, the veteran historian of international relations Ian Hill Nish (born 1926) published a two-volume *History of Manchuria, 1840–1948*, of which the first volume surveys the region's history and the second reprints select historical sources.[7]

Research on various aspects of Manchurian history has been large but fragmented. The present book stems from a seminar, which I have taught at Tel Aviv University for over a decade. To bring the story of Manchuria to my students, I had to collect and systematize the historical literature as well as follow the latest publications on the subject; and because no textbook on Manchuria existed, I gradually wrote one. Many of the sources on which the present book is based, therefore, have been debated in class, and my interpretation of them is indebted to those discussions. As this concise history is meant to be a textbook, I have mostly aimed to refer readers to publications in English. When important sources in Chinese or Russian are cited, their titles are translated into English in the bibliography.

No historian works on Manchuria as a whole: I, too, specialize in one facet of the story, the relations between Chinese and Russians in this region.[8] My aim here has been to synthesize the most important scholarship so as to offer readers a new resource: an up-to-date history of Manchuria from the seventeenth century to the present, combining the perspectives of politics, culture and economy. Beyond any professional bias towards Russia, I also hope to demonstrate that Manchuria's history has been intertwined with the history of Russia's advance towards the Far East since the early Qing and especially from the late nineteenth century.

Russian–Chinese relations have not been limited to the Northeast (there has always been contact and military friction between the two states over Xinjiang) and, in turn, the history of the Northeast did not always involve Russians. Some aspects of life in Manchuria did not involve any foreigners, whereas in some periods the most important outside factor in the region were the Japanese. Indeed, Japan will often be mentioned here. However, it cannot be denied that from the late nineteenth century on Russia made an enormous impact on life in Northeast China. Although we do not have space to discuss it here, the impact of proximity to China was also important on the Russian side of the border. While Russian–Chinese relations will be a recurring theme, this book centres on the Northeast itself.

Before considering the name Manchuria, let us look at the Russian word for China: 'Kitai', comparable with the English Cathay, the name of (northern) China as used in medieval Europe. Kitai evolved from the ethnonym of the Qidan 契丹 (also Khitan, or Kitan) people, and was probably brought to Russia via India in the fifteenth century.[9] The Qidan founded the Liao state in 916; in 1125 they were defeated by the Jurchen people. The Jurchen (Chinese: Nüzhen 女真, or Ruzhen), founders of the Jin dynasty (1115–1234) also defeated the Song dynasty of China (960–1279), putting an end to the period that retrospectively became known as the Northern Song. After the Jin conquered the capital Kaifeng in 1126, taking emperor Huizong 徽宗 as prisoner, the Song moved their capital south to Hangzhou.[10] The third northern people to invade China after the Qidan and the Jurchen were the Mongols: Genghis Khan (?1167–1227) vanquished the Jurchens, sacking Beijing in 1215. The Mongol Yuan dynasty (1271–1368) was followed by the Han Chinese rule of the Ming dynasty (1368–1644), but the Ming were succeeded by the Qing dynasty (1644–1911) of the Manchus, who accordingly were the fourth northern nomadic people to conquer China, in whole or in part. As for 'Cathay', until the early seventeenth century some Europeans thought that a Christian community by this name existed somewhere in Central Asia and was distinct from 'China'.

When Russia first made contact with the Manchu Empire in the Far East in the seventeenth century, neither side had any knowledge of previous contacts between them, not even the fairly recent time when both Russia (1240–1478) and Yuan-dynasty China were under Mongol rule. At first the Russians did not realize that their adversary along the Amur River was subject to Peking's rule and instead believed the enemy to be a small kingdom ruled by a 'Bogdoiskii Khan'. For their part, the Qing called their enemy *Luosha* or *Luocha* 羅刹 (this term is usually interpreted as a reference to demons mentioned in Buddhist scriptures, although some scholars have suspected here a calque from the Russian *lovets*, a now obsolete word for 'hunter').[11] These 'Luocha' were actually Cossacks, whom the Qing did not initially identify with the distant continental Russians in Moscow, for the latter were known to them as *Eluosi* 俄羅斯.[12]

As we begin our study of this region, it is important to remember how large and how relatively empty it was. The territory of Manchuria as of 1895 was 390,000 square miles, i.e. 1,010,100 square km. This would be over 10 per cent of the current size of the People's Republic of China, more than twice the size of Japan, or almost twice the size of France. Writing in 1932, Owen Lattimore described Manchuria as having the size of France and Spain combined. Manchukuo, which included territory beyond the three provinces of the Northeast, measured 1,303,143 square km in 1940,[13] making Manchukuo the seventh largest country in the world. The three north-eastern provinces alone today measure 789,000 square km, or 8 per cent of the territory of China, and this is also the percentage of the Northeast population within the country. However, fewer than 2 million people lived in Manchuria in 1842, when its territory was larger than the (narrowly defined) 'Northeast' today. The Manchu people were about 5 million strong nationwide in 1900, while the total for Manchuria had by then risen to 17 million. More than 122 million people lived in the Northeast according to the PRC census of 2010.

'Manzhou' 滿洲 was originally an ethnonym,[14] a Chinese transcription of the Manchu word *Manju*, meaning the Manchus as an ethnic group. It will be of no use therefore to infer meaning from the two Chinese characters (which would be something like 'full continent'). Yet even the origin of the Manchu use of this name is obscure, as we shall see below. *Manzhou* functioned as a Chinese toponym from about 1877 (it appeared on maps from the early 1900s) to the early 1950s. The Western geographical term 'Manchuria', however, emerged through Jesuit maps drawn at the Qing court in the early eighteenth century. The term was copied by the Japanese, possibly through Russian maps, in the 1790s, and brought to Europe by the German Japanologist in Dutch service, Philipp Franz von Siebold (1796–1866).[15]

By the 1830s 'Manchuria' had succeeded the older toponym 'Tartary', which Europeans began to use for the homeland of the Mongols, whom they called 'Tartars' in the thirteenth and fourteenth centuries.[16] The name 'Tartars' had evolved either from the Chinese *Dada*, which was used for northern nomads, or from the Russian application of *tartary* to the conquering Mongols (with the added 'r' conveying the connection to Tartarus, the Latin for 'hell'). In the seventeenth century Western Tartary signified the Mongol lands, whereas Eastern Tartary was applied to the territory of the Manchus.[17] These appellations have nothing to do with the Tatars, a Turkic people in Asian Russia, with a centre in today's Republic of Tatarstan on the River Volga. Although the name 'Manzhou' never enjoyed wide currency in Chinese, it met with disapproval in the PRC and the name 'Manchuria' dropped out of international usage by the 1950s, as it was too closely associated with the Manchukuo state. A regional 'Manchurian' identity is extant under another name today in the collective notion of Dongbei, Northeast China.

Qing Manchus called themselves *qiren* 旗人 (bannermen) in Chinese: a non-ethnic appellation, rather than the later *Manren* 滿人, or the now standard form, *Manzu ren* 滿族人. The system of the 'eight banners' evolved in the early seventeenth century from the Manchu clan organization. Not only the Manchus, but also the Han Chinese, Mongol and tribal forces who had joined them were divided into detachments called after the colour of their flag. Initially there were four 'plain' banners (yellow, white, red and blue) and, after 1615, also four 'bordered' ones of the same colour.[18] By 1642, the total number of banners reached twenty-four. In the late Qing, ethnic Manchus made up more than half of the banners and Han Chinese about a third (the Mongols were next with about a seventh, followed by the native peoples of Manchuria). Until the end of the Qing, bannermen, somewhat similarly to Russian Cossacks, were born into military service. Enjoying privileges that set them apart from (and evoked the jealousy of) most Chinese, they were not permitted to take up another occupation. In the early years, a Manchu boy would be assigned to a banner at age three; later in the Qing a bannerman's service lasted from age 16 to 60.[19]

The first two emperors of the Qing imagined the bannermen as 'universal functionaries', to be trained both in the Chinese classics and in the traditional skills of riding and archery.[20] By the end of the Qianlong 乾隆 reign in the late eighteenth century, however, in an effort to counter the decline of the Manchu language and traditions among the Manchu bannermen, the emperor launched a reform, by which they were urged to study Manchu, riding and archery, instead of Chinese.

Notes

1 The same policy is adopted here for China's capital city, which is referred to as Beijing or Peking for the late imperial and republican periods, but exclusively as Beijing from 1949.
2 Juha Janhunen, *Manchuria: An Ethnic History* (Helsinki: The Finno-Ugrian Society, 1996).
3 Evelyn S. Rawski, *Early Modern China and Northeast Asia: Cross-Border Perspectives* (Cambridge: Cambridge University Press, 2015). Cf. Nianshen Song, 'Northeast Eurasia as Historical Center: Exploration of a Joint Frontier', *The Asia-Pacific Journal*, vol. 13, 43:1 (2 Nov. 2015), who proposes the notion of North-east Eurasia instead of the problematic 'Manchuria'.
4 Cf. Yongtao Du and Jeff Kyong-McClain, eds, *Chinese History in Geographical Perspective* (Lanham: Lexington Books, 2013).
5 A pioneering treatment from the perspective of political geography was W. A. Douglas Jackson, *Russo-Chinese Borderlands: Zone of Peaceful Contact*

or Potential Conflict? (Princeton: D. Van Nostrand, 1962). An excellent historical anthropology of China's border with tsarist Russia, then with the Soviet Union and after 1991 with the new states of Kyrgyzstan and Tajikistan, is Steven Parham, *China's Borderlands: The Faultline of Central Asia* (London and New York: I. B. Tauris, 2017). An attempt at a cultural history of China's north-eastern border, Victor Zatsepine, *Beyond the Amur: Frontier Encounters between China and Russia, 1850–1930* (Vancouver and Toronto: UBC Press, 2017) is, however, far less successful.

6   Alexander Hosie, *Manchuria: Its People, Resources and Recent History* (Boston: J. B. Millet, 1910).
7   Ian Nish, *The History of Manchuria, 1840–1948*, in 2 vols (Folkestone: Renaissance Books, 2016).
8   See articles cited below, and Mark Gamsa, *Harbin, City between Russia and China: A Cross-cultural Biography*, forthcoming at University of Toronto Press.
9   A. I. Kobzev, 'Kitaistika i summa sinologiae', in *Arkhiv rossiiskoi kitaistiki*, vol. 1 (Moscow: Nauka – Vostochnaia literatura, 2013), pp. 15–16.
10 On the Liao, see Michal Biran, 'The Mongols and Nomadic Identity: The Case of the Kitans in China', in Reuven Amitai and Michal Biran, eds, *Nomads as Agents of Cultural Change: The Mongols and their Eurasian Predecessors* (Honolulu: University of Hawaii Press, 2015), pp. 152–81.
11 Anna Di Toro, *La percezione della Russia in Cina tra XVII e XVIII sec.* (Rome: La Sapienza Orientale, 2012), p. 189; on the loss of information about earlier contacts, see pp. 38, 41, 165–6.
12 At least by 1686, Emperor Kangxi knew the Russians on the Amur were subjects of Ivan and Peter, if indeed he wrote the letter to them cited in Susanna Soojung Lim, *China and Japan in the Russian Imagination, 1685–1922: To the Ends of the Orient* (London and New York: Routledge, 2013), p. 17 (ibid., p. 24, says it is unclear whether the 14-year-old Peter got the letter).
13 Peter Duus et al., eds, *The Japanese Wartime Empire, 1931–1945* (Princeton: Princeton University Press, 1996), p. xiii.
14 Many other linguistic explanations are offered in Immanuel C. Y. Hsü, *The Rise of Modern China*, 6th edn (Oxford: Oxford University Press, 2000), pp. 24–5.
15 Mark Elliott, 'The Limits of Tartary: Manchuria in Imperial and National Geographies', *Journal of Asian Studies*, vol. 59, no. 3 (Aug. 2000), pp. 603–46. Elliott is mistaken in the population figures he gives for 1900 in this important article: it was about 17 million, rather than '170 million total, of whom 150 million Han', p. 636, the result of miscalculating 1,700 *wan* from a Chinese source.
16 See, on Tartary, Jürgen Osterhammel, trans. Robert Savage, *Unfabling the East: The Enlightenment's Encounter with Asia* (Princeton: Princeton University Press, 2018).

17 The *Oxford English Reference Dictionary*, eds Judy Pearsall and Bill Trumble, 2nd rev. edn (Oxford University Press, 2002), pp. 1476, 1477, regards 'Tatar' as merely a variant of 'Tartar', but ignores the historical association of Tartary with Mongolia and the subsequent application of the term to Manchuria.
18 The yellow, white and blue flags were bordered with red, and the red flag with white.
19 See Edward J. M. Rhoads, *Manchus & Han: Ethnic Relations and Political Power in Late Qing and Early Republican China, 1861–1928* (Seattle and London: University of Washington Press, 2000).
20 Pamela Kyle Crossley, 'Manchu Education', in Benjamin A. Elman and Alexander Woodside, eds, *Education and Society in Late Imperial China* (Berkeley: University of California Press, 1994), pp. 340–78, quoting p. 363.

1

The Ethnic Mosaic of the Northeast

Qing garrisons were established not only in Manchuria, but also near many cities in mainland China. Bannermen (Manchus, Han Chinese and others) lived in these military outposts with their families, while being permanently supported by state salaries. Until 1735, the garrison towns in Heilongjiang were Aigun (Chinese name Aihui 愛輝), Mergen (founded in 1688; now Nenjiang 嫩江) and Qiqihar 齊齊哈爾. In Jilin these were Ninguta 寧古塔 (founded in 1654; Chinese name Ning'an 寧安), Boduna (伯都納, also transcribed Potune; now Songyuan 松原), Alechuka (now Acheng 阿城 district of Harbin), Sanxing 三姓 (now Yilan 依蘭) and Hunchun 琿春. All were located along the major rivers of Manchuria: the Amur, Nonni (Nenjiang; the river and town share the same name), Sungari (Songhuajiang 松花江), Hurka (old name of Mudanjiang 牧丹江) and Tumen 圖們江. Attracted by the comforts of life in the capital Beijing, most of the Manchus who were not stationed in the garrisons had left their home region by the seventeenth century.[1] Despite the long official ban on Han Chinese settlement in Manchuria, still to be discussed, the number of Chinese colonizers there constantly rose.

Frontier tribes

Among the indigenous nomadic peoples of Manchuria, the Solon (Chinese: Suolun 索倫) and the Daur tribes (Chinese: Dawoer 達斡爾) were historically and linguistically affiliated with the Mongols. They also lived next to each other, mainly in the basin of the Nonni River, between the two garrison towns of Qiqihar and Mergen (today's Nenjiang). This is the region in Heilongjiang where the biggest community of Daurs is now extant at the Daur Autonomous Banner, Morin Dawa 莫力達瓦, located on the border with Inner Mongolia (another five to six thousand Daurs presently live in Xinjiang, where their ancestors were sent out from Manchuria in Qing service in 1763). To the north of it is the Elunchun 鄂伦春 Autonomous Banner in Inner Mongolia. The Daur language is still spoken in these parts.

The Qing incorporated the Solon and the Daur into the Buteha banners (Buteha 布特哈, now called Zhalantun 札蘭屯, is a town in Hulunbuir 呼倫

貝爾, Inner Mongolia), in which native chiefs were supervised by Manchu commanders. The natives who joined the Qing banners became known as the 'new Manchus'. Under the Qing tribute system, the indigenous peoples were required to submit fur and ginseng to the imperial court but otherwise carried out regulated trade with Chinese merchants.[2] From the last decade of the Qing to Japanese conquest in the 1930s, the Chinese policy was to 'sinicize' natives by turning them from hunting nomads to farmers and replacing their horses with cattle. The ecological change that followed Han Chinese immigration and settlement further reduced their hunting options.[3] The Oroqen in Heilongjiang, however, readily adopted Russian names and clothing and much to the alarm of Qing border officials joined the Russian Orthodox Church and married Russians. Beyond the Russian border, they often became naturalized as Russian subjects.[4]

The Oroqen (also Orochen; Chinese: Elunchun) were also partly organized within the Buteha banners in the Qing, although many of them remained in scattered groups in the Xing'an 興安 (or Khingan) ranges south of the Amur and the Argun rivers. Since 1957, China has classified the Solon, the Tungus Evenki (also known as Khamingan) and the smallest community of Reindeer Evenki (herders in the Argun River area, who now number about 250) under a single term, Ewenke 鄂温克. Accordingly, these groups, who are largely concentrated in Inner Mongolia, have been considered as a single national minority, while the Oroqen and the Daur are classified separately.[5]

The Khamingan and Reindeer Evenki had actually moved into China from the Russian Far East between the late nineteenth century and the 1920s; in China today, they still use many Russian words in daily life and attach symbolic importance to eating bread.[6] In Russia, various groups of Tungus peoples, including Evenki, Even (most of whom live among the Yakut people in Russia's Sakha Republic) and Nanai, are spread across Siberia and the Russian Far East with a total of 72,229 persons counted in the census of 2010. In China, the same year's census registered 30,875 Evenki, 8,659 Oroqen (Elunchun) and 5,354 Hezhe 赫哲.[7] The Evenki, Oroqen and Hezhe languages are hardly spoken in China by now, but the Solon still is.[8]

Until the early twentieth century, shamanism characterized the religious and social life of Evenki, Oroqen and Hezhe in both Siberia and China, as well as of the Manchus, who also belong to the Tungus peoples. Indeed, the word 'shaman' reached European languages in the late seventeenth century from the language of the Siberian Tungus. A hereditary shaman, initiated after an illness, would enter a trance and dance while being possessed by spirits. Shamanism was classified as superstition and violently outlawed in both Soviet Russia and the PRC, and it could not be revived once more tolerant policies replaced persecution in both countries. Instead, 'neo-shamans' have emerged in Russia and professional performers have begun acting out shamanist ceremonies for the ethnic tourist industry in China.[9] In 1994, two US anthropologists met a man they described as the last shaman of the Oroqen near Huma River 呼瑪河, a tributary of the Amur in Heilongjiang.[10]

The cession to Russia of lands beyond the Amur and the Ussuri in 1860 (which will be discussed in Chapter Five) disrupted the tribute system as the basis for the native people's relations to the Qing Empire. Some of them, such as groups of Oroqen, the Hezhe (whom the Chinese traditionally called Yupi dazi 魚皮韃子, Fishskin Tatars; Russians called them Gol'dy or Nanai) and the Giliaks (Chinese: Feiyaka 费雅喀), found themselves living in Russia. Their numbers in that country subsequently dwindled due to recurring epidemics, of which smallpox claimed the heaviest toll. The Giliaks, who relied on fishing for their livelihood, came to Russian attention mainly as the native inhabitants of Northern Sakhalin, where they are known today as Nivkhi. A chapter in Anton Chekhov's (1860-1904) travel account *Sakhalin Island*, the longest piece of prose by the famous playwright and short-story writer, provided an ethnographic overview of their situation as of 1890.[11]

The Hezhe, another fishing people who turned to hunting in winter, also lived on both sides of the Amur and Ussuri Rivers. In China, those who concentrated near Sanxing, the Songhua River port in Heilongjiang, were closest to the Manchus culturally. Owen Lattimore visited them there, describing their shamanist rituals.[12] In 1921, Russian writer Vladimir Arsenyev (1872-1930) published an account of his friendship with a Gol'd (Hezhe), whom he had hired as a guide in the exploration of the Russian Ussuri Province between 1902 and 1910. The guide's name was Dersu Uzala. The book was translated into several languages, enabling readers beyond the region to discover the Hezhe through Arsenyev as they had the Giliaks through Chekhov.[13] A Soviet-Japanese film based on the book, *Dersu Uzala* by director Akira Kurosawa, won the Academy Award for the best foreign language film in 1975.

In the film, Dersu saves Arsenyev's life during a snowstorm near Lake Khanka; Arsenyev and his men reciprocate by rescuing the drowning Dersu during their second expedition. But Dersu was losing his eyesight and could not stay on as a hunter in the taiga. Arsenyev therefore brought his friend to live with him in Khabarovsk. Unable to adjust to city life, Dersu tried to return to the taiga but was soon robbed and killed. Much has been written on the factual background, fiction and art of *Dersu Uzala* as both literature and cinema.[14]

The native peoples inhabiting the banks of the lower Amur had also been in contact with the Ainu people of Sakhalin, who crossed the Strait of Tartary into the mainland to trade in Chinese brocades. A centre of this trade was a

Figure 1 A Gol'd village on the Amur, north of Khabarovsk. Photograph by William Henry Jackson (1843–1942), 1895. Library of Congress.

town called Deren, described in the travel report of the first Japanese to survey Sakhalin in 1808, Mamiya Rinzō (1775–1844). From Sakhalin, Mamiya had continued into mainland Qing territory.[15] These trade and communication networks were disrupted later in the nineteenth century; the vanished town Deren is an example of Qing presence in the territories beyond the Amur, which passed to Russia after 1860. This was presence which Soviet historians were at pains to deny, all the more once Communist China began recalling such losses in the 1960s.

The UNESCO *Atlas of the World's Languages in Danger* calls the Hezhe language 'severely endangered', citing an estimate of 3,000 speakers of all 'Nanai languages' in Russia as of the year 2002 and only about twenty speakers in China.[16] The 'Oroch' language of the Oroqen is considered 'critically endangered' both in Russia, where it is rarely spoken even by the elderly people in 'two isolated groups in Khabarovsk region', and in China, where the estimate is 4,000 speakers 'in the official Oroqen nationality'.[17]

The steep decline in the population of these native peoples in Russia and China belies the efforts made in Russian and Chinese historiographies to enlist them as tools in their ideological propaganda: Russians had always claimed that the Far Eastern minorities welcomed them as protectors from Chinese exploitation, while Chinese historians have cast them in the opposite role as defenders of the border from Russian aggression.[18] In reality, natives were exploited by both Russians and Chinese. There was also a third nationalist player in the game, for whom the Amur basin was important: in Japan, the Kokuryūkai (Amur River / Black Dragon Society) was founded in 1901 to defend the Amur from Russian incursion. This society was active in Manchuria after 1905, surviving until the end of World War Two.[19]

Notes

1 Shao Dan, *Remote Homeland, Recovered Borderland: Manchus, Manchoukuo, and Manchuria, 1907–1985* (Honolulu: University of Hawaii Press, 2011), p. 23.
2 See more in Loretta E. Kim, *Ethnic Chrysalis: China's Orochen People and the Legacy of Qing Borderland Administration* (Cambridge MA: Harvard University Asia Center, 2019).
3 Patrick Fuliang Shan, *Taming China's Wilderness: Immigration, Settlement and the Shaping of the Heilongjiang Frontier* (Farnham and Burlington: Ashgate, 2014), pp. 92–103.
4 Ibid., pp. 104–11.
5 Aurore Dumont, 'Declining Evenki "Identities": Playing with Loyalty in Modern and Contemporary China', *History and Anthropology*, vol. 28, no. 4 (2017), pp. 516, 520.
6 Ibid., pp. 518–19, 523–4.
7 Data following Alexandra Lavrillier et al., 'Human–Nature Relationships in the Tungus Societies of Siberia and Northeast China', *Études mongoles et sibériennes, centrasiatiques et tibétaines*, vol. 49 (2018), at pp. 6, 10–11.
8 Dumont, 'Declining Evenki "Identities"', p. 523. Ping Chen, 'China', in Andrew Simpson, ed., *Language and National Identity in Asia* (Oxford: Oxford University Press, 2007), at p. 165, gives 'only about a dozen remaining speakers' of Hezhe, all over 60 years old. Cf. 'Hunters of the Hinterlands: The Oroqen, Daur, Ewenki, and Hezhen', in Colin Legerton and Jacob Rawson, *Invisible China: A Journey Through Ethnic Borderlands* (Chicago: Chicago Review Press, 2009).
9 Lavrillier et al., 'Human–Nature Relationships', pp. 9–10, 13 (and p. 12, on the Solon language).
10 Kun Shi and Richard Noll, 'Chuonnasuan (Meng Jin Fu): The Last Shaman of the Oroqen of Northeast China', *Journal of Korean Religions*, vol. 6 (2004), pp. 135–62. This shaman, born in 1927, died in 2000.
11 Anton Chekhov, trans. Brian Reeve, *Sakhalin Island* (Richmond: Alma Classics, 2013), ch. 11.

12 Owen Lattimore, 'Byroads and Backwoods of Manchuria', *National Geographic Magazine*, vol. 61, no. 1 (Jan. 1932), p. 129.
13 See V. K. Arsenyev, trans. Malcolm Burr, *Dersu the Trapper* (Kingston NY: McPherson, 1996), and now also Vladimir K. Arsenyev, trans. Jonathan C. Slaght, *Across the Ussuri Kray: Travels in the Sikhote-Alin Mountains* (Bloomington: University of Indiana Press, 2016).
14 An interesting interpretation of the film is Olga V. Solovieva, 'The Erased Grave of Dersu Uzala: Kurosawa's Cinema of Memory and Mourning', *Journal of Japanese and Korean Cinema*, vol. 2, no. 1 (2010), pp. 63–79.
15 Tessa Morris-Suzuki, 'The Telescope and the Tinderbox: Rediscovering La Pérouse in the North Pacific', *East Asian History*, no. 39 (Dec. 2014), pp. 41, 49. Deren was located to the north-east of today's Komsomolsk-na-Amure.
16 Christopher Moseley, ed., *Atlas of the World's Languages in Danger*, 3rd edn (Paris: UNESCO Publishing, 2010), cited from http://www.unesco.org/languages-atlas/index.php
17 Ibid.
18 Ed Pulford, 'The Nanai, Hezhe and Mobilized Loyalties along the Amur', *History and Anthropology*, vol. 28, no. 4 (2017), pp. 531–52.
19 Sven Saaler, 'The Kokuryūkai (Black Dragon Society) and the Rise of Nationalism, Pan-Asianism, and Militarism in Japan, 1901–1925', *International Journal of Asian Studies*, vol. 11, no. 2 (2014), pp. 125–60.

2

The 'Rise of the Manchus' and Their Later Fortunes

Manchu society was marked by predominance of the clan, whose members believed they were descended from a common ancestor. Authority was vested in the clan heads and the elder men of each household. The prized martial skills of archery and horsemanship, along with the Manchu language, were the only subjects taught in Manchu schools until the end of the eighteenth century. The vertical Manchu script was borrowed from the Mongolian (compare the 'borrowing' of Chinese characters in Japan). In contrast to Chinese, Manchu has tenses and verb inclination and is not a tonal language.

In 1583 the first leader of the people then not yet called Manchu, Nurhaci (1559–1626), began uniting all the Jurchen tribes under him. In 1616 he founded a dynasty he called the Later Jin 金 and proclaimed himself its emperor. Thereby a direct historical connection was also established with the Jurchen Jin dynasty, founded in 1115, which as we recall had defeated the Song in 1125 and was in turn destroyed by the Mongols in 1234. Only at this stage did Nurhaci rebel against the Ming, which until then had endorsed him.[1]

In 1621 Nurhaci conquered the Ming cities Shenyang 瀋陽 (Mukden) and Liaoyang 療陽. After his death from battle wounds in 1626, his son, known in Chinese as Hong Taiji (洪台極, modernized Chinese form 皇太極; born 1592, ruled 1636–43), continued to expand his lands. In 1627 Hong's forces occupied Korea, forcing its king to switch his loyalty and submission of tribute from the Ming Empire to the new rising power in the region, a relationship formalized by 1637.[2] In 1635 Hong (reversing the move made by his father) forbade the use of 'Jurchen' and instead introduced the name 'Manchu' for his people. The meaning of 'Manchu' has long remained obscure; it is now sometimes glossed as a clan belonging or connected to the Amur River, although the historian of the Manchus, Mark Elliott, insists that 'the origin and meaning of this word remain unclear'.[3] In May 1636 Hong also abolished the name Jin for his dynasty, calling it Qing 清 instead: among other factors, this was a name more understandable (and less painfully memorable) to the Chinese. This step was early evidence of the Manchu ability to embrace new identities at key moments in their history: the next would be becoming patrons of Confucian culture, as well as of Tibetan Buddhism, as rulers of the Chinese state.

A year after Hong Taiji's death, the regent of the incipient dynasty, Dorgon, achieved final victory over the Ming in 1644, keeping power until his own demise in 1650. Emperor Shunzhi 順治 (born 1638) then took up rule as the first emperor of the Qing dynasty, but he died in an epidemic in 1661. One of his sons shaped Chinese history by ruling over China for the next sixty years as the Kangxi 康熙 emperor, from age 13 in 1662 to his death in 1722.

Throughout the Qing period, from 1644 to 1911, the Manchu dynasty regarded Manchuria as its birthplace and sacred ancestral land (*long xing zhi di* 龍興之地; the place where the dragon arose). As we shall see, already the Kangxi emperor sent missions to the Changbaishan 長白山, the Manchurian mountain he decreed to be sacred. Imperial cultivation of Manchu identity reached a peak with Kangxi's grandson the Qianlong emperor, who also ruled for almost six decades (1736–95; he died in 1799). He was a prolific poet in both Chinese and Manchu and glorified the Manchu myth of origin in a lengthy 'Ode to Mukden' (1743). This enduring nostalgia for Manchuria is surprising considering how well the Manchus blended into Chinese culture. It is also one of many recent discoveries, which refute the earlier theory of their full assimilation.

To conclude that the Manchu patronage of Confucianism and Buddhism was simulation, while their cultivation of Manchurian loyalties was real, would be simplistic. Rather, the Manchus combined their genuine identity as rulers of China with commitment to 'the Manchu Way', implying adhesion to their group belonging and complete loyalty to the emperor. Even as the Manchus developed a sense of self-identification with China (Zhongguo 中國) as a polity, promoting the idea of China as a multi-ethnic state long before this conception would be embraced by regimes in the twentieth century, they did not begin to view themselves as Han.[4]

The Willow Palisade and segregation of Manchuria

The first Qing emperor Shunzhi planted the first line of the Willow Palisade (Liutiao bian 柳條編) in 1661, the last year of his rule. This was an extension of the Great Wall consisting of a fence of trees, interspersed by a total of thirty-four gates or checkpoints, and protected by a deep trench on the outer side. Unlike the Great Wall, the aim of this barrier was strategic, not military defence. At the gates, there was always a tower, manned by a military staff whose duty was also to keep their section of the Palisade in good repair. The scheme was completed by the Kangxi emperor in 1681. The total length of the walls was 1,584 km, divided into three sections. The northern line went from Shanhaiguan 山海關 (the Mountain and Sea Pass), the gate of the Great Wall through which the Manchus had entered to conquer China, today a tourist attraction along the Great Wall about 300 km east of Beijing, to Kaiyuan 開原 in Liaoning (north-east of Shenyang) and further to the north-east, passing the town of Jilin. Another line stretched from Kaiyuan south-west to the Yalu River.

From 1653 to 1668, the Qing actually encouraged Chinese migration to Manchuria, but thereafter successive Manchu emperors placed a ban (*fengjin* 封禁) on Han settlement in this vast region, aiming to prevent 'sinicization' of the land from which China was conquered. The Palisade was also meant to prevent Han Chinese from entering Jilin to collect ginseng and furs, to block access to the large imperial hunting grounds in Shengjing 盛京 (later: Liaoning) province and delimit a neutral zone between the Qing and the Mongols on the north-west and Korea on the south-east.[5] In addition, a historian of Sino–Mongol relations has proposed regarding the Palisade as part of the Qing strategy of segregating the peoples under their rule.[6]

Interestingly, stockades of tree trunks were also erected around Moscow as a defence against the Crimean Tatars, who burned the city in 1571 (thereafter, a stone wall was built). The Palisade was not considered the outer border of China, for its purpose was to separate Manchuria from the rest of the empire. In 1740 Qianlong expelled all the unregistered migrants then present in Manchuria. Although an almost complete ban on Han Chinese emigration beyond Shanhaiguan had already been announced in 1680, in 1750 the emperor again forbade it, thereby closing off Manchuria; a ban on Han settlement in Mongolia soon followed.[7] However, by the mid-eighteenth century the Palisade was no longer an effective barrier and by the end of that century it was in disrepair. The Willow Palisade was finally abandoned in 1920; a recent travelogue describes a search for its utterly forgotten traces.[8]

Han settlement and exile

Despite the gradual erosion of Manchu identity over their two centuries of rule in Beijing, only after 1870 did the danger of continuous Russian incursion into the sparsely populated territory of Manchuria force the Qing government to abandon its long-standing policy and (gradually and hesitatingly) begin to open it for Chinese settlement. This step was designed both to strengthen defence of the new borders and engender revenues for the state, which were much needed after the damage of the Taiping rebellion (1851–64). Han Chinese settlement of Manchuria had already begun under orders of the first

Figure 2 A 'Manchurian' (Manchu) archer. In the distance houses razed by Boxers in search of Christians. Photograph by C. H. Graves (1867–1943), 1902. Library of Congress.

emperor of the Ming, Hongwu 洪武, in the late fourteenth century. A large majority of those settlers reached no farther north than contemporary Liaoning, with only a minority settling in Jilin. When the Manchus conquered the Liaoning cities from the Qing in the 1620s, they expelled into China (within the Great Wall) a Han Chinese population said to have numbered 'over a million' people. Edicts banning the Han Chinese from going beyond the Shanhai Pass were issued repeatedly during the eighteenth century, but even then the Qing government had to make concessions to the Han presence there.[9]

While it was maintained as a Manchu imperial reserve, Manchuria served as a place of exile. As was also the case with Siberia, Manchuria's remoteness and harsh climate made it suitable for that purpose. Under the Qing, Heilongjiang became the worst destination of the penal system, second only to Xinjiang in the Far West. Exile to Xinjiang began after its conquest in the mid-eighteenth century, and, although it soon surpassed the Northeast in importance (possibly, because the Palisade was no sufficient deterrent for escapes back into China), it did not entirely replace the banishment to Manchuria, which lasted to 1870.[10] Criminal convicts were enslaved to bannermen, or otherwise put to forced labour; scholars and officials were exiled to Ninguta, now in south-east Heilongjiang, or to Heilongjiang's capital Qiqihar, where they then acted as agents for the spread of high Chinese culture among the garrison Manchus.

How the Manchu people disappeared, but reappeared again

In the seventeenth and eighteenth centuries many Han Chinese bannermen adopted Manchu names, leading their descendants to declare themselves Manchu during the high Qing. After the 1911 revolution, however, they were quick to shed their banner connection. Ethnic Manchus were also lying low, afraid to reveal their origins even to their children and grandchildren. Soon after the revolution, Manchus were hunted down and killed: at least 20,000 men, women and children were massacred in the Manchu garrison of Xi'an in Shaanxi; the Manchu quarter in Nanjing, too, was burnt down and its residents were massacred.[11] The Manchu language, not even spoken by the last members of the imperial family, practically disappeared.

Despite efforts by the Qing emperors to cherish Manchuria as the birthplace of the dynasty, by the end of the eighteenth century everybody in Jilin town spoke Chinese (80 to 90 per cent of the population being Han), whereas the most northern garrison town Aihui (Aigun) was among the few places to preserve the spoken Manchu language by the early twentieth century. Spoken Manchu might have died out because Manchu women received no schooling; what they passed on to their children was the Chinese they heard in daily life. Other factors also contributed to the disappearance of the language. Nonetheless, there were still communities of Manchu speakers in the Qiqihar area in Heilongjiang in the 1980s. Pioneering PRC scholars did fieldwork there, along the Amur River and in the Shenyang area, to publish textbooks of 'contemporary Manchu'.[12] As of 2007, there were 'less than 100 people who still speak Manchu, out of a population of 10 million'.[13] In 2010, the UNESCO Atlas indicated 'Dawujia village in Aihui County of Heihe Prefecture of Heilongjiang Province' as the location where about ten persons were estimated to speak 'Amur Manchu'; at another location, 'Sanjiazi village in Fuyu County of Heilongjiang Province', a variant called Nonni Manchu was also spoken by only ten persons.[14]

While Manchu is all but extinct in the Northeast, a closely related language is spoken by the Xibo 錫伯, about 190,000 people inhabiting the Qapqal Xibo Autonomous County in Xinjiang. Although not recognized as Manchus and treated as a separate ethnic minority in the PRC, the Xibo (also: Xibe or Sibe) were originally a north-eastern people close to the Manchus, whom the Qing relocated to Xinjiang in the mid-eighteenth century.[15]

Although approximately five million Manchus were living in 1910, the first and second PRC censuses in 1953 and 1964, as well as the minority survey in 1978, indicated the number of Manchus in China as only about two and a half million. Beginning from the 1980s, however, the Manzu 滿族 emerged as the second or third largest ethnic minority in the PRC after the Zhuang 壯 people in the extreme south.[16] According to the census of 1982, they numbered 4,299,159, with the main concentration in Liaoning, Heilongjiang and Jilin.[17] This number more than doubled to reach 9,821,180 in the census of 1990 and then rose more steadily to the 10,410,585 recorded in 2010. By the 1990s, many Han Chinese in the Northeast passed themselves off as Manchu because of the government policy that permitted national minorities to have more than one child. To be registered as Manchu, it is enough to have had a single Manchu ancestor on either the maternal or the paternal side, going three generations up; accordingly, it suffices to be one-eighth Manchu to be recognized as a 'complete' one by the Chinese state.[18]

An important point here is that the Manchus of Qing times are not quite the same as the 'Manzu' in the PRC today, as the latter include the descendants of other banner people, such as Han, Mongol and native tribes. All of these have been allowed to register as 'Manzu' since the early 1950s.[19] It was not until 1985 that the first Manchu autonomous county was established with a capital seat in Xinbin 新賓, near Fushun 撫順 in eastern Liaoning, and several more have been created since.[20]

Notes

1 Nicola Di Cosmo, 'Nurhaci's Gambit: Sovereignty as Concept and Praxis in the Rise of the Manchus', in Zvi Ben-Dor Benite et al., eds, *The Scaffolding of Sovereignty: Global and Aesthetic Perspectives on the History of a Concept* (New York: Columbia University Press, 2017), esp. pp. 114–15.
2 This process is analysed in detail in Yuanchong Wang, 'Claiming Centrality in the Chinese World: Manchu–Chosŏn Relations and the Making of the Qing's "Zhongguo" Identity, 1616–1643', *The Chinese Historical Review*, vol. 22, no. 2 (2015), pp. 95–119.
3 Mark Elliott, 'Ethnicity in the Qing Eight Banners', in Pamela Kyle Crossley et al., eds, *Empire at the Margins: Culture, Ethnicity, and Frontier in Early*

Modern China (Berkeley: University of California Press, 2006), p. 57, n. 9. Ibid., p. 39, says: 'there is every reason to believe that Manchu was an invented name with little prior currency'. Earlier opinion explained it as 'abbreviation of Manjusiri, the name of Nurhaci's remotest forefather': see Erich Hauer, 'Why the Sinologue Should Study Manchu', *Journal of the North China Branch of the Royal Asiatic Society*, vol. 61 (1930), p. 158. See also Donald F. Lach and Edwin J. van Kley, *Asia in the Making of Europe*, vol. 3, book 4 (Chicago: University of Chicago Press, 1993), ch. 22: 'China's Periphery'.

4   See Gang Zhao, 'Reinventing *China*: Imperial Qing Ideology and the Rise of Modern Chinese National Identity in the Early Twentieth Century', *Modern China*, vol. 32, no. 1 (Jan. 2006), pp. 3–30; and Shao Dan, *Remote Homeland, Recovered Borderland*, pp. 15–17.

5   For an interpretation of these policies, see chapter 4, 'Internal Frontiers and Intensified Land Use in China', in John F. Richards, *The Unending Frontier: An Environmental History of the Early Modern World* (Berkeley: University of California Press, 2003).

6   Uradyn E. Bulag, 'Rethinking Borders in Empire and Nation at the Foot of the Willow Palisade', in Franck Billé et al., eds, *Frontier Encounters: Knowledge and Practice at the Russian, Chinese and Mongolian Border* (Cambridge: Open Book Publishers, 2012), pp. 33–53.

7   Christopher M. Isett, 'Village Regulation of Property and the Social Basis for the Transformation of Qing Manchuria', *Late Imperial China*, vol. 25, no. 1 (June 2004), p. 130.

8   Michael Meyer, *In Manchuria: A Village Called Wasteland and the Transformation of Rural China* (London and New York: Bloomsbury Press, 2015), pp. 52–62.

9   Quentin Pan, 'Early Chinese Colonization in Manchuria', *The China Critic*, 7 Nov. 1929, pp. 889–92.

10 See Joanna Waley-Cohen, *Exile in Mid-Qing China: Banishment to Xinjiang, 1758–1820* (New Haven and London: Yale University Press, 1991).

11 See on these events Rhoads, *Manchus & Han*, pp. 187–205.

12 Chia Ning, 'Manchu Language Resources in the People's Republic of China: A Comprehensive Review', *China Review International*, vol. 16, no. 3 (2009), pp. 316–17.

13 Ping Chen, 'China', p. 148, n. 7.

14 Christopher Moseley, ed., *Atlas of the World's Languages in Danger*, cited from http://www.unesco.org/languages-atlas/index.php. A visit to the 'last native speakers of Manchu' in Sanjiazi 三家子 is described in Meyer, *In Manchuria*, pp. 132–4.

15 See the report from Sanjiazi by David Lague, 'China's Manchu Speakers Struggle to Save Language', *New York Times* (16 March 2007); Andrew Jacobs, 'Manchu, Former Empire's Language, Hangs On at China's Edge', *New York Times* (11 January 2016).

16 14,150,000 (about 91 per cent) of the Zhuang, China's largest minority, are concentrated in Guangxi province, where they make up over 30 per cent of

the population. The other main minorities besides the Manchus are the Uyghurs (a Turkic Muslim people, mostly living in Xinjiang; over 11 million), Hui (Chinese Muslims; about 10.5 million) and Miao (also known as Hmong; almost 9 million).

17 Judith Banister, 'An Analysis of Recent Data on the Population of China', *Population and Development Review*, vol. 10, no. 2 (June 1984), p. 263.
18 Matthew Hoodie, 'Ethnic Identity Change in the People's Republic of China', *Nationalism and Ethnic Politics*, vol. 4, nos. 1–2 (1998), p. 124. See also Thomas Scharping, 'The Integration of Manchuria: Political Change, Demographic Development and Ethnic Structure from the Early Qing Period to Present Times (1610–1993)', in Lutz Bieg et al., eds, *Ad Seres et Tungusos: Festschrift für Martin Grimm* (Wiesbaden: Harrassowitz, 2000), esp. p. 352.
19 Shao Dan, *Remote Homeland, Recovered Borderland*, pp. 12, 207.
20 Ibid., pp. 211–15.

3

Russian Expansion into Asia and the Way to the Treaty of Nerchinsk

The Russian Empire was born with the conquest of Kazan, formerly a Muslim Khanate, by Ivan the Terrible (1530–84) in 1552. Tsar Ivan began the Russian advance into Siberia in the 1570s. After the defeat of Khan Kuchum by the Cossack force under Ermak, near modern Tobolsk on the Irtysh River in 1581, the conquest of Siberia was soon completed. Imperial expansion was led by fur hunters, who forced the local population to pay them tribute (*yasak*).[1] The prominence and symbolism of fur, associated with the tsar or the emperor, was shared in early modern Russia and China.[2]

After the conquest of Siberia, the Russians began to send out expeditions to gather information about China. The first of these, under Ivan Petlin, left from Tobolsk in 1618. Travelling through Mongolia, it reached Peking,[3] which is why Russia and China celebrated the 400th anniversary of their diplomatic ties in 2018. The Russians had to depart in four days, however, as soon as it became clear that they had not brought tribute. Petlin carried a letter from the Wanli 萬曆 emperor of the Ming (ruled 1573–1620) back with him to Russia, inviting the tsar to join the tribute system. This letter (along with another, to the same effect, received in 1642) lay untranslated for half a century; by the time it was finally read in 1675 a new dynasty sat on the throne in China.[4] Petlin's travel account was important for European knowledge about China and was translated and published widely. After the death in 1598 of Ivan's childless and retarded son Fedor, Russia went through a period of instability dubbed the 'Time of Troubles'. At its end, the Romanov Empire was founded in 1613.[5]

As a northern bordering state, relations with Russia were handled in China by the Lifanyuan 理蕃院,[6] the Court for Frontier Dependencies (alternative translations are Court of Colonial Affairs, or Barbarian Control Office), an organ originally established in 1638 to manage Qing relations with Mongolia and Tibet. Russia thus was not included in the Board of Rites (Li Bu 禮部), which managed the tribute system for the neighbouring states in East and South East Asia that accepted elements of Chinese and Confucian culture. This situation was maintained until the Zongli yamen 總理衙門 (predecessor of the Chinese Foreign Office) was created in 1861. The

Lifanyuan was staffed only by Manchus and Mongols, as Han Chinese were excluded from it.[7]

Meanwhile, the Russian occupation of Siberia proceeded rapidly. In 1628 they passed Lake Baikal, and in 1643 the expedition of Vasilii Poiarkov reached the Amur River. The Russians tried to impose the *yasak* on the natives, who reported their arrival to the Manchus, to whom they were already paying tribute. In 1650 a brutal expedition under Erofei Khabarov (after whom, two centuries later, Khabarovsk would be named) came to the Amur and the fort of Albazin was founded. In 1652 the first battle between Khabarov and a Qing army took place: the Russians won.

In 1656 a new mission headed by Fedor Baikov arrived in Peking. Baikov refused to perform the kowtow ceremony (literally 'knocking the head', which must consist of the ritual three kneelings and nine prostrations), to partake of the emperor's gift of tea boiled with butter and milk after the Tibetan fashion,

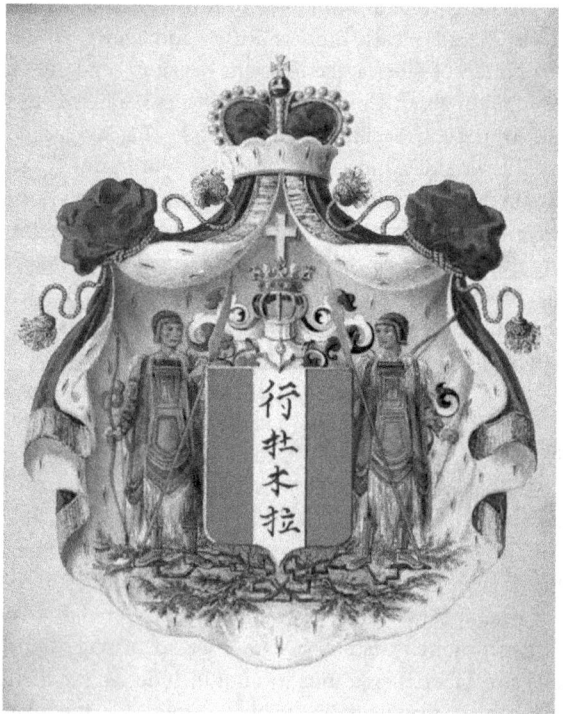

Figure 3 Coat of arms of the Princes Gantimurov. Obshchii gerbovnik dvorianskikh rodov Vserossiiskoi imperii (General Armorial of the Noble Families of the All-Russian Empire), part 17. St Petersburg, 1904.

or to hand over the tsar's presents to anyone but the emperor himself. Incidentally, the kowtow, which later proved a major obstacle in China's relations with the West, had a parallel in the Russian *chelobit'e* (prostration before the tsar), which would only be abolished by the Europeanization measures of Peter the Great. In September Baikov's diplomatic mission ended in failure and he was turned out of China's capital. He did, however, compile an elaborate report which included a description of Peking life, the first to reach Russia.

Soon thereafter, in 1658, the Manchus won a battle against Russia on the Amur. But the Amur problem was not raised in negotiations with the Russian missions in Peking, as neither side was sure at this point who was its enemy along that river. The Albazin fort, razed by the Qing army in 1659, was partially rebuilt by 1666, while Russia continued to squeeze tribute from the natives. As the Russians initially demanded less than the Qing, some Tungus leaders began to switch sides and seek Russian protection.

The conflict came to a head with the defection to Russia of the Tungus chieftain Gantimur (about 1610–85) in 1667: he was eventually baptized, settled in Nerchinsk and in 1684 given the title of Prince Gantimurov. His Russian-speaking descendants still bear that unique surname today.[8] The next Russian mission was headed by the Romanian exile Nicolae (Nikolai) Milescu (1636–1708), known in Russia as Spafarii. A well-travelled European diplomat and translator of the Bible into Romanian (who had been mutilated in punishment for his part in a plot to usurp the throne of Moldavia), Milescu joined the service of Tsar Aleksei Romanov (1645–76) in Moscow in 1671. He was to remain in Russia until his death.[9] At a time when the Qing had become alive to the fact that *Luocha* and *Eluosi* both referred to Russians, Milescu enabled the court in Moscow to understand that the *bogdoiskie* on the Amur and *kitaiskie* in Peking also represented the same country.

Leaving Moscow in March 1675, Milescu reached China's border in early 1676 and was met by a Manchu envoy on the Nonni (Nenjiang) river in Manchuria. These preliminary negotiations lasted fifty days, as the Qing demanded the return of Gantimur, an end to Russian raids across the Amur and agreement to all the established rites of tributary envoys. Milescu's aim was to ensure bilateral trade and the visits of Chinese diplomats to Russia; as to the border problem, the tsar had only instructed him to enquire about possible Russian prisoners in China and bail them out for no more than thirty roubles per head.

Reaching Peking in May, Milescu eventually kowtowed to Kangxi, but rejected the demand to deliver Gantimur. In late August a statement was read out to him conveying Kangxi's refusal to write to the tsar unless it was to accept him as a tribute-bearing monarch. Milescu had spoken in Latin with the Jesuit missionary Ferdinand Verbiest (1623–88), but did not believe what the priest told him of the Qing emperor's plan to drive out the Russians from the Amur. Instead he reported back to Moscow that the Manchus were no match for the Russians. The Jesuits may have translated the letters of previous emperors, which Milescu had brought with him to China. He also reported on the Russians he saw in Peking – the Cossacks, who had joined the banners – describing them as traitors.[10] In Chinese records, Milescu's conduct was denounced as insolent.[11] His *Description of China*, which was apparently completed on his return journey to Russia but remained in manuscript until 1910, was largely a translation of *Novus Atlas Sinensis* (1655) and *De Bello Tartarico* (1654) by the Jesuit Martino Martini (1614–61), a copy of which he received from Verbiest, with only the chapter on the Amur being new. Were it published in Russian at the time, it would have been the only book on China in that language (besides Petlin's report) until the 1770s.[12]

By the time Milescu returned to Moscow in January 1678, Russian interest in expansion to the East was dampened by the death of Tsar Aleksei two years previously. Aleksei's son Fedor spent most of his six-year rule, until his death in 1682, in court struggles. When Fedor died without heir, the Russian crown passed to his brothers, the sickly 15-year-old Ivan V and the 10-year-old Peter I (the future Peter the Great). Their elder sister Sophia Alekseevna ruled as a regent on the brothers' behalf from March 1683. A renewed Qing assault on Albazin began in June 1685, after a thorough preparation that included the foundation of Aigun as a Manchu military stronghold. When the Russians surrendered within days they were allowed to retreat. Some forty-five men were then either taken captive or willingly went with the Qing army to Peking, where they were settled, married to Manchu women (the widows of condemned criminals) and were taken into service in the Yellow banner as Eluosi qiren 俄罗斯旗人.

A few of these men taught Russian at the School of Russian (Eluosi wenguan 俄罗斯文館), created in 1708, but their descendants were soon assimilated.[13] Nonetheless, the presence of the so-called Albazinians in Peking later allowed Russia to establish a large religious mission in the city, which served all the purposes of diplomatic representation. In August 1685 the former occupiers of Albazin (669 men) returned there, collected the harvest and rebuilt the fort. A new Manchu siege began in July 1686. It was partially lifted in November, when only sixty-six of the men remained alive inside. The siege ended in August 1687, after news of Sophia's readiness to negotiate the border with the Qing had been received in Peking: by this time only about twenty men were alive, and the disease raging in the fort had spread to the Manchu soldiers.

In 1687 the nobleman Fedor Golovin (1650–1706), later one of Russia's leading diplomats, was delegated to the negotiations with China, accompanied by a Pole who had received Latin education in Cracow. The Mongols detained Golovin by laying siege to his delegation in Selenginsk (a town founded by Cossacks to the south of Lake Baikal in 1655; now Novoselenginsk in the Buryat Republic) from January to March 1688. But in summer 1689 the two delegations finally met in Nerchinsk (a town founded as recently as 1653 on the bank of Shilka River, about 300 km east of Chita). The Qing side, including military forces and Buddhist priests, numbered about ten thousand and the Russians about two thousand men. In Nerchinsk, Golovin, his Polish interpreter from and into Latin, Andrei (before his conversion to the Russian Orthodoxy in 1682: Ian) Belobotskii, who was a theological writer and translator, and a French and a Portuguese Jesuit on the Chinese side, Gerbillion and Pereira, negotiated from 22 to 27 August 1689 the first treaty ever concluded between China and any European state.[14]

This treaty fixed the borders between Russia and the Qing to run along the Stanovoy mountain range and along the Argun River, which meant a full Russian retreat from the Amur and the razing of Albazin. Some recent research has argued that state borders were only vaguely delimited at Nerchinsk, and that the more important element of the treaty was the mutual agreement reached on preventing populations in the border area from shifting their allegiance to the other side.[15] A large Qing army had surrounded Nerchinsk, yet both parties, as well as the Jesuits who were later rewarded by Kangxi, were satisfied: in return for what they then considered insignificant territory (they would change their mind about the Amur region by the 1850s), the Russians got a promise of future trade under precise regulations. As historian Peter Perdue stresses, China and Russia were both content in excluding any claims for the area by a third party, the Mongols.[16]

An important factor in the background of the Qing's strategic considerations was the revolt of Galdan (ruled 1676–97), khan of the Junghars of western Mongolia (in today's northern Xinjiang), who invaded Outer Mongolia in 1687. It was vital for Kangxi to prevent his enemy receiving Russian aid. Soon after the signing of the Nerchinsk treaty, Galdan's request for aid was rejected by Moscow, and in 1696 Kangxi personally led a military campaign – his last, for he died the following year – which resulted in Galdan's defeat.[17] Nerchinsk itself became the main commercial centre of Eastern Siberia, the base from which trade caravans to China set out. However inaccurately charted, these borders remained in force for the next 170 years. Through the Jesuits, the text of the treaty, like the maps of Manchuria already mentioned, also reached Europe and Japan (it was translated in Nagasaki in 1805).[18]

On the day when the Nerchinsk treaty was signed, 27 August 1689, the future Peter the Great, then 17 years old, overthrew his sister Sophia in Moscow. He was to rule until 1725, a contemporary of Kangxi; and the two monarchs have been compared as the early modernizers of their realms.[19] Incidentally, at another end of the world, 1689 was also the momentous year of the English 'Glorious Revolution' (replacement of James II by his daughter Mary II, who then ruled with her Dutch husband William III), the beginning of Protestant constitutional monarchy in Britain.

Notes

1. Alexander Etkind, 'Barrels of Fur: Natural Resources and the State in the Long History of Russia', *Journal of Eurasian Studies*, vol. 2, no. 2 (July 2011), pp. 164–71, republished (with the same mistake on the conquest of Kazan being 'in 1522' instead of 1552) as part of ch. 5 in his *Internal Colonization: Russia's Imperial Experience* (Cambridge: Polity, 2011).
2. Evelyn Welch, 'Between Italy and Moscow: Cultural Crossroads and the Culture of Exchange', in *Cultural Exchange in Early Modern Europe*, chief ed. Robert Muchembled, in 4 vols (Cambridge and New York: Cambridge University Press and European Science Foundation, 2006–7), vol. 4, pp. 59–99 (section on 'furs and falcons' as Russian imperial gifts in the fifteenth century). For China, cf. Jonathan Schlesinger, *A World Trimmed with Fur: Wild Things, Pristine Places, and the Natural Fringes of Qing Rule* (Stanford: Stanford University Press, 2017).
3. This version of the events is challenged by Su Fenglin, 'Questions Regarding Past and Present Sino-Russian Cultural Exchange', in Iwashita Akihiro, ed., *Eager Eyes Fixed on Eurasia*, in 2 vols (Sapporo: Slavic Research Center, Hokkaido University, 2007), vol. 2, pp. 93–109. Su says Petlin did reach China but not necessarily Peking, and doubts the authenticity of the letters he brought back.
4. Here and below I am much indebted to R. K. I. Quested, *Sino-Russian Relations: A Short History*, 2nd edn (London and New York: Routledge, 2005).
5. Ivan IV (the Terrible), the first to crown himself as tsar of Russia, had killed his able son Ivan in 1581. He was succeeded by Fedor I (1557–98), followed by Boris Godunov (ruled 1598–1605).
6. Compare with the Sibirskii prikaz (Department of Siberia), which Russia created in 1637. On the Lifanyuan, see Dittmar Schorkowitz and Chia Ning, eds, *Managing Frontiers in Qing China: The Lifanyuan and Libu Revisited* (Leiden: Brill, 2016).
7. Joseph W. Esherick, 'How the Qing Became China', in Esherick et al., eds, *Empire to Nation: Historical Perspectives on the Making of the Modern World* (Lanham: Rowman & Littlefield, 2006), p. 232.

8 A. R. Artemyev, 'The Gantimurov Princes in Russian Service', *Journal de la Société Finno-Ougrienne*, vol. 84 (1992), pp. 7–20.
9 On Milescu, see the ongoing research of Daniela Dumbrava.
10 Andrey V. Ivanov, 'Conflicting Loyalties: Fugitives and "Traitors" in the Russo-Manchurian Frontier, 1651–1689', *Journal of Early Modern History*, vol. 13, no. 5 (2009), p. 353.
11 Di Toro, *La percezione della Russia in Cina*, pp. 49–50.
12 Gregory Afinogenov, *The Eye of the Tsar: Intelligence-Gathering and Geopolitics in Eighteenth-Century Eurasia* (PhD diss. Harvard University, 2015), pp. 50–5.
13 In post-Soviet Russia and China, the interests of Russian Orthodox circles combined with root-searching among Chinese who considered themselves descendants of the 'Albazintsy', resulting in a flurry of Russian publications about them and offers of spiritual Orthodox guidance to the persons involved. Much of this was the initiative of Dmitrii Napara, a Russian resident of Beijing. Jasper Becker, *City of Heavenly Tranquility: Beijing in the History of China* (London: Allen Lane, 2008), pp. 301–2, incorporated information from Napara to report on the presence in present-day Beijing of an exotic community consisting of 'the descendants of five Cossacks, Romanov, Khabarov, Kristov, Jakovlev and Dubinin, who had been brought to Beijing in 1685 by the Manchu emperor Kangxi'.
14 Among many accounts of Russia's first claims to the Amur and its acceptance of Qing control of the region in the Treaty of Nerchinsk, cf. John J. Stephan, *The Russian Far East: A History* (Stanford: Stanford University Press, 1994), ch. 4. Latin would be replaced by French as the language of international diplomacy after the Peace of Utrecht in 1713.
15 Ivanov, 'Conflicting Loyalties'. Cf. the discussion in V. S. Frank, 'The Territorial Terms of the Sino-Russian Treaty of Nerchinsk, 1689', *Pacific Historical Review*, vol. 16, no. 3 (Aug. 1947), pp. 265–70.
16 Peter C. Perdue, 'Boundaries and Trade in the Early Modern World: Negotiations at Nerchinsk and Beijing', *Eighteenth-Century Studies*, vol. 43, no. 3 (Spring 2010), pp. 341–56.
17 Immanuel C. Y. Hsü, 'Russia's Special Position in China during the Early Ch'ing Period', *Slavic Review*, vol. 23, no. 4 (Dec. 1964), pp. 689–93.
18 David Mervart, 'The Many Lives of Father Gerbillion's Sino-Russian Treaty: An Attempt at a "Global" Intellectual History', paper presented at the East Asian Seminar, University of Zurich, 26 Sept. 2014.
19 Laura Hostetler, 'Imperial Competition in Eurasia: Russia and China', in *The Cambridge World History*, chief ed. Merry E. Wiesner-Hanks, in 7 vols (Cambridge: Cambridge University Press, 2014–15), vol. 6, part 1, eds Jerry H. Bentley et al., pp. 297–322.

4

Qing–Russian Relations in the Eighteenth Century

The previous chapter demonstrated how the changing relations between China and Russia impacted on Manchuria even when they played out in Peking or in Nerchinsk. In terms of international relations, the eighteenth century was not an eventful age for Manchuria compared to the earlier and later periods. The present chapter supplies the necessary link between Russia's military confrontation with Qing China over parts of Manchurian territory in the seventeenth century, the story sketched out above, and the annexation of these territories by Russia in the nineteenth century, which will be related in Chapter Five.

Throughout the reign of Peter the Great, Russia was busy with European wars, especially those against Sweden. The tsar's orientation to the West was evident in his foundation of a new capital in St Petersburg in 1703. Trade with China was restricted to caravans, not exceeding 200 men, which were permitted to arrive in Peking once in three years. To ensure the smooth implementation of the conditions agreed to in Nerchinsk in 1689, the Dutch merchant Isbrand Ides (1657–1708) was sent by the tsar to Emperor Kangxi in 1692 and was well received at the Qing court. Upon his return, Ides recommended goods to the tsar that he thought were suitable for export to China. He also wrote the first account in a European language of the Tungus and Mongol peoples he had seen in the Transbaikal area on the mission's route to China (the original Dutch text, published in 1704, was quickly translated into other European languages).[1]

Ten caravans had gone from Nerchinsk to Peking by 1719. The standard route passed by Selenginsk and Kalgan (today's Zhangjiakou 張家口).[2] For the needs of the caravans, a hostel (called Eluosi nanguan 俄羅斯南館) and a church (Eluosi beiguan 北館) were established in Peking. The latter became a permanent base of the Russian Orthodox Mission after the Treaty of Kiakhta in 1727. Russia imported tea, silk, tobacco, cotton, as well as luxury objects such as porcelain and lacquered furniture from China. A particularly interesting item in this shopping list was rhubarb. The word comes from the Greek for 'Barbarians beyond the Volga'; modern Russian has the similar *rabarbar* (the older Russian term was *reven*); the Chinese name is *dahuang*

大黃. Especially during the eighteenth century, the root of this plant was used in European medicine as a laxative, though not so much in Russia itself, which maintained a monopoly on its trade. Re-exported via Kiakhta to Europe, Chinese rhubarb fetched a high price in England and France, where pharmacists pounded it into powder. Spreading from elite to popular usage in Europe, rhubarb also gradually evolved from medicine to food, eventually to be consumed in jams and pies, the form in which we encounter it today.[3]

Russian exports to China included fur, cloth (either made in Russia or of English, German and French origin) and leather, as well as 'glassware, hardware, tin, camels, horses, hounds and horned cattle'.[4] In the eighteenth century Russia developed its own variety of chinoiserie, the fashion which had made Chinese silk, porcelain and lacquered *objets d'art* highly attractive to the royal courts and nobility of Europe. So a pattern was established, by which Russia depended on tea and other Chinese goods far more than China needed Russian furs or any other Russian products.

The most important Qing-period description of Russia was the outcome of an unusual mission, sent by Kangxi in 1712–15 to the Volga region to negotiate with the khan of the Torghuts, who had left Ming China in the late 1620s, and whom the Qing now needed as allies against the Junghars.[5] The mission's report, *Yi yu lu* 異域錄 (Record of a Foreign Land), was written by Tulišen 圖理琛 (1667–1741), a high-ranking Manchu official. It was published in the original Manchu and then in a Chinese version (probably self-translated by Tulišen) in 1723. It was subsequently translated into Russian (twice), French, German and English.[6] The Qing mission spent much time in Selenginsk, going on to visit Udinsk (now Ulan-Ude), Irkutsk, Saratov and Tobolsk (where Tulišen had conversations with governor of Siberia, Prince Matvei Gagarin).[7] From 1719 to the death of Kangxi in 1722 (also the last years of Tsar Peter's rule) Russian–Chinese relations were strained by the Qing attempt to conquer Jungharia. This region, which includes the valley of Yili 伊犁, lies in northern Xinjiang between Tianshan Mountains 天山 in the south and the Altai in the north. The tsar was willing to support the Junghars against the Qing in return for gold-mining rights, which he needed to finance his incessant warfare in Europe. These tensions were an early prelude to the 'Yili Crisis', which would develop in the region in the 1870s.

In summer 1719 Peter sent Lev Izmailov (1685–1738) as envoy to Peking with a proposal to change the terms of Russian–Chinese trade, as the caravan system was becoming unprofitable. It was also the tsar's plan to make the Swede Lorenz Lange (*c*. 1690–1752), who had already travelled to China, Russia's consul in Peking – an unprecedented appointment, had it come to pass. Izmailov and his retinue were constrained to kowtow to the old Kangxi. Nevertheless, the embassy of 1720 was a failure. Although Lange was given several audiences with the emperor and was allowed to live at the Russian hostel for seventeen months (thereby becoming the first-ever Western resident representative at the Chinese court), he was expelled during the Jungharian crisis in July 1722.[8] Something of a pioneering book agent, Lange had brought publications of the Russian Academy of Sciences with him, which became the first Russian books in China. He returned to Russia with the first Chinese books, still preserved in St Petersburg today. His journal of the stay at the Chinese court in 1721–2, published in French in 1726, was translated repeatedly in the course of the eighteenth century. But the function of a foreign 'consul', as a new study points out, could not at the time be fitted into the categories of Chinese bureaucracy.[9]

Tsar Peter had insisted on establishing state monopolies on most categories of goods in the trade with China, which remained in force (though were not always effectively implemented) until 1728. After Peter's death his illiterate widow Catherine I, who ruled briefly until her own death in 1727,[10] began new negotiations with China. These were conducted by the court's envoy, a favourite of Tsar Peter, Count Savva Vladislavich (1669–1738), known in Russian as Raguzinskii since he came from the multinational Ragusa republic (1358–1808; now the southernmost end of Croatia). He was instructed to perform the kowtow and do everything else needed to accommodate the Qing in order to achieve stable trade relations and the appointment of Lange (who again joined the mission) as consul. Savva Vladislavich arrived in Peking in October 1726 and stayed until the following April. After difficult negotiations an agreement was reached and both delegations then travelled to the frontier in order to have it demarcated. In August 1727, the Bura agreement was signed, fixing the Argun River border, and in November 1727 the two sides signed the Treaty of Kiakhta. By that time Catherine had been succeeded by Peter's grandson, Peter II, born in 1715, who would 'rule' only until dying of smallpox, aged 14, in 1730. He was followed by Empress Anna.

The town of Kiakhta was founded in 1727, as was the border post Tsurukhaitui, on the right bank of the Argun. The treaty of that year established Kiakhta and Tsurukhaitui as new trading centres, confirmed Qing control over the Khalkha Mongols,[11] relaunched the Russian trade caravans to Peking, agreed on mutual punishment of future fugitives from Chinese and Russian justice and also allowed a Russian clerical mission to arrive in Peking every ten years. Lange, who never became 'consul', returned to China with some of the caravans. The Outer Mongolian border was fixed in the Kiakhta treaty just as the Manchurian border had been fixed in Nerchinsk. However, the eighteenth-century treaty was more specific in attempting to resolve a list of potential problems. Until 1772, trade with China was also conducted through Nerchinsk, but from then and until 1851,

Figure 4 The tea trade in Kiakhta. Photograph by Jules Legras (1866–1939), 1890s.

when Russian–Chinese trade across the Xinjiang border became possible, Kiakhta remained unique in its standing and functions.

The treaty of Kiakhta determined Russian–Chinese relations until the mid-nineteenth century. While the treaty envisaged a dual track of commerce (both by triennial caravans and by trade in the border towns), the caravans disappeared by 1755 whereas Kiakhta itself grew quickly in importance. The treaty was considered a success by the Chinese because it settled the Mongolian question. But the nomads who moved with their herds between territories now firmly defined as belonging to the Russian or Qing Empires faced difficult choices about taxes (defined as tributes) to be paid to one side or another, and some resettled as a result.

In 1729 the Yongzheng 雍正 emperor (fourth son of the Kangxi emperor; ruled 1723–35) mounted an attack on Jungharia. To ensure himself of Russian neutrality, in the same year the emperor dispatched the first Manchu delegation to the Russian court, which was also the only delegation sent by the Qing to any Western country until the second half of the nineteenth century. The delegation, led by Tuo Shi 托時 and Man Tai 滿泰, had intended to congratulate Peter II, but as the tsar was dead it was received in Moscow, temporarily the capital of Russia in 1728–31, by his successor, the niece of

Peter the Great, Anna Ioannovna (ruled 1730–40) in January 1731. She was the second of four women who ruled over eighteenth-century Russia.[12] With updated letters of introduction another delegation, headed by De Xin 德新, arrived in St Petersburg in 1732. In June they visited the Academy of Sciences, receiving a book on China by a member of the Academy: *Museum Sinicum* by the German scholar from Königsberg, Gottlieb Siegfried Bayer (1694–1738).[13] Immanuel C. Y. Hsü (1923–2005), the eminent historian of China, pointed out the unique standing of Russia in Chinese eyes: as attested by the kowtows performed by both Qing delegations in front of the empress, it was the only country China conceived as its political equal.

With no strong ruler until the rise to power of Catherine II, Russia concentrated on maritime exploration rather than overland expansion. Russian explorers first crossed the Bering Strait into Alaska in 1732 (the territory, exploited by the Russian-American Company from 1799, was to be sold to the USA in 1867). In East Asia the Mongol troubles continued, however, as Khalkha Mongols constantly crossed the Russian border to escape from the Manchus. Quarrels over fugitives caused the Qing occasionally to suspend trade in Kiakhta. They knew they were in a good bargaining position because Russia was much more dependent on this trade. Between 1755 and 1758 the Qing finally conquered Jungharia along with the Yili area, killing a third of the Junghar population (which had numbered about a million) in punitive expeditions. The Grand Lama (Khutuktu) of Khalkha was killed, too, and as the Qing took full control of Outer Mongolia they approached the Russian border. Relations with Russia soured, while Junghar as well as Outer Mongol refugees crossed over to the Russian side.[14] By contrast the Torghuts, to whom Tulišen was delegated in 1712, returned to China in a perilous journey with much loss of life in 1771, soon after Catherine the Great had attempted to draft them into the Russian army against the Ottoman Empire. The last Mongol confederation to submit to the Qing, they were settled in Tianshan and elsewhere in Xinjiang. Those of them who remained in Russia are today known as the Kalmyks; most are resident in the Republic of Kalmykia within the Russian Federation, on the western shore of the Caspian Sea.

In 1762 the German princess who would become known in Russian history as Catherine the Great replaced her husband Peter III (1728–62), a German-speaking grandson of Peter I who had been deposed and strangled only six months after ascending to the throne earlier in the same year. Catherine was to rule until 1796. In 1765 the Qing broke off relations with Russia, until in 1768 another favourable agreement on trade tariffs and border control was signed as a supplement to the Kiakhta treaty. This increased the profitability and importance of the Kiakhta trade for both sides.

However, Russian merchants petitioned to Catherine, who renegotiated the agreement, reaching a compromise, which was signed in February 1792. The text of this agreement marks the high point of Chinese superiority over Russia: for the first and last time in relations between the two countries, Russia was effectively made to obey the emperor of China. Qianlong's three closures of the Kiakhta trade because of fugitives and border incidents in 1764–8, 1778–80 and 1785–92 were a means of exerting pressure on Russia, which he believed could not do without Chinese rhubarb.[15]

* * *

The School of Russian in Peking, the Eluosi wenguan opened in 1708, which has been mentioned above, was managed by Qing officials with members of the Russian Orthodox Mission as teachers and is not generally considered a success.[16] Nevertheless, it was probably the only foreign language school in Peking until the establishment of the Tongwen guan 同文館 (Metropolitan School of Foreign Languages) in 1862. Russian delegations served periods from seven to sixteen years in the Orthodox Mission, officially enabled by the Treaty of Kiakhta in 1727. Each such delegation had ten members: seven monks and three students. Some of them spent their time drinking, but a few of the students learned excellent Chinese as well as Manchu, Mongolian or even Tibetan, laying the foundations for Russian Oriental Studies. From the perspective of the Qing state, allowing Russians to come to China to study Chinese was probably perceived in terms of spreading the glory of Chinese civilization.

As a result of the Kiakhta treaty, Russia had become the only country with permanent representatives in Peking until 1860 – since its ostensibly religious mission there also fulfilled a diplomatic role.[17]

Notes

1 Jan Borm, 'The French of the Tundra: Early Modern European Views of the Tungus in Translation', *Études mongoles et sibériennes, centrasiatiques et tibétaines*, vol. 49 (2018), pp. 1–14.
2 Mark Mancall, *Russia and China: Their Diplomatic Relations to 1728* (Cambridge MA: Harvard University Press, 1971), p. 197. The route from the frontier to Peking took only seventy days. On the Ides journey, see Lach and van Kley, *Asia in the Making of Europe*, vol. 3, bk 4, pp. 1762–7.
3 Among several studies, this draws especially on Erika Monahan, 'Locating Rhubarb: Early Modernity's Relevant Obscurity', in Paula Findlen, ed., *Early Modern Things: Objects and their Histories, 1500–1800* (London and New York: Routledge, 2013), pp. 227–51.

4 Muping Bao, trans. Gaynor Sekimori, 'Trade Centres (*Maimaicheng*) in Mongolia, and their Function in Sino-Russian Trade Networks', *International Journal of Asian Studies*, vol. 3, no. 2 (2006), pp. 213-14. See also the list of trade items in Martha Avery, *The Tea Road: China and Russia Meet across the Steppe* (Beijing: China Intercontinental Press, 2003), p. 125.
5 See James A. Millward, 'Qing Inner Asian Empire and the Return of the Torghuts', in Millward et al., eds, *New Qing Imperial History: The Making of Inner Asian Empire at Qing Chengde* (London: Routledge, 2004), pp. 91-105.
6 The title of the only extant English translation is worth quoting in full: *Narrative of the Chinese Embassy to the Khan of the Tourgouth Tartars: in the years 1712, 13, 14, & 15*, by the Chinese Ambassador, and published, by the Emperor's authority, at Pekin. Translated from the Chinese, and accompanied by an appendix of miscellaneous translations, by Sir George Staunton [1781-1859] (London: J. Murray, 1821).
7 Di Toro, *La percezione della Russia in Cina*, pp. 166-74. Gagarin (? - 1721), governor of Siberia from 1711, was executed on Tsar Peter's orders for charges of Siberian separatism and corruption.
8 Izmailov's delegation included the young Scottish doctor, John Bell (1691-1780), who in 1763 published *A Journey from St. Petersburg to Pekin, 1719-1722*. Peter C. Perdue, *China Marches West: The Qing Conquest of Central Eurasia* (Cambridge MA: Harvard University Press, 2005) uses the accounts of Tulisen and Bell.
9 Michael Keevak, *Embassies to China: Diplomacy and Cultural Encounters Before the Opium Wars* (Singapore: Palgrave Macmillan, 2017), ch. 6.
10 Distinguish Catherine I (1684-1727), of Polish-Lithuanian peasant origin, from Catherine II (the Great; 1729-96), the German princess who ruled as empress of Russia from 1762.
11 Khalkha is Outer Mongolia; the old name for Inner Mongolia is Chahar. Both are originally names of Mongolian ethnic groups and dialects.
12 Catherine I (1725-27), Anna Ioannovna (1730-40), Elizaveta Petrovna (1741-61), Catherine II (1762-96). On the delegation, see Hsü, *The Rise of Modern China*, pp. 114-16.
13 N. A. Samoilov, *Rossiia i Kitai v XVII - nachale XX veka. Tendentsii, formy i stadii sotsiokul'turnogo vzaimodeistviia* (St Petersburg: Izdatel'stvo SPGU, 2014), p. 98. Königsberg in East Prussia became Soviet Kaliningrad in 1946.
14 John P. LeDonne, 'Proconsular Ambitions on the Chinese Border: Governor General Iakobi's Proposal of War on China', *Cahiers du monde russe*, vol. 45, nos. 1-2 (Jan.-June 2004), pp. 36-8.
15 Che-Chia Chang, trans. Penelope Barrett, 'Origins of a Misunderstanding: The Qianlong Emperor's Embargo on Rhubarb Exports to Russia, the Scenario and Its Consequences', *Asian Medicine*, vol. 1, no. 2 (2005), pp. 335-54.
16 On the school, see esp. P. A. Lapin, *Pervaia shkola russkogo iazyka v Kitae* (Moscow: Vostochnaia literatura RAN, 2009).
17 The main academic study is presently the dissertation by Gregory Afinogenov, *The Eye of the Tsar*.

5

The Treaties of Aigun and Peking (1858–60)

By the mid-nineteenth century overland Kiakhta trade had declined, for reasons we shall go into at a later stage, and competition arose between Russia and Britain in the Far East. Catherine II had been succeeded by her son Paul (Pavel) I, born in 1754, who reigned briefly from 1796 until he was assassinated in 1801. Thereafter, with Paul's son Alexander I (1777–1825), a line of powerful and long-serving tsars began. However, when in 1805 Alexander I sent a large mission to China under Count Yuri Golovkin (1762–1846),[1] its failure added to the sense of Russian inferiority in the relationship with China, the imbalance which had manifested itself in the Kiakhta treaty. When Golovkin reached Urga (the previous name of Ulan Bator), he was informed of the ceremonial requirements for reception at the court of the Jiaqing 嘉慶 emperor (ruled 1796–1820). This made him return to Siberia, much to the displeasure of the tsar.[2]

Later in 1805, the two Russian ships Nadezhda and Neva, making the first Russian circumnavigation of the globe on behalf of the Russian-American Company (founded 1799) under the command of Ivan Krusenstern (1770–1846) and Yuri Lisianskii (1773–1837), entered the harbour of Canton. The Qing customs superintendent allowed them to trade, only to be punished for this transgression as the emperor insisted that Russians had to conduct all their business via Kiakhta.[3]

Alexander I was succeeded by his brother, who ruled as Nicholas I from 1825 until his death in 1855. During this reign Nikolai Murav'ev (1809–81), appointed in 1847 as governor-general of Eastern Siberia, developed ambitious plans to expand Russian imperial rule in the East. Murav'ev feared British occupation of the Amur, which might enable the colonial rival to penetrate farther west into Siberia. Meanwhile China was humiliated by the European powers in the Opium War from 1839 to 1842 and its inability to defend its borders was well noticed in Moscow, too. In 1849, an expedition that Gennadii Nevel'skoi (1813–76) undertook on his own initiative from Kamchatka established the navigability of the Amur as well as proved, by passing through the Strait of Tartary, that Sakhalin was an island rather than a peninsula. The 1804 report of Krusenstern, perpetuating an error made by an earlier French explorer, La Pérouse in 1787, was disproved on both points.[4]

During their navigation down the Amur, Nevel'skoi's party detected no traces of Chinese power and in his next sailing Nevel'skoi warned a group of 'Manchus' he encountered that Russia would not tolerate Qing ships on this river.[5] On 1 August 1850, near the mouth of the Amur, which he had discovered, Nevel'skoi founded an outpost that he baptized Fort Nikolaevsk, in honour of the tsar. In December Nevel'skoi was demoted for insubordination but quickly restored in rank by Nicholas I, who said on that occasion that 'where the Russian flag has been raised, it must not be lowered' (the tsar did forbid Nevel'skoi to provoke the Chinese any further). Until 1853 Russia still recognized the territory north of the Amur as Chinese.

Russia's defeat in the Crimean War against Britain, France and Turkey (1853–6) suggested, however, that the Far East was the only arena in which Russia could still expand and restore its international standing. The ongoing Taiping rebellion made plain China's weakness, while also diverting its military forces from the Manchurian borders. In 1855 Nicholas I died, leaving Russia to his son Alexander II (1818–81). Following that year, Russia expressed to the Qing its claims over the Amur and Ussuri regions; it sent three naval expeditions with Cossack settlers, meeting no opposition. In 1857 the Cossack station Albazin was founded on the place of the old fort, one among sixteen such stations which heralded Russia's return to the Amur. By this time, China had no choice but to acknowledge Russian control of the river.

The Second Opium War, also known as the 'Arrow War' of 1856 to 1858, further exposed China's inability to resist the Western powers. In Aigun, near today's Heihe, the Qing was forced into a treaty with Russia, negotiated in May 1858. Together with the subsequent Peking treaty of 1860, Russia was allowed by these diplomatic means to peacefully annex some 360,000 square miles (932,400 square km) north of the Amur and east of the Ussuri.[6] Russia exploited Chinese ignorance as to its actual strength, while posing as the mediator between China and the allied powers at the end of the Arrow War. The Treaty of Peking also provided for the opening of Russian consulates in Urga in Outer Mongolia and Kashgar in Xinjiang. By concluding this treaty, young Nikolai Ignat'ev (1832–1908) joined the triumvirate of men, who almost independently of the government in St Petersburg had reshaped the map of the Far East: the other two being Nevel'skoi and Murav'ev. For their efforts, both Ignat'ev and Murav'ev were made counts by the tsar. Murav'ev then commemorated his achievements on the Amur by adding Amurskii to his surname.[7]

The vast territory acquired by Russia in both Aigun and Peking amounted to two and a half times the size of England, as Chinese historians would later put it; or as more than the combined territory of France, England, Germany

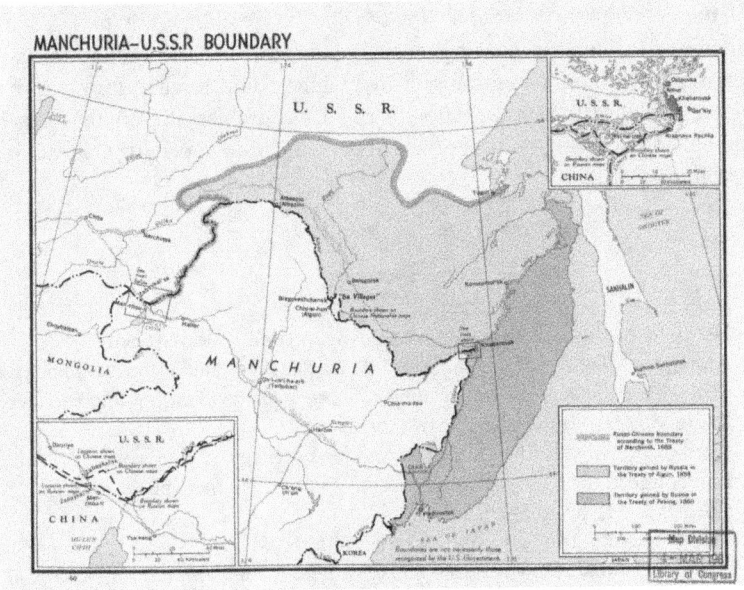

Figure 5 'Manchuria–USSR Boundary'. Map showing Russian territorial gains by the treaties of Aigun and Peking.

and Italy. It could also be described as more than the combined area of Jilin and Heilongjiang provinces. Even today, the Chinese still use the ancient Chinese names for Vladivostok (Haishenwai 海参崴) and Khabarovsk (Boli 伯力). Historical memory in China of the lands lost to tsarist Russia during the era of imperialism is comparable to Mexican awareness of the even larger territory (about half a million square miles), which that country lost to the United States at the end of their war in 1848. Neither Chinese nor Mexicans cherish real hope to recover these lands, but they are not forgotten.

A key justification for the acquisition of this region by Russia was the claim that the Qing had no real presence or control there. In 1409 the Ming dynasty had established a Nurgan Regional Military Commission in Outer Manchuria, a location corresponding to present-day Tyr near the town Nikolaevsk-on-Amur (as the fort founded by Nevel'skoi has been called since 1926). Steles in the Chinese, Mongol and Jurchen languages, commemorating the founding there of the Buddhist Yongning Temple (dedicated to the Bodhisattva Guanyin), were erected in 1413; but the Nurgan commission was abandoned in 1435.[8] The territory which a Chinese historian has intriguingly called 'the Northeastern heritage of the Ming dynasty' was still preserved in the terms of the treaty signed in Nerchinsk, but it was lost in Aigun and Peking.⁹ Archaeologists in the Russian Far East, through the late tsarist and Communist eras, discovered Chinese and Jurchen traces in the region. The latter findings were not too politically problematic, but the former ran into conflict with the state policy of denying or downplaying evidence of the Chinese past.

Notes

1. Not to be confused with the Russian envoy in 1687, Fedor Golovin.
2. Afinogenov, *The Eye of the Tsar*, pp. 275–84. See also Chen Kaike, *Jiaqing shi nian: Shibai de Eguo shituan yu shibai de Zhongguo waijiao* (Beijing: Shehui kexue wenxian chubanshe, 2014).
3. Matthew W. Mosca, 'The Qing State and Its Awareness of Eurasian Interconnections, 1789–1806', *Eighteenth-Century Studies*, vol. 47, no. 2 (Winter 2014), pp. 103–16.
4. Morris-Suzuki, 'The Telescope and the Tinderbox'.
5. G. I. Nevel'skoi, *Podvigi russkikh morskikh ofitserov na krainem vostoke Rossii* (Moscow: Drofa, 2008), pp. 168–72.
6. This is the usual estimate of Russia's territorial gains. S. C. M. Paine, *Imperial Rivals: China, Russia, and Their Disputed Frontier* (Armonk: M. E. Sharpe, 1996), pp. 28–9 (ibid., p. 105, n. 108, gives 185,000 square miles north of the Amur (in 1858) and 130,000 east of the Ussuri (in 1860), a total of 315,000).
7. An excellent account from the perspective of Russian history is Mark Bassin, *Imperial Visions: Nationalist Imagination and Geographical Expansion in the Russian Far East, 1840–1865* (Cambridge: Cambridge University Press, 1999).
8. V. Ts. Golovachev et al., *Tyrskie stely XV veka. Perevod, kommentarii, issledovanie kitaiskikh, mongol'skogo i chzhurchen'skogo tekstov* (St Petersburg: Nauka, 2011).
9. T. C. Lin, 'The Amur Frontier Question between China and Russia, 1850–1860', *Pacific Historical Review*, vol. 3, no. 1 (March 1934), p. 4. This old article is still useful for its detailed summary of the diplomatic history of Russian expansion along the Amur and Ussuri.

6

From the First Sino-Japanese War to the Russo-Japanese War in Manchuria

In early 1870 the Qing diplomats Zhigang 志剛 and Sun Jiagu 孫家谷 visited St Petersburg together with the former American minister in China Anson Burlingame, who died during this visit. The delegation was received at court and met with members of the imperial family. Its arrival in Russia was part of a grand tour of the United States and Europe, in which China's representatives campaigned for equal treatment of their country in international relations.[1] But in summer 1871, following the spread of the large Muslim rebellion against the Qing of Yakub Beg in Xinjiang (which had begun in 1862) to neighbouring Mongolia, the governor-general of Russian Turkestan, Konstantin von Kaufman, decided to occupy the rich and fertile Yili valley. An area of 1,200 square miles or 3,100 square km, Yili included the important town of Kulja, now Yining 伊寧 in North-west Xinjiang, in the Tianshan mountains. Russian Turkestan (like Manchuria, a vanished toponym) comprised Kazakhstan, Turkmenistan, Uzbekistan, Tadzhikistan and Kirgizstan – all territories acquired by Russia from the 1850s to the 1870s. Chinese Turkestan refers to Xinjiang, which means 'the New Frontier'.

By 1878 all of Xinjiang with the exception of Yili had been reconquered from the rebels by the Qing general Zuo Zongtang 左宗棠 (1812–85). In the treaty of Livadia, signed in 1879 at the Black Sea resort where the tsar was then on vacation, Russia tricked a naive Chinese envoy into allowing her to keep most of the Yili area while obtaining extensive trade rights in China, navigation of the Sungari and an indemnity from China. This could have been a repetition of the Aigun scenario twenty years earlier, but now it aroused uproar in China and war with Russia almost broke out in 1880. However, thanks to a growing understanding of international law and awareness of the limits of Russian power after a costly war with Turkey (1877–8), in February 1881 China was able to replace the terms of Livadia with the Treaty of St Petersburg, which ensured the return of Yili. This treaty was signed by China's first minister to Russia Zeng Jize 曾紀澤 (1839–90; served 1880–6) shortly before Alexander II was assassinated in March and his son Alexander III (1845–94) ascended to the throne. The Sino-Russian western frontier was gradually demarcated thereafter, the Qing side aiming to forestall further Russian incursion. Formally ruled by local leaders reporting to the court in Peking, in 1884 Xinjiang was incorporated as a province into the Chinese Empire in a step designed to fend off Russian encroachment. The same concerns, and realization that tribute relations were no longer a safe barrier from Russian intrusion, led the Qing to attempt formal annexation of Mongolia.

In Manchuria, crucial events took place in the 1890s. War between China and Japan over domination of Korea erupted in August 1894.[2] The Japanese had invaded Korea long before, in the 1590s, but they were driven out by Ming China. In 1868 Japan launched the epochal reform, which became associated with the name of the Meiji emperor; Japanese ambition to dominate the less modernized countries of East Asia grew in the following decades. In 1884 the Qing still succeeded in repelling the Japanese from Korea and reliance on Chinese protection helped the Choson dynasty to last longer than any other in Asia, from 1392 to 1910. However, in 1894 Japan captured Pyongyang, forcing the Chinese military out; then, in the battle of the Yalu, it destroyed the Chinese navy. When the Japanese occupied Port Arthur (Chinese: Lüshunkou 旅順口) on 21 November 1894, tens of thousands of Chinese civilians (only thirty-six persons survived) were massacred over a four-day period in retaliation for the killing of Japanese soldiers before the evacuation of the Qing army.[3] The northern Beiyang fleet associated with the powerful minister Li Hongzhang 李鴻章 (1823–1901) faced the enemy alone, as the southern (Nanyang) fleet, based in Fuzhou 福州, stayed out of the war.

China's defeat led to the Treaty of Shimonoseki in April 1895: in addition to the island of Taiwan (which had only become a province of China in 1885), this ceded to Japan the Liaodong peninsula and control over Port Arthur. However, somewhat similarly to the actions taken by the European powers against Russia in the Congress of Berlin at the end of the Russo-Turkish war in 1878, Russian pressure on Japan in a coalition with France and Germany, known as 'the triple intervention', brought about the return of Liaodong to China within two weeks of the Shimonoseki treaty. The Russian fleet in Vladivostok had made visible preparations to enforce this demand. In return for evacuating Liaodong, Japan was given larger reparations. Russia obviously harboured its own designs on Manchuria.

The importance of the war was manifold. It signalled a dramatic change of the balance of power in East Asia, with Japan's rise to the role of the first modern Asian power (as will be demonstrated by its alliance with Britain in 1902); a humiliation for China which, coming from an Asian neighbour, was perceived differently than previous defeats by Western powers. The repercussions would include rising Chinese animosity towards Japan, the Russo-Japanese war (1904–5) and the Japanese annexation of Korea (1910–45). The implications for Manchuria were a stimulus for Russia to extend its railway through this territory to prevent Manchuria from falling under Japanese influence. The war also ended the period of treaty-port diplomacy and ushered in the 'scramble for concessions': Germany occupied Jiaozhou Bay (胶州湾) on the south coast of Shandong in mid-November 1897, and the following year it began to build the port town of Qingdao 青岛 there; Britain took Weihaiwei 威海衛 port (now Weihai, on the northern coast of Shandong), previously a Japanese base, in 1898.[4]

Russia began constructing the Chinese Eastern Railway in August 1897. According to Chinese records, in January 1898 Russian forces violently evicted the Chinese population from Liaodong peninsula.[5] In March a large bribe, delivered by the Russian Finance Ministry to the Qing ministers Li Hongzhang and Zhang Yinhuan 張蔭桓 (1837–1900), facilitated China's agreement to lease Lüshunkou and nearby Dalianwan to Russia for twenty-five years.[6] In the early summer of 1898 the foundations of Harbin were laid: as we shall see, this Russian-built city in China became key to Russia's enterprise in Manchuria. The tsar declared the port of Dal'nii (meaning Distant) open for trade on 30 July 1899, after its original inhabitants had been evicted with compensation paid. The summer of 1900 saw the Boxer uprising spill into the Northeast, triggering Russian military occupation of Manchuria. The scheduled evacuation of Russian forces from the three eastern provinces was still incomplete by the time the Japanese fleet attacked Port Arthur in February 1904.

Interlude: The Boxers

The Boxers were so called because of the martial arts they practised. An anti-foreign mass movement, which by then was supported by the Qing court, in June 1900 they besieged the legations quarter in Peking. By mid-August, however, they were defeated by the allied troops of eight powers. The victors imposed a huge indemnity on China in December 1900 and their troops did not leave Peking until the following September. The uprising, which had first erupted in Shandong, also reached Manchuria: in summer 1900 Blagoveshchensk, capital of the Amur District, was shelled by Chinese fire from a village near Aigun on the opposite bank of the Amur.

When in 1858 Russia and China signed the Treaty of Aigun, Nikolai Murav'ev announced the Glad Tidings (*blagie vesti*) of Russia's immense territorial acquisitions. The Russian military post Ust'-Zeisk, founded in 1854 opposite the Manchu garrison of Aigun, was accordingly renamed Blagoveshchensk. The original Chinese name of the town, Hailanpao 海蘭泡, still appears in brackets in Chinese atlases, which do not fully acknowledge the toponymic innovations of 1858.

In July 1900 the Chinese population of Blagoveshchensk was rounded up and ordered to swim to the Chinese shore of the Amur. Between two to four thousand people died in this notorious incident. More Chinese were killed in villages around Blagoveshchensk. A settlement of Manchu and Han peasants collectively known as 'the sixty-four villages', whose safety on the Russian side of the border had been guaranteed by the Treaty of Aigun, was wiped out. Russian civilian losses in Manchuria during the summer of 1900 were far smaller in comparison.[7]

Over 100,000 Russian troops were brought into Manchuria to protect the Chinese Eastern Railway from the Boxers, as well as to exclude other powers from a region perceived as a Russian sphere of influence. By November 1900 Manchuria was under Russian military control. Conveniently, Russia's potential imperialist rival was then preoccupied in the Boer War (1899–1902);[8] partly in reaction to the Russian advance in Manchuria, however, Britain was to conclude an unprecedented alliance with Japan in 1902.

The treaty that ended the Boxer uprising was signed in Beijing in September 1901, imposing on the Qing an indemnity of 450,000,000 taels (one for each Chinese subject, the equivalent of £67.5 million) to be paid within thirty-nine years until 1940. The highest amounts were due to Russia, then to Germany, France, Britain, Japan, USA etc. From February 1901 Russia attempted to force China to accept its de facto control of Manchuria and in addition to grant it the right to build a new railway from Manchuria to Peking. But the Qing procrastinated, hoping that the powers would not permit Russia to realize its plans. This is indeed what happened.[9] In April 1902 Russia finally promised to withdraw from Manchuria in three stages (first to evacuate from Liaoning, then from Jilin and Heilongjiang) by October 1903, although it also presented numerous demands to the Chinese side.

Claims have been made that the Russian occupation of Manchuria brought about many civilian casualties and induced famine in Heilongjiang. Similarly to the issue of the Chinese casualties of the Russo-Japanese war, soon to be discussed, this subject has not yet been well researched and certainly merits further inquiry. Along with its reluctance to evacuate Manchuria, Russia aroused Japanese suspicion by its activity at the mouth of the Yalu River in Korea. Meanwhile, a number of moderate ministers in the tsarist government had been replaced by militants.

The Russo-Japanese War

From the mid-1890s to the outbreak of the war, alarmed by apparent Russian expansion into Korea and Manchuria, Japan made offers to Russia to delimit their spheres of influence in both regions.¹⁰ On 8 February 1904, Admiral Togo unexpectedly attacked the Russian fleet in Port Arthur (as Japan would do in Pearl Harbor in 1941), declaring war only two days later. The success of this operation was limited and it even failed to convince the Russians that Japan was indeed starting a war. But on 13 April bombs planted by the Japanese succeeded in sinking the warship Petropavlovsk. Admiral Stepan Makarov, the commander of the Russian fleet, who had defended Port Arthur since Togo's attack, was on board and went down with his crew.

Japanese forces stationed in Korea crossed the Yalu (the river separating Korea from Manchuria) into Liaodong peninsula by the end of April. Their first victory was achieved on the Yalu in early May, the first ground battle in the modern era in which an Asian nation defeated a Western power. On 26 May the Russians were forced to evacuate Dal'nii (later Dairen/Dalian), never to return. A battle involving 300,000 soldiers near the city of Liaoyang in late August was inconclusive but led to the retreat to Mukden of Aleksei Kuropatkin (1848–1925), supreme commander of the Russian land and naval forces in the East Asia.

The next confrontation took place in Shahe 沙河, 15 km south of Mukden, in October 1904; the Russian failure on this occasion resulted in the recall of Admiral Evgenii Alekseev (1843–1917), the tsar's viceroy for the Far East. The large-scale battle of Mukden, lasting three weeks from 19 February to 10 March 1905, with 600,000 soldiers involved, ended with Russian defeat and Kuropatkin's resignation. After a siege was imposed on Port Arthur in July 1904, it finally surrendered to the Japanese admiral Nogi Maresuke (1849–1912) at the cost of many lives on 2 January 1905. Nogi lost thousands of his soldiers to achieve his goal, including his two sons. He was the Japanese commander who first captured Port Arthur in 1894 (created baron thereafter, he was elevated to the rank of count after 1905). An icon of Japanese patriotism, he committed ritual suicide (*seppuku*) together with his wife after the death of Emperor Meiji in 1912.

The Trans-Siberian Railway, begun in 1891, was still unfinished in the stretch connecting Manchuria with the Transbaikal Province when the war with Japan broke out, so it could not ensure the efficient transfer of Russian troops: instead, Lake Baikal had to be crossed on the ice in winter, or on ferries in other seasons. The Russian Baltic fleet, with forty-two ships and a crew of 12,000 men, embarked from the port of Liepāja (German: Libau) in today's Latvia in October 1904. On its long route, it created an incident near the eastern British coast by firing at fishing boats, mistaken for Japanese.¹¹ The larger part of the fleet circumnavigated the Cape of Good Hope, while the other took the shorter route via the Suez Canal. Arriving at Tsushima Straits between Korea and Japan only in the following May, after a long wait in Madagascar for other ships that had left Russia in February, the now united Baltic fleet was destroyed there by a Japanese attack. About five thousand Russians died in Tsushima; over six thousand, including the commander of the fleet, Admiral Zinovii Rozhestvensky (1848–1909), became POWs in Japan. The name Tsushima became etched in the Russian memory as the tragic symbol of the Russo-Japanese War. Indeed, Tsushima is considered the most important naval battle since Trafalgar, Admiral Nelson's defeat of the Franco-Spanish fleet in October 1805 (exactly a century earlier). Togo (1848–1934) was an admirer of Nelson.

In the meantime, a revolution began in Russia, peaking with the so-called Bloody Sunday in St Petersburg on 22 January 1905, less than three weeks after the fall of Port Arthur: the police fired at a procession of workers carrying a petition to the tsar with the request for free elections, leaving 150 dead and many more injured. While both Russia and Japan were exhausted by the war, the tsar was not easily convinced to acknowledge defeat and had to be reminded of his weakness by a final Japanese attack and invasion of Sakhalin in July. The peace treaty was signed with the mediation of President Theodore Roosevelt in Portsmouth, New Hampshire, on 5 September 1905. In recognition of his role, Roosevelt (1858–1919; US president from 1901 to 1909)[12] was awarded the Nobel Peace Prize in 1906. The Russian delegate Sergei Witte (1849–1915), who before being unseated as Minister of Finance in 1903 had promoted Russia's entry into Manchuria, was rewarded with the count title by Tsar Nicholas.

Russia lost all of South Manchuria and the stretch of the railway from Port Arthur to Changchun 長春. Japan, in addition to regaining the territory it had originally won in the war of 1894–5 (but had then been forced to cede) in Manchuria, also obtained the southern half of Sakhalin and a free hand in Korea. Sakhalin was first occupied by Russia in 1853. After long negotiations with Japan, it was confirmed as Russian territory in 1875 (the Kuril archipelago, fifty-six islands between Kamchatka and Hokkaido, was passed to Japan in exchange). From 1905 to 1945, the southern part of Sakhalin was held by Japan; at the end of World War Two, it lost the whole island to the Soviet Union, along with the Kurils, which are still disputed by Russia and Japan today. Thanks to Witte's negotiating skills, Russia avoided paying reparations and the peace treaty was internationally seen as a Russian success. It also freed the regime's hand to deal with 'the enemy within', although, following a long general strike, the tsar was still forced to sign the October manifesto, by which some powers were granted to the Duma, a newly created parliament. In Japan, popular anger at the perceived unfairness of the treaty led to huge-scale demonstrations and riots.

Wartime damages to Manchuria and the missing Chinese perspective

China announced its neutrality in the war on 12 February 1904 (two days after Japan had declared war on Russia). In the course of 1903, the Qing, like Japan, had tried to hasten Russian evacuation of Manchuria. If the Chinese did support one of the belligerents, it was Japan rather than Russia. In the alien territory, where it had to wage war, the Russian command was initially above hiring Chinese as spies, but eventually it was forced to do so by the war's circumstances. As Chinese and Japanese often looked the same to them, one way the Russians devised to distinguish the neutral Chinese from the enemy was to pull the 'pigtail', the Chinese queue: if it came off, it had obviously been glued on and its bearer was Japanese.

Both sides executed Chinese they suspected of spying against them; one such execution conducted by the Japanese army was described in a famous introduction to the first story collection by modern China's leading writer Lu Xun 魯迅 (1881–1936), *Call to Arms*, published in 1923.[13] Both armies also violated Chinese neutrality in various ways, including entering territory which was supposed to remain outside of the conflict. The Chinese involved in espionage for the Japanese typically came from among the Manchurian bandits popularly known as *hong huzi* 紅胡子 (to whom we shall return).[14] Thousands of Chinese may have worked for Japan in the war, most of them as coolies rather than spies. Chinese merchants and villagers also sold supplies to both parties.

Figure 6 'Chinese Camp Peddlers', stereoview card, from 'Stereoviews of the Siege of Port Arthur', 1905, by T. W. Ingersoll (1862–1922). Lafayette College, East Asia Image Collection.

Most of the warfare was conducted in southern Manchuria. From March 1898 to January 1905, Russia was the dominant power in Guandong 關東, the southern part of Liaodong peninsula. During the war, Chinese villages were transformed into Russia army bases and their inhabitants had to evacuate them. Because of the deteriorating situation at the front, the Russians frequently had to move on from one village to the next. Houses were dismantled and used for fire. Livestock and all produce were used to feed the soldiers. Normally compensation was paid, but this did not solve the problem of forced relocation. Over 20,000 Chinese lives were lost because of the war, in one frequently cited estimate. But, as research has focused on the Russo-Japanese conflict and the international diplomacy surrounding it, little is known about the experience of ordinary Chinese who had found themselves at the crossfire.[15] In the cities and towns of Manchuria, at the time, missionaries assisted 'great numbers of peasants, expelled from their homes by the operations of the rival armies'.[16] In Shanghai, the famous educator Cai Yuanpei 蔡元培 (1868–1948) launched newspapers like *Eshi jingwen* (*Alarming News on Russian Actions*) in late 1903 and *Jingzhong ribao* (*Alarming Bell News*) in 1904, spreading nationalist indignation against Russian occupation of Manchuria while satirizing the 'neutral' stand of the Chinese government in the Russo-Japanese War.[17]

Notes

1. Jenny Huangfu Day, *Qing Travelers to the Far West: Diplomacy and the Information Order in Late Imperial China* (Cambridge: Cambridge University Press, 2018), ch. 2. On this, and other visits by Qing diplomats to St Petersburg up to 1910, see more in Samoilov, *Rossiia i Kitai*.
2. See S. C. M. Paine, *The Sino-Japanese War of 1894–1895: Perception, Power, and Primacy* (Cambridge: Cambridge University Press, 2003).
3. Benjamin A. Elman, 'Optical and Cognitive Illusions: The MIT Visualizing Cultures Controversy in Spring 2006', *Positions: East Asia Cultures Critique*, vol. 23, no. 1 (Feb. 2015), pp. 16, 21, mentions newspaper reports on the Port Arthur massacre, concluding that the event 'deserved more attention'.
4. See Robert Bickers, *The Scramble for China: Strangers in the Middle Kingdom, 1832–1914* (London: Allen Lane, 2011).
5. Paine, *Imperial Rivals*, p. 191.
6. The secret correspondence about this was published by the Bolsheviks: 'Perepiska o podkupe kitaiskikh sanovnikov Li-Khun-chzhana i Chzhan-in-Khuana', *Krasnyi arkhiv*, vol. 2 (1922), pp. 287–93. Zhang Yinhuan was soon demoted and exiled.
7. See Gamsa, *Harbin, City between Russia and China*, ch. 1.

8 Uprising against the British by the descendants of Dutch settlers in South Africa. The Boers lost the war, but received self-government in 1907. South Africa became independent in 1961.
9 Cf. Hsü, *The Rise of Modern China*, pp. 401–4.
10 See esp. John W. Steinberg et al., eds, *The Russo-Japanese War in Global Perspective: World War Zero*, in 2 vols (Leiden: Brill, 2005–7); Rotem Kowner, *Historical Dictionary of the Russo-Japanese War*, 2nd rev. and enlarged edn (Lanham: Rowman & Littlefield, 2017).
11 See Constantine Pleshakov, *The Tsar's Last Armada: The Epic Journey to the Battle of Tsushima* (New York: Basic Books, 2002); and cf. Nicholas Papastratigakis, *Russian Imperialism and Naval Power: Military Strategy and the Build-up to the Russo-Japanese War* (London: I. B. Tauris, 2011), ch. 8.
12 Distinguish Theodore Roosevelt from his distant cousin, Franklin D. Roosevelt (1882–1945), who was president between 1932 and 1945.
13 See Lu Xun, trans. Julia Lovell, *The Real Story of Ah-Q and Other Tales of China: The Complete Fiction of Lu Xun* (London: Penguin Books, 2009), pp. 16–17.
14 See Evgeny Sergeev, *Russian Military Intelligence in the War with Japan, 1904–05: Secret Operations on Land and at Sea* (London and New York: Routledge, 2007).
15 Paine, *Imperial Rivals*, p. 245. See also ch. 20, 'Suffering of the Innocent', in Dugald Christie, *Thirty Years in Moukden, 1883–1913* (London: Constable, 1914). Gotelind Müller-Saini, 'Chinesische Perspektiven auf den Russisch-Japanischen Krieg', in Maik Hendrik Sprotte et al., eds, *Der Russisch-Japanische Krieg 1904/05: Anbruch einer neuen Zeit?* (Wiesbaden: Harrassowitz, 2007), pp. 203–39, purports to fill in the lacking Chinese perspective, but instead generalizes about alleged changes in Chinese political opinion based on a sampling of articles and cartoons in the press, most of which were borrowed from Japanese sources and reflected a pro-Japanese position. One of these cartoons, dated 23 Feb. 1904, refers to the shelling by Russian fire of '20,000' Chinese residents in Yingkou. Not much more research is available in Chinese: a brief article such as Peng Fa, 'Shilun Ri-E zhanzheng shiqi Zhongguo putong minzhong de xintai' (Tentative Discussion of the Attitude of the Chinese Masses during the Japan–Russia War), *Lanzhou xuekan*, no. 1 (2007), pp. 187–9, only celebrates the greatness of the Chinese nation in the face of adversity.
16 Daniel T. Robertson, *The Story of Our Mission: Manchuria* (Edinburgh: United Free Church of Scotland, 1913), p. 126, says that 5,000 refugees were lodged by the missionaries in Mukden alone, while 'in Liaoyang and Kaiyuan similar work was carried on'.
17 Rudolf G. Wagner, 'China "Asleep" and "Awakening." A Study in Conceptualizing Asymmetry and Coping with It', *Transcultural Studies*, no. 1 (2011), pp. 4–139, at pp. 24, 29, 98–9.

7

The Chinese Eastern Railway

There seems, at first sight, to have been little ideology tied to the Russian expansion into Manchuria – perhaps because its long-term strategy was never formulated. This absence contrasts with the ideologies of other colonial powers. The American geopolitical vision was based on the 'manifest destiny' of the United States to move westward in pursuit of its frontier; America was thus a country 'colonizing itself'. The idea of 'manifest destiny' was taken a step further in the 'frontier thesis' of historian Frederick Jackson Turner (1861–1932). British imperialist ideology relied on the notion of spreading civilization, 'the white man's burden', as most famously articulated by writer Rudyard Kipling (1865–1936); similarly, French imperialists had their *mission civilisatrice* and the Germans, too, saw themselves as culture bearers, *Kulturträger*.

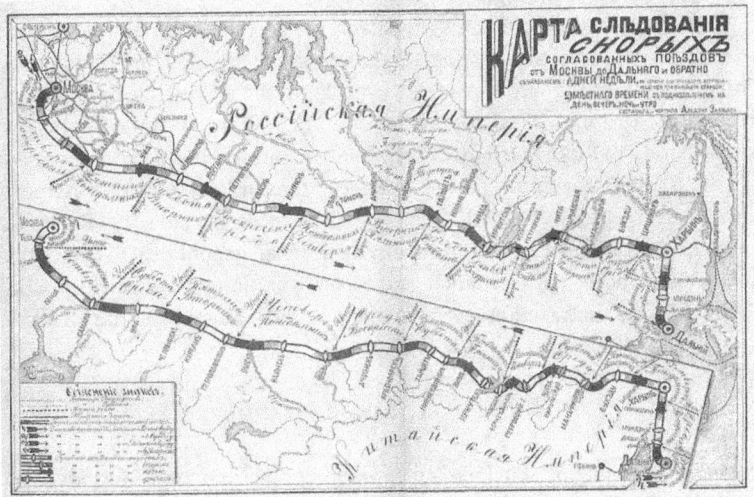

Figure 7 The Trans-Siberian Railway. Russian map (by Al'dona Zabello), showing the journey from Moscow to Harbin and Dal'nii. 1903.

One basic question, on which opinion in Russia itself was divided, was: should Russia expand into China at all before it had made the most of its recent acquisitions in the Far East? Alexander II had sold Alaska, Russia's isolated colony, to the United States in 1867, the better to concentrate resources on the newly acquired Amur and Maritime regions. The Trans-Siberian Railway, too, was designed to advance the integration of Siberia and the Russian Far East in the tsarist empire. Construction of the Ussuri Railway had begun in 1893, yet many voices opposed the extension of the railway into Manchuria by the late 1890s, considering this a digression from the original goal. The project of the Trans-Siberian Railway was only completed in October 1916, when the Amur Railway, begun in 1907, connected the town of Sretensk in the Transbaikal Province with Khabarovsk by passing entirely through Russian territory north of the Amur River.[1]

A prime mover in this expansion or diversion of the railway line was the Minister of Finance between 1892 and 1903, Sergei Witte. Because he promoted a policy of peaceful economic penetration, he opposed the Russian military invasion of Manchuria in 1900. The huge investments in Manchuria, made by the Ministry of Finance under Witte, drew much criticism for neglecting the Russian Far East.[2] As 'peaceful' expansion did not bring the desired dividends, however, by summer 1903 Witte was ready to annex Manchuria to Russia so as to prevent foreign powers from competing with the Russians there. This shift in policy did not prevent him losing his ministerial position in August.[3]

On the ground, Chinese migrant workers in the Amur and Maritime provinces met with the hostility of parts of the Russian population. As Chinese labour migration reached a peak in the 1890s, local publicists frequently trumpeted xenophobic opinion. There was an obvious contradiction in Russia's reliance on Chinese manpower in a project designed to strengthen Russian power and influence in the Far East (outside observers were also surprised by the willingness of Chinese workers to assist Russia in the colonization of their own country). One Russian geopolitical vision of the early 1900s conceptualized Manchuria and parts of Mongolia as 'Zheltorossiia', a Yellow Russia that would serve as a buffer between Russia and the Orient.

Russian–Chinese Harbin

Now the capital of Heilongjiang province, Harbin was founded as headquarters for the construction of the Trans-Manchurian (Chinese Eastern) Railway by tsarist Russia in 1898. Following the October Revolution, this colonial city became a refugee centre. From then to the end of the 1940s, it housed the largest Russian community ever to exist in East Asia. After a period of direct Russian administration until 1917, Harbin came under the authority of north-eastern warlord regimes, was then occupied by Japan and was held for a year by the Red Army (1945–6), before finally passing to Chinese Communist rule.[4]

The first official census of Harbin in February 1913 still indicated 43,691 Russians and 23,639 Chinese (the total of 68,549 residents meant that other nationalities were only negligibly represented), but by 1916 the figures had already changed to 45,481 Chinese, 34,115 Russians and about 2,000 Japanese (the total Harbin population, probably including Fujiadian, stood at 81,602).[5] The Chinese majority in Harbin was maintained ever since, while Fujiadian 傅家甸, Harbin's satellite town of Chinese workers also known as Daowai 道外, 'beyond the [railway] track', became a de facto part of the city long before being formally integrated into 'Great Harbin' under Japanese rule. The tens of thousands of refugees from the Russian Revolution, who arrived in Harbin between 1918 and the mid-1920s, prolonged Harbin's existence as 'a Russian city in China' (as its Russian residents perceived this, though the Chinese were in the majority) while also swelling unemployment and crime.

The introduction of railways in China, initially as a foreign initiative and under foreign ownership, redefined the importance of towns and cities, brought commerce to previously remote spots and eventually transformed towns situated at railway junctures into provincial capitals.[6] Besides Harbin, examples of this process are Shijiazhuang 石家莊, formerly a 'village of the Shi family', which became the capital of Hebei province, and Changchun, the juncture of the CER and South Manchuria Railway (SMR), which became capital of Manchukuo and then of Jilin province.[7] Hankou 漢口, now part of Wuhan 武漢, the capital of Hubei 湖北 province at the confluence of the Yangtze River and its largest tributary the Han (Hanjiang 漢江), emerged to importance by being both a trade port with several foreign concessions and a railway terminus of the Peking–Hankou railway line, which a Belgian firm completed in 1905. This was a common effect of railways worldwide, but in China and elsewhere in Asia they were also a tool in the colonial enterprise known as 'railway imperialism'. At the same time, railways were harbingers of modernity: in the republican period, Wuhan considered itself the most modern inner Chinese city. Crossing borders, railways were also vehicles of internationalism.[8]

Harbin is rare in China in being a new city built by a foreign power. Other such cases were Dalian, first developed by the Russians from 1899 to 1905 and by the Japanese from then until 1945, and Qingdao, founded by Germany; another example of grand city-building in Asia during the age of imperialism is New Delhi, built by the British between 1912 and 1931.

Figure 7a Kitaiskaia ulitsa (Chinese Street; now Zhongyang dajie), Harbin's main avenue. Hotel Moderne can be seen on the right. Undated postcard. Courtesy of Olga Bakich.

Moreover, all of Harbin's inhabitants were newcomers: contrary to the common situation, in which colonial regimes faced an indigenous population, the Russians who came to Harbin found themselves sharing the emerging town with Chinese migrants from Shandong and Hebei. Some of these did not settle in Harbin itself, but in the neighbouring town of Fujiadian (officially called Binjiang 濱江). While the name Harbin probably comes from Manchu, none of the Han Chinese peasants whom the Russians met on the spot in 1898 could explain its meaning or origin. As a result, the Russians thought the place name was Chinese, and vice versa.[9]

This is only one illustration of the abyss in communication between the speakers of Russian and Chinese in Harbin. As a partial solution to the problem, they relied on the Russian–Chinese pidgin known as *moia-tvoia*, which was brought to Harbin from the Russian Far East. Also, many Chinese and Russian words entered the vocabulary of both sides. A few of these may still be heard in Harbin today: for example, *subotang* 蘇波湯 (from the Russian *sup*) for a Russian-style soup and *baza'er* 八雜兒, literally 'eight mixed', for bazaar.[10]

There was an obvious linguistic imbalance in Harbin, as Russians did not need to know more than a few basic Chinese words to supplement pidgin in their daily shopping, while for the Chinese knowing Russian was essential to make any progress in the city. The imbalance was reflected in the education system: in Harbin Russian schools, Chinese was taught very inadequately until the Chinese authorities made it compulsory, as late as 1929. A first Chinese guidebook for Harbin, published in the same year, commented that the city institutions and especially the Chinese Eastern Railway still largely continued to work in Russian; hence anybody planning to settle in this city should count on learning Russian to guarantee his future.[11] Contrary to the linguistic policies pursued by British and French imperialists, little effort was made to teach Chinese children Russian. However, affluent Chinese parents in Harbin hired private Russian teachers for their children, and there was much demand among the Chinese for study in the Harbin Polytechnic (founded in 1920, this is now the Harbin Institute of Technology) and the Law Faculty (founded in the same year), where studies were conducted in Russian.

The situation was different along the many stations that made up the CER route between Manzhouli 滿州里 in the west and Suifenhe 綏芬河 in the east. The far smaller proportion of Russians among the local population forced them to interact more with the Han Chinese and other Asian ethnicities in these locations. Still, one might reasonably have expected Harbin to become a centre of Russian sinology, since a number of sinologists arrived there following the Russo-Japanese War, establishing a Society of Russian Orientalists (1908–27), which published its own journal, and a Society for the Study of the Manchurian Region (1922–8). The Institute of Oriental and Commercial Studies, founded in Harbin in 1925, did train a number of young people in Chinese language and culture. However, these sinologists had rather little contact with the Chinese population. Hardly any Chinese literature was translated into Russian in Harbin, or for that matter Russian literature into Chinese.

Most Russians in Manchuria were determined to live in China as if they were still in Russia, and the self-sufficient society they created in Harbin allowed them to maintain this attitude for a long time. The attitude of the Chinese to the Russian presence may be described as pragmatic: most attempted to make the best of it economically while it lasted and did not mourn its eventual disappearance. Chinese travellers arriving in Harbin on their way to Europe were impressed by its architecture and tended to emphasize the city's exotic character. The Russians faced little nationalist enmity – less so than in Shanghai – beyond the general disdain of Chinese towards foreigners.

The period of Harbin as a mixed city has left other legacies. More than anywhere else in China, people in Harbin today eat bread, especially the local specialty: the large loafs called *lieba* 列巴, after the Russian word for bread, *khleb*. They also consume sausages and ice cream; and while all of China cracks melon seeds, in the Northeast the same cracking technique is applied to sunflower seeds, an old Russian favourite.[12] Beer and Russian kvass are popular beverages, marketed as special local products: the brand Harbin Beer (哈爾濱啤酒, or Hapi in short) is advertised 'since 1900' and 'the oldest beer brewed in China', while a plastic can of *gewasi* 格瓦斯 (kvass) is decorated by the picture of a Russian church.

In daily life much of the intercourse between the two communities did revolve around food, of which Chinese were the purveyors. The peaceful coexistence of Russians and Chinese in Harbin worked well as long as relations between them were mainly limited to the economic realm and few direct inroads were made by either side into the other's way of life. However, the epidemics of pneumonic plague in 1910–11 (which left from 42,000 to 60,000 dead in Manchuria; including about 8,000 in Fujiadian and 1,500 in Harbin) and 1920–1 (9,300 dead in Manchuria; 3,125 in Harbin and Fujiadian) were episodes in which both sides' fundamental differences and negative images of each other were revealed. For the Russians, the Chinese were the natural source of infection during epidemics, while the Chinese feared Russian doctors no less than the unknown disease.[13]

The Russian population of Harbin began leaving it, both for the Soviet Union and for Shanghai, after the Japanese invasion in 1932 and the sale of the Chinese Eastern Railway to Manchukuo in 1935. After the establishment of the Communist regime in 1949, the remaining foreigners departed or were forced out of Harbin, so that by the late 1950s it had become an almost entirely Chinese city, albeit with lingering memories of the Russian and Japanese presence. We shall revisit Harbin in the chapter on Heilongjiang, below.

Notes

1. See Chia Yin Hsu, 'A Tale of Two Railroads: "Yellow Labor", Agrarian Colonization, and the Making of Russianness at the Far Eastern Frontier, 1890s–1910', *Ab Imperio*, no. 3 (2006), pp. 217–53.
2. This is echoed in Igor V. Lukoianov, 'Russian Imperialism in the Far East at the Turn of the Twentieth Century: The Collapse of S. Iu. Vitte's Program of Economic Expansion', in Kimitaka Matsuzato, ed., *Imperiology: From Empirical Knowledge to Discussing the Russian Empire* (Sapporo: Slavic Research Center, Hokkaido University, 2007), pp. 225–44.
3. Ibid., pp. 243–4.

4 On the history of Russian–Chinese relations in Harbin, see my *Harbin, City between Russia and China*.
5 Chong-Sik Lee, *Revolutionary Struggle in Manchuria: Chinese Communism and Soviet Interest, 1922–1945* (Berkeley and Los Angeles: University of California Press, 1983), p. 27. All demographic data should be regarded with circumspection. While Chinese migration into Harbin constantly increased, the decline in the Russian population between 1913 and 1916 may be traced back to the mobilization of World War One.
6 See now Elisabeth Köll, *Railroads and the Transformation of China* (Cambridge MA: Harvard University Press, 2019).
7 David D. Buck, 'Railway City and National Capital: Two Faces of the Modern in Changchun', in Joseph W. Esherick, ed., *Remaking the Chinese City: Modernity and National Identity, 1900–1950* (Honolulu: University of Hawaii Press, 2000), pp. 65–89.
8 Kate McDonald, 'Asymmetrical Integration: Lessons from a Railway Empire', *Technology and Culture*, vol. 56, no. 1 (Jan. 2015), pp. 115–49.
9 Gamsa, *Harbin, City between Russia and China*, ch. 3.
10 Other such words are *bulaji* (plat'e, a dress), *weideluo* (vedro, bucket), *gelan* (kran, tap), *balizi* (politsiia, police). See more in Olga Bakich, 'Did You Speak Harbin Sino-Russian?', *Itinerario*, vol. 35, no. 3 (Dec. 2011), pp. 23–36.
11 Liaozuo sanren (Liu Jingyan), *Binjiang chenxiao lu* (Beijing: Zhongguo qingnian chubanshe, 2012), pp. 167–8.
12 See 'cracking seeds', one of the images in the photo-essay by Cyrus Chen, 'Manchuria in Dongbei', *Cross-Currents*, no. 11 (June 2014).
13 Mark Gamsa, 'The Epidemic of Pneumonic Plague in Manchuria 1910–1911', *Past and Present*, no. 190 (Feb. 2006), pp. 147–83.

8

The Japanese Sphere of Influence and the South Manchuria Railway

The common conception about the Japanese occupation of China is that it began with the Mukden Incident on 18 September 1931 and the establishment of Manchukuo in the following spring; this then led to the invasion of China in 1937. However, the southern part of Liaodong peninsula, where Japan replaced Russia in controlling the Kwantung (Guandong) Leased Territory, was under continuous Japanese administration from 1905 to 1945. What happened in 1931 was therefore the culmination of a process, begun with the Japanese victory in 1905. In contrast to the 'total empire' of the Manchukuo era, this period is known as the 'Japanese informal empire' in China. We shall focus on it here before looking closely at the Manchukuo period in chapter 11.

The outcome of the Russo-Japanese War in Manchuria was surprising: in July 1907, Russia and Japan already reached an agreement on the demarcation of spheres of influence in China. This was confirmed in July 1910 and renegotiated in 1915.[1] As part of the rapprochement between the two countries, in October 1907 Japan dedicated a military cemetery and a monument to the fallen Russian soldiers in Port Arthur. The memory of the sacrifice that the war had required from the Japanese nation stimulated Japan's colonization of southern Manchuria. At the same time, the army pursued plans to use the South Manchuria Railway as a Trojan Horse in preparation for a future confrontation with Russia over northern Manchuria.[2] After World War One, Japanese ideologues also began to see Manchuria in terms of *Lebensraum* for their country.

South Manchuria was the laboratory of Japanese imperialism. This does not mean that the actual invasion in September 1931 was planned for that specific moment. Rather, it was the unexpected result of a long build-up, which had been challenged by the growth of Chinese nationalism. In November 1906 the SMR Company (Mantetsu, in Japanese) was founded, with a head office in Tokyo, officially to manage the railway taken over from Russia, but in fact to assist in the eventual colonization of Manchuria while using the railway as its main instrument. It is often regarded as 'the largest Japanese company in history',[3] while a global historian has called the SMR

Figure 8 South Manchuria Railway: Most Important Link between the Far East and Europe. Japanese lithographic print, dated between 1907 and 1919. University of Southern California Digital Library.

'the most lucrative railroad colony in history'.[4] The first SMR president from 1906 to 1908, Gotō Shinpei (1857–1929), had been educated in Germany, obtaining a doctorate from Munich University in 1891. Before his posting to Manchuria he was an administrator and then civil governor in Japanese-controlled Taiwan. He became the leader of the drive characterized by scholars as 'imperial utopianism', or 'techno-imperialism', his own slogan being 'invasion / military preparedness in civil garb'. There is some similarity between Gotō's colonizing vision and that of the Russian Minister of Finance, Witte: in Gotō's master plan, Japan was to earn the support of the Chinese in

Manchuria by investing in local social and cultural facilities. Gotō's declared aim was also to settle 500,000 Japanese in Manchuria; in practice, the SMR favoured cheap Chinese labour over encouraging Japanese immigration.[5] Gotō went on to serve as Japan's Minister of Transport, Home Minister and finally Mayor of Tokyo.

In February 1905 the Japanese announced that Dal'nii was henceforth to be known as Dairen. The SMR was centred on two trunk lines: the first stretching about 700 km from Dairen to Changchun, and the second (built from 1908 to 1911; about halfway between these two ends) around 260 km from Mukden to Andong 安東 (original name of the busy port on the Yalu on the Chinese-Korean border, renamed Dandong 丹東 in 1965), where it connected with the Korean railway line leading to the port of Pusan. About 105 towns along the railway were under SMR jurisdiction. The company became involved in every aspect of the economy in South Manchuria, investing especially in heavy industry such as the coal mining in Fushun, east of Shenyang, and the iron works in Anshan 鞍山, south of Liaoyang.

Equipment of the best quality was purchased for the Manchurian industry in the USA, and the locomotives also came from America; later during World War One the SMR began producing locomotives itself. Exploiting new opportunities as they occurred, the company enjoyed huge revenues. It attracted the most talented young professionals from Japan by offering high salaries. The SMR also maintained its own schools, hospitals, farms and the Yamato hotel chain. Of particularly high profile, as symbols of science and modernity, were the SMR hospitals in Dairen and Mukden, although they served overwhelmingly Japanese residents rather than the Chinese. The SMR trains were the most comfortable and most exactly on time in all of Manchuria, outperforming the Russians.

Aware they were lagging behind, Russians officials in Manchuria attempted to emulate the wide-ranging study of the region's agricultural potential and natural conditions, carried out by the SMR Research Department, but they were far less systematic in their efforts. This department of the SMR was established directly by Gotō Shinpei as early as 1907 and lasted until 1945. It has been called 'the largest research institute in the world' as of the 1930s.[6] Its academic staff did not want to see itself as serving Japanese imperialism, adhering instead to the SMR's announced principle of 'Japanese-Chinese amity'. The department experienced a crisis after the Mukden Incident in 1931, when much against the will of many researchers it had to take orders from the Kwantung Army. Created as a Japanese garrison in 1906, the latter was redefined as an army in 1919 and was headquartered in Mukden from 1928.

Open conflict between the convictions of SMR staff and the Japanese army erupted only in 1942 and 1943, when thirty members of the SMR

Research Department were arrested. After the war, some former SMR researchers supported the People's Republic of China. But a recent study of the SMR Employees Association casts doubt over the usual identification of the Mantetsu elite (in particular, its Research Department) with liberal positions; Japanese chauvinism prevailed among them, too.[7]

The city of Dalian/Dairen, which in the 1920s was the second largest port in China after Shanghai,[8] became the first landing port of labour migrants from Shandong, many of whom did not go any farther, finding employment as dock workers. In Chinese historical writing, these workers, not their Japanese employers, are credited with the development of the city (the same issue has faced historians of Harbin). In Western historiography, too, it is now fashionable to speak of the 'early modern development' of China prior to foreign colonial intervention. An opponent of this thesis, however, is the historian James Reardon-Anderson, who argues in his important book, *Reluctant Pioneers*, that there was no native development of Manchuria before modernization was introduced by Japan and Russia: the soybean trade, for example, had been carried out for generations using inadequate techniques, through personal networks and with no long-term investment. This trade rose dramatically only after the Japanese acquisition of Dalian.[9]

By the early 1930s, about 250,000 Japanese already lived in Dalian (Dairen); almost all of them connected with the SMR. The Russian population

Figure 8a A small transport of soybeans, Manchuria. Undated Japanese postcard. Lafayette College, East Asia Image Collection.

of Dal'nii had to leave the city after the Russo-Japanese War, but some Russian émigrés did settle in Dairen in the early 1920s. The demographic majority in the city was, of course, Chinese. In the 1920s the Japanese launched an 'industrial Manchuria' programme to exploit the great economic potential of local natural resources, especially soybeans (Chinese *huangdou* 黃豆) and coal. We will return to the soybean industry as the trademark of Manchuria in the 1920s. Japan was already the most important export destination of the Manchurian market in the 1920s, long before the invasion in 1931; it was also the largest foreign investor in Manchuria. At the same time, especially from the mid-1920s, there was growing nationalist agitation by the Chinese against Japanese colonialism in South Manchuria.

Notes

1 See Peter Berton, *Russo-Japanese Relations, 1905–1917: From Enemies to Allies* (Abingdon and New York: Routledge, 2012).
2 Y. Tak Matsusaka, 'Japan's South Manchuria Railway Company in Northeast China', in Bruce A. Elleman and Stephen Kotkin, eds, *Manchurian Railways and the Opening of China: An International History* (Armonk: M. E. Sharpe, 2010), pp. 41–2.
3 Emer O'Dwyer, 'Mantetsu Democracy', *Modern Asian Studies*, vol. 47, no. 6 (Nov. 2013), p. 1812, n. 1.
4 Jürgen Osterhammel, trans. Patrick Camiller, *The Transformation of the World: A Global History of the Nineteenth Century* (Princeton: Princeton University Press, 2014), p. 445.
5 Matsusaka, 'Japan's South Manchuria Railway Company in Northeast China', pp. 45, 49.
6 Joshua Fogel in Itō Takeo, trans. Joshua Fogel, *Life along the South Manchurian Railway* (Armonk: M. E. Sharpe, 1988), p. xxv.
7 O'Dwyer, 'Mantetsu Democracy'.
8 Ramon H. Myers, 'Japanese Imperialism in Manchuria: The South Manchuria Railway Company, 1906–1933', in Peter Duus et al., eds, *The Japanese Informal Empire in China, 1895–1937* (Princeton: Princeton University Press, 1989), p. 117.
9 James Reardon-Anderson, *Reluctant Pioneers: China's Expansion Northward, 1644–1937* (Stanford: Stanford University Press, 2005).

9

Chinese Migrant Society in the Northeast

The migration of Han Chinese to Manchuria during the nineteenth and twentieth centuries is one of the largest in the world. Han Chinese now make up about 90 per cent of the population in the region, almost as high as their proportion within the whole of China. For peasants in China's densely populated northern provinces, Manchuria had been a constant attraction long before the immigration boom, which came in response to the employment offered by the Russians in Manchurian railway construction from the late 1890s. The official Qing ban on Han settlement had never been effective: despite prohibitions and restrictions, the population of Fengtian province doubled between 1683 and 1734.[1] Still, the gradual lifting of the ban by the Qing government after 1860 served as a strong impetus for the growth of Chinese migration to the Northeast, as it was accompanied by a new policy of encouraging settlement in government-approved areas through grants of land, loans and rewards. Before immigration was permitted, the Han Chinese were illegal squatters or subtenants on bannermen lands, and migration was mostly limited to the Liaodong area. Once settlement became legal, it also extended to northern Manchuria. The last region officially opened for Han settlement was Heilongjiang, in 1905.

The Han Chinese population of Manchuria totalled more than 1,665,000 in 1842, concentrated mainly in contemporary Liaoning. It had doubled by 1872 and reached 5,046,000 by 1890. This amounted to a sweeping sinicization of Manchuria. The arrival of Han Chinese transformed Manchuria, and the language they spoke had already become the lingua franca of the region by the late eighteenth century. By the end of the Qing, civil governments were created in the three north-eastern provinces so as to attend to the needs of the settlers. The Russian demand for cheap labour in the Far East was met by Chinese migrant workers: the so-called coolies, whom Chinese intermediaries delivered by ships from the ports of Tianjin and Zhifu 芝罘 (Chefoo, today part of Yantai 煙台 in northern Shandong) to Vladivostok. The origin of *coolie* was mistakenly attributed to the Chinese for hard labour, *kuli* 苦力, but it actually derives from India rather than from China. After a brief interruption during the Boxer uprising, the coolies kept on arriving in Manchuria and, at the height of construction, tens of thousands of Chinese workers toiled for the CER.

Figure 9 Chinese workers on the CER. Undated Russian postcard. Author's collection.

The Chinese term for the immigration into Manchuria, widely known in the Northeast today, is *chuang guandong* 闖關東, which may be translated as 'breakthrough to the east of the pass'.² The character *guan* refers to Shanhaiguan, the largest pass through the Great Wall, in present-day Hebei, which allowed access by land from North China to Manchuria. This is the same gateway (also known as *tianxia di yi guan* 天下第一關, First Pass Under Heaven) which the Chinese General Wu Sangui 吳三桂 (1612–78) opened for the Manchu army to facilitate its final defeat of the Ming dynasty in 1644. While *Guandong* here means the Northeast, the same term is also used for the southern part of Liaodong, a territory that was leased to Japan after 1906 and lent its name to Japan's Guandong (Kwantung) Army.³

Between 1876 and 1879 alone, drought and famine in North China, above all in Shanxi province, caused the deaths of 9 to 13 million people. These disasters triggered a mass migration to Manchuria.⁴ In the late nineteenth century, over 95 per cent of all newly arriving migrants to Manchuria came from the two provinces of Zhili 直隸 (modern Hebei) and Shandong. Approximately 85 per cent of the migrants were men; most were unmarried, and the remainder had left their families behind. Most did not come with the intention of staying: at least two thirds of all migrants returned to their home provinces after one to four years of work in Manchuria.

From the 1890s to 1941 about 25 million migrants arrived in Manchuria, of whom 8 million remained there.⁵ As noted, this was one of the largest migrations in world history and is certainly the least studied of them. Only the migration of Europeans to the Americas was significantly greater in size (between 55 to 58 million people from the 1840s to 1940; 65 per cent reached the USA and the rest mainly Canada, Argentina and Brazil), followed by the migrations of Indians (over 29 million) and southern Chinese (over 19 million) to South East Asia, the Indian Ocean Rim and the south Pacific.[6]

The migrants to Manchuria reached their highest numbers in the late 1920s and 1930s. They left a region that suffered from overcrowding, floods and droughts, to which were added the ravages of warlord armies. In the terminology of 'push' and 'pull' factors, their migration cannot be classified only as 'push' because it was not primarily a case of an escape by the poorest peasants, nor was it limited to the poorest regions of the home provinces; it was also a community response to the 'pull' of a land considered as full of opportunity. Wages in Manchuria were higher than elsewhere in North China and more arable land was available there.

Nevertheless, migration was felt to be a painful process of separation from China proper, rather than an optimistic move towards a new future, and was seen as a necessity. Hence Reardon-Anderson's choice of the title, *Reluctant Pioneers*. Most migrants would leave Shandong in the late spring (March–April) and once every two to four years they would return (beginning already from October to December) to spend the Chinese New Year with their families. Their identity was anchored in the places they had left, with their ancestral temples and graves. As a Scottish missionary in Manchuria put it, in 1913: 'the Manchurian, then, is a Chinaman. Asked where his ancestral home is, he mentions some prefecture not in Manchuria but on the other side of the Great Wall'.[7] The 'pioneer spirit', associated with the American West, or with Zionists arriving in British-mandate Palestine, was conspicuous in its absence: the place the migrants reached meant little to them. Unlike, for example, the Russian migration to Siberia in the late nineteenth century, the men from Shandong made the far shorter trip to Manchuria unaccompanied by families and (until the new policies of Zhang Zuolin in the 1920s) unassisted by government settlement programmes. Unlike Siberia, Manchuria did not become a melting pot for migrants from various ethnic groups and regions; nor was there a mass movement to the Manchurian frontier. Rather, the migrants mostly populated Liaoning.

This process is known as 'commuting', 'seasonal' or 'circular' migration. Research on the migrants often calls them 'sojourners', a term which would also be appropriate to describe Chinese migration beyond Manchuria to the Russian Far East, but would be less apt for Chinese emigrants to the USA, who largely went there to stay. For the average young male in Shandong, a period of 'service' for the family in Manchuria was a transitional stage to adulthood. After a few years at most, the migrants were expected to return, marry and go on living in their village. The migration of women to Manchuria has been even less noticed or studied, although it is clear that no settler community could have formed without them. Statistical data for Dairen port in 1928 and 1929 indicate that women made up about 17 per cent of the arrivals.[8] An article in the *National Geographic Magazine* in 1929 described migrants, both men and women, walking to Manchuria as well as filling the Japanese steamers that circulated between Tianjin or Qingdao to Dairen.[9]

The migrants initially travelled in carts, junks or on foot, but the process was transformed by steamers and especially by the railway. To buy tickets and be able to start out at a new place, migrants borrowed money and usually remained in debt for several years later (a similar system operated among Chinese emigrants to the USA). Arriving in Manchuria, some migrants headed for the cities while others settled in the empty countryside. There they founded villages, often named after the leading family whose head would have brought over many clan members after his own arrival.

The migrants introduced their local culture into the cities of the Northeast: whether the popular Shandong theatre or the maize cakes (the cheap Shandong addition to the *mantou* 饅頭, the steamed buns most commonly eaten in Manchuria). Local associations were created for migrants according to their county of origin. Moving to the city brought rural migrants into a more varied environment (including possible contact with foreigners), but even in Harbin some streets became settled by people from the same county in Shandong, who spoke the same home dialect. Peasants in the villages preferred to minimize their outside contacts and, rather than obtain their needs from other villages, used the general stores, which opened chains throughout Manchuria. Unwilling to enter into direct contact with foreigners, peasants sold their grain through brokers.

Migrants in Manchuria hoped that if they died they would not be buried there. It was the duty of their relatives, comrades or fellow villagers to send their body back to the native village. There are descriptions of such processions, which passed through Shanhaiguan, several coffins piled above each other and a caged cockerel on top; the bird was supposed to keep the soul awake, so it would not wander off before burial. The bodies of those whose friends or family could not afford the transport were stored in sheds in anticipation of the eventual shipment. The sight of these 'open tombs' shocked foreigners, who did not understand the reasons for such treatment of the dead. 'The surest sign that [...] the transition from sojourner to settler was complete, was when the village established a graveyard.'[10] Another such sign was the establishment of schools for the education of the next generation.[11]

The workers crowded into single-storey dwellings dominated by the *kang* 炕: a heated brick bed still in use in North China and Korea. All migrants sent back significant parts of their wages to their families in the home village, either through the efficient postal system or via personal contacts. The minority who did not do so were subject to group pressure and their families in Shandong were also badly regarded by their peers.[12] While the normative attitude to emigration in Chinese culture was negative, the phenomenon was quite widespread in the south. The people of the coastal Shandong province were the only population in northern China to emigrate in large numbers, and besides Manchuria they also settled in Korea and Japan. The Shandong migrants in Manchuria did not tend to enter trade unions or take part in strikes, relying instead on familiar *laoxiang* 老鄉 ('fellow villagers') networks. Priding themselves on their ability to bear hardship (*chiku nailao* 吃苦耐勞), they were accustomed to the harshest of conditions, including exploitation by both Chinese and foreign employers. This explains their reluctance to lend support to the anti-Japanese resistance, or indeed their undiminished readiness to live and work in Japanese-occupied Manchuria. We shall return to this question when we discuss wartime collaboration.

The population of the Northeast today takes pride in the ethos of *chuang guandong*, which, retrospectively, has acquired the aura of settling the wilderness, which it had not possessed at the time. A successful television series using this expression as its title re-enacted the drama of settlement for contemporary viewers in the 2000s. Belonging to the Shandong 'pioneers' has the additional prestige of distinguishing their descendants today from more recent immigrants, whom the Communist government settled in the Northeast in the 1950s.

Notes

1 Richard L. Edmonds, 'The Willow Palisade', *Annals of the Association of American Geographers*, vol. 69, no. 4 (Dec. 1979), pp. 599–621, at p. 614. This article was collected in Edmonds, *Northern Frontiers of Qing China and Tokugawa Japan: A Comparative Study of Frontier Policy*, University of Chicago, Department of Geography; Research Paper No. 213 (1985).
2 Two important studies in Chinese are Liu Dezeng, *Chuang guandong: 2500 wan Shandong yimin de lishi yu chuanshuo* (Jinan: Shandong renmin chubanshe, 2008), and Fan Lijun, *Chuang guandong: lishi yu wenhua yanjiu* (Beijing: Shehui kexue wenxian chubanshe, 2016).
3 Of course, Guandong should be distinguished from Guangdong, the province in the south of China.

4 See Kathryn Edgerton-Tarpley, *Tears from Iron: Cultural Responses to Famine in Nineteenth-Century China* (Berkeley: University of California Press, 2008). Cf. Reardon-Anderson, *Reluctant Pioneers*, pp. 109–10.
5 Cf. Adam McKeown, 'Chinese Emigration in Global Context, 1850–1940', *Journal of Global History*, vol. 5, no. 1 (March 2010), p. 100, on 'over 30 million people who travelled from Hebei and Shandong to Manchuria'. Like many other historians, McKeown is indebted to data presented in Thomas R. Gottschang and Diana Lary, *Swallows and Settlers: The Great Migration from North China to Manchuria* (Ann Arbor: Michigan, Monographs in Chinese Studies, 2000), the main study in English to date.
6 Adam McKeown, 'Global Migration, 1846–1940', *Journal of World History*, vol. 15, no. 2 (June 2004), pp. 155–89.
7 Robertson, *The Story of Our Mission*, p. 19.
8 Tsao Lien-en, *The Chinese Migration to the Three Eastern Provinces* (Shanghai: Bureau of Industrial and Commercial Information, Ministry of Industry, Commerce and Labor, National Government of the Republic of China, 1930), pp. 38–9.
9 Frederick Simpich, 'Manchuria, Promised Land of Asia', *National Geographic Magazine*, vol. 56, no. 4 (October 1929), pp. 379–428, at p. 391.
10 Reardon-Anderson, *Reluctant Pioneers*, p. 142.
11 Cf. Elizabeth R. VanderVen, *A School in Every Village: Educational Reform in a Northeast China County, 1904–31* (Vancouver and Toronto: UBC Press, 2012).
12 See Gottschang and Lary, *Swallows and Settlers*.

10

Manchuria in the 1920s, Banditry and Warlord Rule

Migration data into Manchuria show 208,940 arrivals in 1921 and about 350,000 in 1922. In 1921 a little more than half of the migrants, 109,780, arrived in Manchuria in the early spring and boarded trains to return home in time for the Chinese New Year. In 1923 Wang Yongjiang 王永江, civil governor of Fengtian under the regime of Zhang Zuolin 張作霖 (which will be our next subject), launched a new Colonization and Development Plan, designed to encourage migrants to bring their families into Manchuria and remain there.[1]

Wang's regulations defined these people as *nanmin* 難民 (refugees) rather than *yimin* 移民 (migrants): Chinese tradition was accustomed to the relief of refugees, but had a difficulty acknowledging migration, which was associated with vagrancy (*youmin* 游民, *liumin* 流民). According to the plan, permanent settlers received funds to build houses (migrants had normally lived in temporary rented rooms), which would become their own after five years. To advertise the plan, agents were sent to the ports in North China from which migrants set out, and the towns in Manchuria where migrants searched for work. Parallel to these steps, all immigrants received reduced rail fares.

Wang hoped to send 70 per cent of the migrants to Heilongjiang, to set up farms and work mainly in sugar beet production in Hulan 呼蘭, or in cattle-raising, mining or forestry. Other migrants were recruited to the large and successful textile mill outside Shenyang (opened in January 1923 to compete against Japanese production, with a large investment by Zhang Zuolin himself), mining in north Liaoning or Jilin, or the construction of a new 193 km-long railway line from Shenyang to Hailong 海龍 in south Jilin. In 1923 as many as 472,900 migrants arrived, of whom 235,200 stayed; the proportion remained about the same in later years.

In 1928 the number of annual immigrants to Manchuria reached 1,089,000, and about 40 per cent of arrivals stayed for three years rather than return every year.[2] A writer for the *National Geographic Magazine* in 1929, who notably called Manchuria 'Promised Land of Asia', claimed the annual estimate at the time was of a million and half arrivals, with as many as two million expected to arrive in the course of 1929 alone.[3] He added that 'before

1926 half the immigrants were seasonal laborers ... now most of them, with their families and household goods, come to stay'.[4] The programme to encourage immigration continued throughout the 1920s, with growing target figures being set. The result, until the Fengtian economy collapsed in 1928, was that people leaving other warlord-controlled areas in China were populating Manchuria.

While Wang's policy encouraged migration, famine and warlordism in Shandong between 1927 and 1929 resulted in a wave of true refugees (*nanmin*, rather than *yimin*) to Manchuria in those years. Even then, few headed to the frontier areas, where uncultivated land was still available. The reasons for this were not only the wish not to move too far from Shandong, but also the high price of the land and lack of protection from banditry in the remote regions. Even in this late period, migrants arriving in Manchuria declared their intention to return home within three years at most.[5]

By 1928 Manchuria's share of Chinese foreign trade reached 32 per cent; almost all trade was export, in particular soybeans, the single crop most suitable for the Manchurian climate. The soybean trade went through two booms in 1909–13 and 1921–7. In 1929 Manchuria produced as much as two thirds of the world's soybean supply. Soy was being used as soybeans, fertilizer (beancakes) and lubricant (bean oil was used to lubricate arms but also as a sauce for cooking).[6] The soybean trade had been the most important export component of Manchurian economy since the late nineteenth century, but it first assumed international dimensions in the Russo-Japanese War, when the Russians bought soy for their arms factories and the Japanese fed the beans to their troops. After 1905, Japan greatly developed the soybean industry in South Manchuria, exporting the beans from its port in Dairen. Japan went on to obtain a near monopoly over Manchurian soybeans after the 1917 revolution in Russia, although the CER, which exported through the port in Vladivostok, recovered some ground in the soybean trade during the second half of the 1920s. Despite the worldwide depression, which began with the Wall Street Crash of October 1929 and lasted to 1934,[7] in 1931 a record in soybean export was achieved. It declined sharply by 1935, both because of floods and droughts and because China boycotted the Manchukuo soybeans after 1932.

Unlike in Asia, in the West, perhaps with the only exception of Italy, soy was seldom used for food.[8] Otherwise, the soybean 'made its way into soap, cheese, salad material, explosives, enamels, varnishes, linoleum, waterproofing, paints, printing inks, lubricating oils, flour, macaroni and crackers',[9] or, to cite the list compiled by a later enthusiastic reporter, was used to make steering wheels for cars, buttons, salad oil, sugar, bottles of Vitamin B, fountain pens, 'and a score of other articles – all from soybeans!'[10] Ironically, while soybeans are still grown in the Northeast today, and although China doubled its soybean production between 1995 and 2005, its 'imports have soared 1,000 percent, to the benefit of producers and shippers in Brazil and Argentina';[11] forests in Latin America are being cleared to plant soybeans for China. The main producer of soy since the 1940s has been the USA.

Banditry

All through the first half of the twentieth century, Manchuria was known for its bandits. These could be former legal or illegal miners, or soldiers in government anti-bandit expeditions; they also included former convicts and exiles, military deserters, unsuccessful settlers, and peasants either impoverished by those same robbing bandits (later: by the marauding warlord soldiers), or perhaps combining agriculture work with robbery in the off season. Before the dynasty's fall in 1911, they could also include rebels against the Qing state and, after the invasion of 1931, rebels against Japanese rule.

The colloquial term for Manchurian bandits is *hong huzi*: literally, 'red beards'.[12] The origin of the term is obscure. According to one folk etymology, the 'red beards' originated as a Chinese image for the Russian Cossacks (compare with *hongmao gui* 紅毛鬼, a term coined for Europeans in the nineteenth century and applied especially to the Dutch); another explanation claimed the term referred to the red cloth, which bandits supposedly attached to the barrels of their guns, or wore as masks. The auspicious colour red had associations with violent uprisings, as manifested by the Boxers and other rebel groups in North China, such as the Red Spears (Hongqiang hui 紅槍會). For the Russians, *khunkhuz* had become a catchword for all suspicious-looking Chinese.

The classical cover used by bandits was the tall *gaoliang* 高粱, a plant used to prepare a fiery liquor, but also for food and animal fodder. With some exaggeration, Peter Fleming (1907–71), the travel writer and brother of the author of James Bond, wrote: 'Practically everything in Manchuria is made of kaoliang. It serves as raw material for many manufactured articles, from hats to houses; also as fodder and fuel. Men eat it as a form of flour, and drink a spirit distilled from it.' He also noted 'its political significance as a stimulus to banditry in the summer and autumn'.[13] A novel by the Shandong-born writer Mo Yan 莫言, *Hong gaoliang* (1986), was translated into English as *Red Sorghum* (this was also the title of the successful film, based on the book, by director Zhang Yimou in 1987; Mo Yan was awarded the Nobel Prize in Literature in 2012). The Chinese traditionally associated bandits with 'mountains and forests' (*shanlin* 山林).

In the Russo-Japanese War, bandits fought on behalf of Japan, chiefly because the Russian army would not hire them. Their activity also became a steady factor in international politics, as both Russians and the Japanese justified their occupation of Manchuria by the need to pacify the region. Banditry in Manchuria increased during and after the Russo-Japanese War; according to one estimate, the number of bandits tripled again, from 20,000 in 1920 to 60,000 in 1931. Banditry was most rampant in the mountainous region of Jilin, with an estimate of 7,900 (twenty-four major bands) in the whole province in 1925, compared to about 1,300 (six bands) in Fengtian.[14] In the countryside, Manchurian villages were often attacked by the bandits demanding supplies and protection money. Villages therefore built defence walls, which the local peasants would patrol, a kind of civil guard in the absence of police protection. The village self-defence forces were associated with northern secret societies, the common Chinese social and religious associations, typically the Big Swords (Dadaohui 大刀揮) and the Red Spears. Koreans, too, were involved in banditry, which had a patriotic side when it was directed against the Japanese.[15]

In the cities, bandits specialized in kidnapping for ransom. After a person disappeared, his family would receive notice with the kidnappers' demands within a few days. The bandits' representatives in the towns were often respectable merchants, who worked with the bandits to guarantee themselves from attack by them. Foreigners ('foreign tickets', *waipiao* 外票, in the bandit jargon) were a most tempting target; and much of the information we have on the bandits in Manchuria comes from the memoirs of their captives.[16]

The Northeast warlords – Zhang Zuolin (1875–1928)

'Warlords' is the collective name given to regional military leaders in the republican era, especially after the death in 1916 of Yuan Shikai 袁世凱, himself a military leader who had seized supreme power in China by quickly ousting Sun Yat-sen (1866–1925), the president of the new republic declared in 1912. Although Sun's successor Chiang Kai-shek (1887–1975) launched the Northern Expedition against the warlords by setting out from Guangdong in July 1926, his power did not extend further to the north than Peking (or Peiping, the official name of the city after Chiang had transferred the national capital). Even after he established a central government in Nanking in 1928, the remote provinces of China remained subject to warlord rule.

Official history writing in the PRC has long described the warlords as an unmitigated evil. However, recent research has pointed out that some of them also contributed to the provinces they controlled, even instituting advanced constitutions. The better among these regimes enjoyed some popular support. While they also caused much damage by fighting against each other and vying to control the national government, it would be an anachronism to expect Chinese politicians in the early twentieth century to have acted out of ideology. Political alliances in China had always been made on the basis of personal interests and connections.[17]

The term warlord (*junfa* 軍閥) was introduced into Chinese from the Japanese in the late 1910s and began displacing the older *dujun* 督軍 (supervisors, identified with the civil bureaucracy rather than the military) by the mid-1920s.[18] The 'warlord' label, much like that of the 'rebel' in imperial China, is retrospectively applied in a pejorative sense; and as the warlords and rebels were eventually defeated, they were not those who wrote history. There is also the widespread perception, strongly conditioned by the propaganda of both the Kuomintang (KMT) and the Communist Party of China (CCP), that China must be united. In reality, patriotic slogans claiming to have the best of 'China' in mind were adopted throughout the century by all participants in the political game, warlords included. Figures such as Chiang Kai-shek and Mao Zedong (1893–1976) may also be described as 'warlords' to the extent that they won and retained power by reliance on their armies more than on their ideas. Indeed, after the end of the Northern Expedition in 1928, the Communists called the KMT 'new warlords', while the KMT called the Communists 'bandits'.

Born to a poor family in south Liaoning in 1875, at the age of 30 Zhang Zuolin led a bandit group that reportedly fought the Russians for Japanese money during the Russo-Japanese War.[19] He became the de facto ruler of Manchuria after occupying Mukden following the 1911 revolution. In 1916 he formally established himself as the Civil and Military Governor of Fengtian. In 1918 his power was acknowledged by Peking as he was appointed Governor-General of the Three Eastern Provinces. In October 1920 Zhang created the Special Administrative Region of the Three Eastern Provinces, with his own seat of power in Mukden, and in May 1922 he declared the Three Provinces independent.

In 1920 Zhang established a huge arsenal of the Three Eastern Provinces in Mukden. Among his many industrial plants were the large textile mill near Shenyang and an automobile factory. He owned banks, grain and oil companies (all in Mukden) and in practice could draw on all the revenues of Manchuria. Like the KMT, Zhang also derived revenue from the cultivation of opium; under the name of Bureau for Opium Suppression, offices for the sale of opium permits were established all around Manchuria in the mid-1920s. Zhang is reputed to have been an addict himself. He lived in a chateau with his five wives, travelling in a luxury armoured car with bodyguards.

Figure 10 Zhang Zuolin's former residence in Shenyang, 2017. Photograph by H. Sinica.

In the summer of 1920 Zhang joined forces with another northern warlord to end the rule of Duan Qirui 段祺瑞 (1865–1936) in Peking. But when warlord Wu Peifu 吳佩孚 (1874–1939) brought down the new prime minister, in whose appointment Zhang had been involved, a conflict between him and Zhang became imminent. Their armies fought from 28 April to 4 May 1922 in what became known as the first Fengtian–Zhili War. On 4 May Zhang's army was defeated and could barely prevent the enemy from entering Manchuria.

A key figure in Zhang's regime was his finance minister Wang Yongjiang (1872–1927), an experienced Liaoning administrator, who hailed from a scholarly family.[20] He first became Zhang's Director of Police Affairs in 1916 and was made the Fengtian Director of Finance in the following year. He realized a currency reform (the switch to the silver standard and creation of the Fengtian dollar), the regulation of the tax collecting system and settlement of Fengtian's debts. In recognition of these achievements, Zhang in 1921 appointed Wang as Acting Civil Governor of Fengtian along with his post as Director of the Finance Bureau. But as historian Ronald Suleski has described it, Wang was constantly frustrated to see up to 80 per cent of the budget he had created for Zhang's treasury to be assigned to military aims. He therefore pressed to separate the civil and military branches of the administration in all the Three Provinces.

Following the military defeat in 1922, Wang threatened to leave his job, claiming an eye infection that needed treatment in Dalian. Although Zhang requested him to stay in Shenyang, Wang left for Dalian in June and from the hospital there conducted negotiations until his demands were accepted by Zhang in July. Wang returned to Shenyang as victor and was appointed both Finance Director and a full Civil Governor of Fengtian on 6 August. In the spring of 1923 Wang launched his Colonization and Development Plan, and in the summer of 1924 he unified three large banks and created a central Official Bank of the Three Provinces, under his own directorship, with the intention of putting an end to uncontrolled withdrawal of state funds by the military. In August 1924 Wang also published a study of the origins of the *Book of Changes*.

However, in autumn 1924 Zhang Zuolin was tempted once again to enter into North China with his army: the so-called Second Fengtian–Zhili War. This time the Zhili clique and the government in Peking, which was recognized by the outside world as representing China, were defeated. Wu Peifu fled,[21] while Zhang ended up sharing political power in the capital of China with the 'Christian general' Feng Yuxiang 馮玉祥 (1882–1948), a figure close to the Communists and the Soviet Union, who had fought on Wu Peifu's side in the previous round but now was bribed by the Japanese to turn on Peking. Zhang's commanders also took control of the local administration of Zhili (Hebei), Shandong, Jiangsu and Anhui, while the forces of his son Zhang Xueliang marched on to Shanghai.

But in October 1925 fighting broke out again. The Fengtian army lost most of North China to the rival warlord armies of Wu Peifu, Feng Yuxiang (who switched sides, rejoining Wu) and Sun Chuanfang 孫傳芳 (1885–1935). Rather than retreat to Manchuria, Zhang Zuolin gathered his forces for a last attack on Peking. In November one of his commanders, Guo Songling 郭松齡, revolted (backed by the Soviets), and in coalition with Feng Yuxiang, he attacked Zhang Zuolin's capital seat Shenyang. Zhang managed to suppress the rebellion and had Guo executed on 23 December 1925.

While all this fighting was going on, Manchuria was being drained of its resources. Fengtian was placed under martial law. As compulsory conscription began, carts and animals were requisitioned, taxes were increased, new ones invented and the banks pressed for 'donations'. Opposition to Zhang's military adventures was growing. Asked to print more money, Minister Wang refused. Zhang overruled him, ordering the central bank to print millions of Fengtian dollars, which then quickly plummeted in value. Zhang's commanders began demanding the Official Bank for money without Wang's permission. Once the Guo revolt plunged everything into chaos, Wang resigned, leaving Shenyang in February 1926 for his family home in Jinzhou 錦州, where he died the following year.

Already in April 1926 Zhang appointed Mo Dehui 莫得惠 (1883–1968), a former administrator in Harbin, as the new Civil Governor, who immediately issued bonds and pressured the population to buy them. In October 1927 Mo moved on to the government in Peking, but the Fengtian economy and the Fengtian dollar collapsed in that winter. Amid spiralling inflation, strikes broke out, businesses went bankrupt, and with the collapse of the Colonization and Development Plan, Shenyang became filled with unemployed migrants. Meanwhile in December 1926 Zhang Zuolin created the Anguojun 安國軍 (Army to Pacify the Country), a union of all the northern warlords under his command. Zhang Zongchang 張宗昌 (1881–1932), known as 'Dogmeat General' from Shandong, who had been his subordinate and ally, as well as warlords Yan Xishan 閻錫山 (1883–1960) from Shanxi and Sun Chuanfang, were declared Zhang Zuolin's deputies. While Manchuria suffered from the results of his military adventures, in April 1927 Zhang ordered the raid of the Soviet Embassy in Peking, executing one of the first leaders of the Chinese Communist Party, who had taken refuge there, Li Dazhao 李大釗 (born 1888; a former librarian of Peking University, whose assistant was Mao Zedong). The KMT 'white terror' against Chinese Communists began in the same month with the purge carried out by Chiang Kai-shek in Shanghai. Zhang soon proclaimed himself head of the central government in Peking.

However, by May 1928 Zhang's army was being pushed out of Peking by Chiang Kai-shek. In the Jinan 濟南 Incident of 3 May, Japanese troops, which had landed in Shandong supposedly for the protection of Japanese citizens there a year earlier, executed seventeen negotiators on behalf of the KMT, ending the progress of the Nationalist Army into Manchuria. The 'tragedy' (can'an 慘案) of 3 May became an official 'humiliation day' in republican China.[22]

On 3 June 1928 Zhang left Peking on a train, which exploded early on the morning of the following day, killing him. A bomb had been planted in a tunnel under the rails of the SMR line (above the passing train of the Peking–Mukden line). The Japanese, Zhang's long-time sponsors, feared that once Zhang was defeated by the KMT, the Nationalist Army would follow him into Manchuria. Swayed by anti-Japanese public opinion, Zhang had begun adopting nationalist rhetoric. He also began building a railway line with US funding, which would have rivalled the SMR. Nonetheless, Japan's prime minister Tanaka Giichi (1864–1929) managed to convince Zhang to return to Manchuria. Tanaka did not know that three officers of the Kwantung Army had made separate plots to assassinate Zhang. Eventually Kōmoto Daisaku (1883–1955) prevailed, carrying out the operation with the help of the *ronin*, Japanese adventurers who engaged in crime in Manchuria, above all in the opium business.[23]

Since 2000, popular historians in Russia have put the responsibility for the Zhang assassination on the Soviet secret agent Naum I. Eitingon (1899–1981), who was later part of the unit that organized the liquidation of Leon Trotsky in Mexico in 1940.[24] Although this scenario appeared to receive corroboration from the opening to the public of Chiang Kai-shek's diaries at the Hoover Institute in 2008,[25] there is ample evidence of Japanese responsibility for the assassination, including letters by Kōmoto himself. Possibly, Joseph Stalin's agents would have got to Zhang if the Japanese had not beaten them to it.

While the assassins tried to attribute the act to the KMT, the fingerprints of the Kwantung Army became immediately clear. Tanaka was disgraced by this action of the military. Although the emperor backed him in seeking to punish the assassins, he was unable to do so and was forced to resign as prime minister on 2 July (he died in September). The assassination became one in a series of independent acts by Japanese officers in the 1920s and the 1930s, 'a culture of insubordination' which, as historian Danny Orbach has argued, led to the invasion of Manchuria in September 1931, targeted politicians in Japan itself and finally resulted in all-out war with China in 1937.[26] Kōmoto refused to return to Japan after the defeat in 1945 and instead remained in China as an advisor to a local warlord. He was arrested by the Communists, interrogated about his various crimes and died in a Chinese prison.

Badly wounded in the explosion of his train, Old Marshal Zhang Zuolin was taken to his headquarters (now the Shenyang Library) and died on the following day. The eldest of Zhang's many sons, Zhang Xueliang 張學良 (the Young Marshal, 1901–2001), succeeded his father as ruler over Manchuria after two weeks during which, to prevent chaos, the press carried fabricated reports on the state of Zhang Zuolin's health. Xueliang had been made colonel at the age of 18, commander of his father's bodyguards at 19 and major general at 22. In the 1920s he developed the Fengtian air force and was made its commander at the age of 24. These aircraft bombed Peking when it was held by Feng Yuxiang in 1925.

On 29 December 1928, Zhang Xueliang announced Manchuria's 'change of flag', i.e. its alliance with the National government in Nanking; at the same time he became the 'sworn brother' of Chiang Kai-shek. This development alarmed Japan, which had heretofore prevented Chiang's Northern Expedition from reaching Manchuria. While he was less careful than Zhang Zuolin in his relations with Japan, Xueliang inherited his father's anti-Soviet convictions. His raid on the Harbin Soviet Consulate in May 1929 (including the arrest of thirty-nine employees whom Zhang Junior, quite justly, suspected of spreading Communist propaganda) was intended to win control over the

CER. Zhang Zuolin had been thwarted in his own previous efforts to achieve the same purpose.

Zhang Xueliang's move resulted in Soviet airstrikes and a limited Soviet invasion of northern Manchuria in November 1929.[27] The settlements of Cossacks and Russian Old Believers in the so-called Three Rivers area in Inner Mongolia were wiped out by the Soviet troops, who massacred a part of the population and forcibly repatriated the other. The conflict ended with renewal of the CER status by the Treaty of Ussuriisk (a town 80 km north of Vladivostok) on 3 December and the Khabarovsk protocol of 22 December 1929. Zhang Xueliang continued to control Manchuria until the Japanese invasion, to which we move next.

Notes

1 Here I rely mostly on Ronald Suleski, *Civil Government in Warlord China: Tradition, Modernization and Manchuria* (New York: Peter Lang, 2002).
2 Ibid., p. 95. Quentin Pan, 'Recent Chinese Colonization in Manchuria', p. 931, shows a decrease in the percentage of migrants remaining in Manchuria in 1928, compared to a peak of 70 per cent remaining in 1927. Yet it was still as high as 58 per cent in 1928.
3 Simpich, 'Manchuria, Promised Land of Asia', pp. 387 (he also estimated the total number of settlers at 30 million), 391.
4 Ibid., p. 395.
5 Reardon-Anderson, *Reluctant Pioneers*, ch. 6, 'Refugees'.
6 A softener for commodities like soap, explosives, celluloid etc.; a replacement for plastic (e.g. in Ford's project of a soya-made car, revealed in 1941 but soon abandoned with the entry of the US into the war). Ines Prodöhl, '"A Miracle Bean": How Soy Conquered the West, 1909–1950', *Bulletin of the German Historical Institute*, no. 46 (Spring 2010), pp. 111–29.
7 For its implications in Manchuria, see Tim Wright, 'The Manchurian Economy and the 1930s World Depression', *Modern Asian Studies*, vol. 41, no. 5 (Sept. 2007), pp. 1073–1112.
8 'Besides its various other uses in the East, in America and in Europe, Italy now consumes soy-bean flour in bread and, to some extent, in macaroni.' Simpich, 'Manchuria, Promised Land of Asia', p. 398.
9 Ibid., p. 413.
10 Willard Price, 'Japan Faces Russia in Manchuria', *National Geographic Magazine*, vol. 82, no. 5 (Nov. 1942), pp. 603–34, at p. 616.
11 'At various times during the 1990s, China imported as much as . . . 28 percent of [the world's] soybean oil.' Jasper Becker, *Dragon Rising: An Inside Look at China Today* (Washington DC: National Geographic, 2006), pp. 180, 240. Cf. Meyer, *In Manchuria*, pp. 155–6.

12 Cf. Mark Gamsa, 'How a Republic of Chinese Red Beards was Invented in Paris', *Modern Asian Studies*, vol. 36, no. 4 (October 2002), pp. 993–1010.
13 Peter Fleming, *One's Company: A Journey to China in 1933* (1934; Harmondsworth: Penguin Books, 1956), p. 120. Cf. Price, 'Japan Faces Russia in Manchuria', p. 606: 'Banditry and kaoliang always reach their greatest height in the same month, June.'
14 Suleski, *Civil Government in Warlord China*, pp. 89–90.
15 A colourful representation of Manchurian banditry, the Korean action film 'The Good, the Bad, the Weird' (2008) confronts Korean bandits and independence fighters with Chinese robber bands and the regular Japanese army.
16 The best known of these is Harvey J. Howard, *Ten Weeks with Chinese Bandits* (London: John Lane at the Bodley Head, 1927).
17 See Frank Dikötter, *The Age of Openness: China Before Mao* (Berkeley: University of California Press, 2008).
18 Arthur Waldron, 'The Warlord: Twentieth Century Chinese Understandings of Violence, Militarism, and Imperialism', *American Historical Review*, vol. 96, no. 4 (October 1991), pp. 1073–1100.
19 The main study on Zhang is still Gavan McCormack, *Chang Tso-lin in Northeast China, 1911–1928: China, Japan, and the Manchurian Idea* (Stanford: Stanford University Press, 1977).
20 The career of Wang Yongjiang is summarized from Suleski, *Civil Government in Warlord China*.
21 F. A. Sutton, known as One Arm Sutton (1884–1944), attributed this victory of the Zhang forces to the guns he [Sutton] had developed and supplied him. Three years earlier, he had offered the same arms to Wu, who rejected them. 'Because of this very weapon he [Wu] would be fugitive, flying from his enemy on a battleship, his impregnable Great Wall stormed, a hundred thousand of his troops left prisoners, all his war material lost, and his reputation as China's greatest general ruined.' Major-general F. A. Sutton, *One-Arm Sutton* (New York: The Viking Press, 1933), p. 213. Sutton reported having been associated with Zhang for five years, apparently starting in 1922, adding that 'this extraordinary man' with 'a fine primitive code of honour' had made him Chief of Staff and Director of Munitions (p. 276).
22 Shuge Wei, 'Beyond the Front Line: China's Rivalry with Japan in the English-language Press over the Jinan Incident, 1928', *Modern Asian Studies*, vol. 48, no. 1 (Jan. 2014), pp. 188–224.
23 Danny Orbach, 'The Military-Adventurous Complex: Officers, Adventurers, and Japanese Expansion in East Asia, 1884–1937', *Modern Asian Studies*, vol. 53, no. 2 (March 2019), esp. pp. 367–71.
24 As in Aleksandr Kolpakidi and Dmitrii Prokhorov, *Imperiia GRU. Ocherki istorii rossiiskoi vneshnei razvedki* (The GRU Empire: Sketches of the History of the Russian Foreign Intelligence), in 2 vols (Moscow: Olma Press, 2000), vol. 1, pp. 182–3. These claims are summarized from a Russian biography of Naum (alias Leonid) Eitington in Mary-Kay Wilmers, *The Eitingons:*

A *Twentieth-century Story* (London: Faber and Faber, 2009), pp. 146–8. However, A. Iu. Sidorov, 'Chzhan Siuelian. Politicheskii portret "Molodogo marshala"' ('Zhang Xueliang: A Political Portrait of "The Young Marshal"'), *Novaia i noveishaia istoriia*, 2008, no. 2, 139–56, here p. 142, n. 11, rejects the version of Soviet responsibility for the assassination as based on no evidence other than hearsay.

25 Emer O'Dwyer, 'Heroes and Villains: Manchukuo in Yasuhiko Yoshikazu's *Rainbow Trotsky*', in Roman Rosenbaum, ed., *Manga and the Representation of Japanese History* (London: Routledge, 2013), p. 141.

26 Danny Orbach, *Curse on This Country: The Rebellious Army of Imperial Japan* (Ithaca NY and London: Cornell University Press, 2017).

27 A new military history of this conflict is Michael Walker, *The 1929 Sino-Soviet War: The War Nobody Knew* (Lawrence: University Press of Kansas, 2017). In Chinese, see Guo Junsheng, ed., *Zhongdonglu yu Zhongdonglu shijian* (Shenyang: Liaoning renmin chubanshe, 2010).

11

The Manchukuo State: Resistance and Collaboration, 1932–45

In January 2017, the PRC Ministry of Education announced that the Sino-Japanese War should henceforth be dated as beginning from the Mukden incident in 1931 rather than from 1937, as has been accepted so far. On 18 September 1931 the Japanese military staged an incident by blowing up the SMR track north of Mukden, to provide an ostensible cause for the army's invasion of Manchuria. Another private initiative by the Kwantung Army, which the government in Tokyo did not dare to resist, the Manchurian offensive was masterminded by Lieutenant Colonel Ishiwara Kanji (1889–1949) and soon assumed a dynamic of its own.

The invasion was unanimously supported in the Japanese press and radio, as old songs of the Russo-Japanese War were revived to hail Japan's 'return' to Manchuria and the racial superiority of the Japanese was affirmed by descriptions of the 'scattering' Chinese soldiers. Thus if the army did not initially have the support of the government, it could still count on favourable public opinion at home.[1] Japan was stricken by the world economic crisis of October 1929, and, as a consequence, the extreme right and the military (who enjoyed a much better image than the politicians, considered corrupt) gained the upper hand in Japanese politics. They intimidated the public with the spectre of the threats that growing Chinese nationalism as well as Communism posed to Japanese interests in Northeast China.

Aggression in China was pursued on another front, too: the bombardment of Shanghai by the Japanese army in January 1932. When forced to respond to the crisis in China, the international community preferred to press Japan on the Shanghai issue, where the Western powers had immediate interests. Indeed, they achieved a ceasefire between the two parties by March (a truce was signed on 5 May). In contrast, Manchuria was too remote to concern the Europeans, whereas the Soviet Union, the bordering country directly affected by the loss of the CER, could not afford to go to war with Japan over this issue.[2] The US reacted to the invasion of Manchuria by announcing the 'non-recognition doctrine' (identified with President Herbert Hoover's Secretary of State, Henry Stimson); it would use the same method to respond to the annexation of the Baltic States by the Soviet Union in 1940.

As the army's plan of outright annexation was not sanctioned by Tokyo, the officers devised the idea of a fake state; the deception, therefore, was aimed at the Japanese government before it was used to trick world opinion. On 6 February 1932 the Kwantung Army entered Harbin. The last emperor of the fallen Qing dynasty, Puyi 溥儀 (1906–67), whom the Japanese had brought from Tianjin to Port Arthur under military escort in November 1931, was appointed president of the new independent state of Manchukuo, founded on 1 March 1932. On 9 March Puyi was inaugurated, but only on 25 August did the Diet in Tokyo announce its decision to recognize Manchukuo and only on 15 September was the new state recognized by the Tokyo government.[3] Puyi probably was not merely forced to take up nominal rule of Manchukuo (as he would claim after 1945), but was motivated to do so by his previous hardship and Chinese offences to the memory of his ancestors. On 5 November 1924 Puyi was expelled from the Forbidden City after the capture of Peking by warlords Zhang Zuolin and Feng Yuxiang. Escaping first to the Japanese legation with the help of his British tutor, Reginald Johnston (1874–1938), he later left the capital for the Japanese concession in Tianjin. In 1928 the Qing imperial tombs in Hebei (and the bodies of Emperor Qianlong and Empress Cixi 慈禧) were desecrated by the soldiers of a local warlord, Sun Dianying 孫殿英, while the Manchu banners were officially disbanded.

In March 1934, Puyi was enthroned as the Kangde emperor in Changchun, the city which in April 1932 had been renamed Xinjing 新京 (Shinkyō) and declared capital of Manchukuo. To this day, Chinese historians always add *wei* 偽 ('false' or 'bogus') before the name Manzhouguo 滿洲國. In the newly created country, the anniversary of the '18 September Incident' was officially celebrated from 1932 on. Four days after the Japanese invasion in September 1931, Chiang Kai-shek announced that China would not fight Japan, but rather referred the conflict's resolution to the League of Nations.

The League's Lytton Committee came to Manchuria, remaining from 21 April to 4 June 1932, to investigate the legality of Japanese rule. The committee had first gone to Tokyo and Osaka, then travelled to Shanghai, Nanking, Hankou, Peking and Mukden. After visits in Changchun, Jilin, Harbin and Qiqihar, the committee members returned to Mukden. They then went to Dairen and finally to Peking, where Lord Lytton wrote his report. The Japanese initially placed high hopes in the committee, which they believed would confer international legitimacy on their actions. However, although the Lytton report, published in October 1932, made an effort to avoid antagonizing Japan, even putting part of the blame on the instability of China and the brutal warlord rule of Zhang Xueliang and recognizing the special interests of Japan in Manchuria, it still rejected the Japanese claim that the

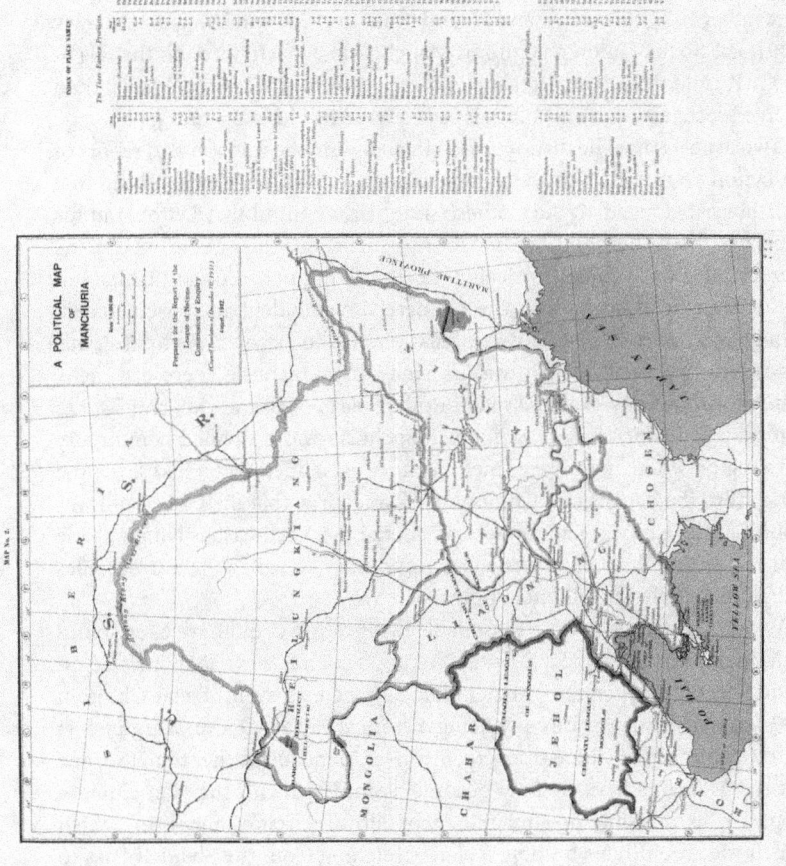

Figure 11 'A Political Map of Manchuria.' League of Nations, 1932.

invasion was an act of self-defence. The committee denied any popular support for the Manchukuo state and called for restoring the status quo ante in Manchuria. After lengthy attempts to conciliate Japan through a diplomatic compromise, the League of Nations finally adopted the report on 24 February 1933, and in March Japan left the League in protest. Manchukuo was recognized internationally by the Vatican (who sent a religious, rather than a foreign relations representative to the new country), El Salvador and the Dominican Republic (both in 1934), Italy (in November 1937), Spain (December 1937), Germany and Poland (both in 1938) and Hungary (January 1939). The Soviet Union recognized Manchukuo de facto through the sale of the CER in March 1935. After the outbreak of World War Two, Manchukuo received recognition from countries conquered by Germany and Japan.

Two aspects must be distinguished in analysing the mission and report of the Lytton Committee: to the extent that these dealt with establishing that Manchuria 'belonged' to the Chinese state, it is doubtful that Lytton and his associates had the tools to make judgment on this question. Japan's counterclaim was valid: historically Manchuria did not belong to China but to the Manchu dynasty, and the Chinese now resident in it were recent immigrants rather than a native population. As the Lytton report put it, this was no 'simple case' of an invasion, since 'in Manchuria there are many features without any exact parallel in other parts of the world'; and (in the summary of historian Zara Steiner) 'Manchuria was a divided community and a region where many races met'.[4] Japan also claimed that it had saved the world from the danger of a Communist Manchuria; that the Great Wall was proof that the Chinese had always considered the Northeast as lying outside their realm; and that China was a chaotic country, to which the normal rules of diplomatic relations did not apply.

What is certain is that no reasonable justification could have been found for Manchuria to become a *Japanese* colony (which is why Japan insisted on the fiction of 'independent' Manchukuo). Indeed, as even official China in 1932 was unable to provide convincing historical, racial or cultural arguments for the legitimacy of Chinese sovereignty over Manchuria other than to argue that the Manchus have by now become assimilated with the Han Chinese people, it is possible to imagine geopolitical circumstances in which Manchuria would have become a state stretching from the Shanhai Pass to Sakhalin. To the extent that the Lytton Committee's mission consisted in determining the treatment of Manchuria's population by Japan, it was right to conclude that this was unfair and based on brute force. But historian Thomas DuBois rightly points out that Manchukuo should be seen in the context of its time, as one of 'many dozens of partially sovereign states, dependent polities' and other 'systems of dependence in a world that formally was no longer willing to tolerate imperialism'; another example, which the League of Nations had sanctioned, was the British mandate over Palestine.⁵

In the Tanggu Truce of 31 May 1933 (signed in Tanggu 塘沽, near Tianjin), Chiang Kai-shek's Nanking government recognized Japanese rule in Manchuria, thereby ending the war and halting Japan's advance in the direction of Peking. Chiang had other problems with the Communists at home, which he considered more urgent; he used the slogan 'unity before resistance' and compared the CCP to an 'inner' disease, which one must cure before attending to an 'external' illness. Even such prominent figures as the public intellectual Hu Shi 胡適 (1891–1962) advocated patience in the face of the occupation of Manchuria. Zhang Xueliang, though he had an army of over 160,000 men under his command, accepted Chiang's orders not to resist the occupation. On the day of the Mukden incident, he was at a theatre in Peking. After attempting briefly to establish a new headquarters in Jinzhou, in March 1933 Zhang travelled to Shanghai, where he entered a hospital in a strenuous attempt to cure his drug addiction. In April he left for Europe, possibly to strengthen his resolve never to use drugs again. He visited Benito Mussolini in Italy and Adolf Hitler in Germany (he also spent some time in Britain), and as a convinced fascist returned to China in January 1934, when he was then detailed by Chiang to fight the Communist forces.⁶ Although Zhang had allied himself with Chiang Kai-shek in 1928 and was in 1934 rewarded by the title of Chiang's 'deputy', he failed to convince him of the necessity to incorporate the Communists in the Nationalist Army and jointly fight the Japanese enemy. In 'the Xi'an Incident' of 12 December 1936, Zhang kidnapped the generalissimo to force him to change his policy.

This dramatic step may have stemmed from Zhang's frustration after fighting costly but ineffective battles against the Communist army, his wish to lead his north-eastern army to victory in Manchuria, and secret contacts between him and the Communists. About 120 Communists had joined Zhang's forces; in April and June 1936 Zhang held talks with the senior Communist leader Zhou Enlai 周恩來 (1898–1976). Alarming rumours that Zhang was planning to pass over to the Communist side brought Chiang Kai-shek to Xi'an in October and again in December 1936.

After the kidnapping, Zhou Enlai and Chiang's wife Song Meiling 宋美齡 (1897–2003)⁷ mediated to bring about Chiang's release in January 1937, thereby enabling formation of the Second United Front between the KMT and the CCP from that year to 1941.⁸ Zhang probably expected the Soviet Union to support his action, but he had to release Chiang once Stalin communicated his protest against the kidnapping, putting direct pressure on the CCP to free Chiang. For his part, Chiang agreed to establish the United Front not to honour a promise given under duress, but because he reasoned that he could then count on continued Soviet assistance. Zhang Xueliang was put under arrest. Transported from place to place in China during the war, from November 1946 he lived in luxurious prison conditions on Taiwan until 1962, and then under comfortable house arrest after the death of Chiang Kai-shek in 1975. He was only (and even then, unofficially) released in 1990, two years after the death of Chiang's son and successor, President Chiang Ching-kuo 蔣經國 (1910–88), and he lived in Hawaii from 1994 to his death at the age of 100 on 15 October 2001.

Chinese labour and Japanese settlers in Manchukuo

Chinese migration to Manchuria declined in absolute numbers in the 1930s, but remained significant.[9] In the 1930s, close regulations were imposed on the admission of migrant Chinese into Japanese-ruled Manchukuo. After the second five-year plan for Manchukuo was adopted in June 1937, there was, however, a new rise in migrant numbers, to reach over 1.4 million in 1940 (an average of 1.2 million migrants a year from 1939 to 1942). The labour conditions of the Chinese 'coolies' were harsh to begin with: they lived in shacks, were controlled by their foremen and earned less than half of the wages of Japanese workers (Korean workers, as Japanese citizens since 1910, also earned more than the Chinese).[10] After war broke out with the attack on Pearl Harbor on 7 December 1941, Manchuria was mobilized to support the Japanese war machine. From February 1942 young men were forcibly conscripted for labour on military projects, and such conscripts made up 71 per cent of all the workforce by 1945. They worked under ruthless conditions of slave labour, which were harshest in the mines. When food rationing began in Manchukuo in late 1941, better quality and larger amounts of rationed products such as rice, flour and sugar were given to the Japanese settlers and military.

The necessity of relying on the labour of Chinese migrants in the construction of Manchukuo was an obvious problem, which administrators wished to solve by encouraging migration from Japan.[11] While there had been some Japanese emigration to Manchuria even before 1932, it was low-key and limited in scope. Commenting on the failure of the Japanese to settle Manchuria up to that time, an American reporter wrote in 1929 that less than 200,000 Japanese lived in Manchuria, and nearly all of these in the Kwantung Leased Territory and the SMR railway zone.[12]

The Japanese did emigrate, but to other destinations: southern Sakhalin, Taiwan, USA (until the Asian Exclusion Act of 1924) and Brazil. In the 1870s they began settling on Hokkaido Island in the north of Japan, previously populated only by the Ainu; in 1885, an emigration programme abroad brought Japanese villagers to work in the sugar cane plantations in Hawaii. Another destination for Japanese emigration was Korea after its annexation in 1910; following the invasion in 1937, Japanese would also move into China proper.

The early 1930s were a time of economic depression and many farmers had been ruined by the fall of the prices for silk and rice. Emigration was seen as a solution to their problem. The first 423 agricultural settlers from Japan arrived in Manchukuo in October 1932 and five more groups (a total of 3,000 households) followed until 1936. They were directed to the areas bordering on the Soviet Union. In 1936 Tokyo announced the ambitious aim of settling 1 million Japanese households in Manchuria (5 million people; a fifth of the Japanese village population at the time) within the next twenty years.[13] This policy became known as 'Millions to Manchuria'.

A huge propaganda machine was set up in Japan for the purpose of making Manchuria racially an extension of Japan. Government propaganda rested on two components: patriotic, in which colonization was advertised as an act proving Japan's world standing and assisting the Japanese nation back at home; and personal, in which Manchukuo was presented as 'an empty land' of opportunities. By the late 1930s, however, the Japanese economy had improved and after the outbreak of war and mobilization in 1937 there were no more land shortages in the villages. Nevertheless, the government did not abandon its colonization project and established two programmes to recruit settlers in Manchuria: the Community Emigration Programme from 1936 and the Patriotic Youth Brigade from 1938.[14]

About 322,000 migrants were brought to Manchuria from 1937 to 1945,[15] mostly from prefectures in east central and northern Japan. They were settled in over a thousand villages; 270,000 settlers (77,600 households, i.e. 3.4 persons per family) were still in Manchuria by August 1945. On the whole, the emigration scheme failed. The 'pioneers' were mainly young men (often the non-inheriting second and third sons in their families at home) and the land given to them was expropriated to this end from the Chinese. The village expropriations immediately aroused local resistance by Chinese peasants. After the male colonists came their 'brides', sent over from Japan.[16] During wartime, 'comfort women' were supplied to the Japanese military (rather than to the agricultural settlers): most were brought over from Korea for the use of the soldiers, while Japanese 'volunteer' prostitutes served the officers.[17]

Resistance

In November 1931 General Ma Zhanshan 馬占山 (1885–1950) ignored China's official policy of non-resistance and held out in a battle against the Japanese army on the Nenjiang River until forced to surrender in January. Ma would rebel again in summer 1932. Other Chinese commanders led a defence of Harbin, which is why this city was not taken by the Japanese until February 1932. In China, exiles from occupied Manchuria formed a Northeast National Salvation Society, a lobby pressuring the government to resist Japan, supporting and publicizing the resistance in Manchuria. However, resistance was dangerous and costly. Residents of the villages where guerrillas hid were massacred by the Japanese. From 1934 to 1937, 5.5 million peasants were relocated (to over 10,000 new hamlets surrounded by barbed wire). In Japanese military operations against the guerrillas about 66,000 Chinese were killed between 1932 and 1940; by 1941, the resistance was crushed.

In post-1949 China it has been important to demonstrate that resistance to Japan was organized by the Communist Party.[18] In the 1930s, the CCP sent Communists from Manchuria for secret training in Moscow, with the aim of preparing them for liberating the Northeast.[19] However, 80 per cent of the CCP members in Manchuria by 1932 were Koreans, showing the party's limited appeal to the local population. One of these was the future leader of North Korea, Kim Il Sung (1912–94), whose family moved to Manchuria when he was 8. From 1940 to 1945 Kim lived in Khabarovsk, where his eldest son and successor Kim Jong Il (1941–2011) was born, initially named Yuri. The motivation of ethnic Koreans to fight against Japan had little to do with Japan's actions in Manchuria and everything to do with its occupation of Korea. However, other prominent Korean figures, later leaders of the South Korean Army, graduated from the Japanese Military Academy in Hsinking (Changchun) and were heavily influenced by Japanese nationalist militarism: one of them was Park Chung Hee (1917–79), the dictator of South Korea from 1961 until his assassination.[20]

Violent Korean patriotism did not manifest itself for the first time in Manchuria in the 1930s. At the Harbin railway station in October 1909, the year before Japan formally annexed Korea as a colony, the Catholic Korean patriot An Chung-gun (in Chinese characters: An Chonggen 安重根) assassinated the Japanese politician Ito Hirobumi (born 1841), who had signed the treaty making Korea into a Japanese protectorate in 1905 and then served as Japan's first Resident-General in Korea. After a trial in Port Arthur, the Japanese hanged An in March 1910, having held him in prison long enough for him to compose a pan-Asian manifesto and to practise Chinese calligraphy (which his guards much admired). During the Manchukuo era the Japanese had a bust of Ito set up between marble columns. The opening of a small museum in honour of his assassin at the new railway station of Harbin in January 2014 triggered official protest from Japan.[21]

Other so-called resistance fighters in the Northeast were former bandits, such as Wang Delin 王德林 (1875–1938), who in February 1932 formed a Chinese People's National Salvation Army in Yanji 延吉 (eastern Jilin) and successfully fought the Japanese in that area before becoming embroiled in conflict with another 'volunteer' army. Such infighting, the heritage of the warlord era, was a major cause of the failure of the resistance; another was poor supplies.[22] Many of the soldiers were recruited not by the CCP, but among members of secret societies, especially the Big Swords and the Red Spears. Because of their non-ideological composition, the CCP opposed these volunteer armies until the 'united front' of 1937. PRC histories have played down their role in the resistance.

Collaboration

From the beginning of the invasion the Japanese could rely on high-ranking collaborators in the Northeast administration. The most cooperative were the landlords in Manchuria, who saw the Japanese as their protectors from the Communist threat. Raised in the Confucian tradition, they were also susceptible to Japanese propaganda emphasizing respect for the Confucian way. In addition, remaining Qing loyalists welcomed the restoration of Puyi, while some Russians hoped that with Japanese help monarchy might return to Russia, too. The civil administrators, frustrated by their conflicts with warlords during the reign of the Zhangs, were also ready to cooperate with the Japanese, while, on the local level, counties formed 'peace maintenance committees'. Several among Zhang Zuolin's former military men accepted positions in the Manchukuo government,[23] which, however, were devoid of real authority. A small number of Chinese forces were used by the Kwantung Army.[24] It is also important to remember that in the SMR zone, the Japanese had been in control and represented power long before 1931.

A more nuanced term than 'collaboration', and one that applied to far greater numbers, would be 'accommodation': this acknowledges that most people inhabit a grey area of daily life and cannot be categorized as either heroes or traitors.[25] Manchuria had only a limited middle class, who would have been more likely to display ideological resistance to the occupation. The idea of resistance appealed most to a small number of young Chinese, who had received patriotic education in the aftermath of the anti-imperialist May Fourth Movement in the 1920s.

The Russians and Jews under Manchukuo rule

At first, the Russians in Manchuria welcomed delivery from the Chinese warlords. However, the new Japanese regime soon initiated methods to put the Russians under its direct control. A special Bureau for the Affairs of Russian Emigrants in the Manchurian Empire (known under its Russian abbreviation BREM) was established in December 1934 under the leadership of Russian collaborators. These included leaders of the Russian Fascist Party, which was active in Harbin from the mid-1920s. After holding its first congress in May 1931, this nationalist and anti-Semitic party blossomed under Japanese rule until the Japanese authorities disbanded it in 1943.[26] The Bureau collected information and compiled intelligence files on every Russian in Manchukuo. The Japanese censored the Russian press and enforced the use of 'Nippon' for Japan in Russian. Similarly, Han Chinese people in Manchuria officially became 'Manchukuokan' (which we might now translate as 'Manchurian'; the appellation 'Chinese' was mostly used for new Han immigrants into Manchuria). The Japanese secret police conducted the extortion and kidnapping for ransom of wealthy members of the émigré community.

The situation of Russians under Japanese rule worsened with the Soviet sale of the CER to Manchukuo in 1935. The railway employees, holders of Soviet passports, were then 'repatriated' to the USSR, where most of them soon perished in the Stalinist purges. About 70 per cent of the Jews had also left Harbin by the mid-1930s. The remainder, increasingly maltreated in Harbin since the kidnapping and murder of Semen Kaspe, the son of the owner of Harbin's Hotel Moderne in December 1933,[27] were co-opted by the Japanese into being part of the Manchukuo propaganda machine by entering the National Council of Far Eastern Jewish Communities in 1937.[28] A Committee of Nationalities set up by BREM in 1940 included representatives from that Council as well as from the Armenian, Georgian, Türk-Tatar and Ukrainian communities.[29]

Ideology and propaganda

At the inauguration of the new state, the Japanese advertised Manchukuo as 'a paradise of five nations': Han Chinese, Manchu, Japanese, Korean (referred to as Chosenese) and Mongol. Because Koreans were treated as Japanese subjects, however, they were replaced on this list by Muslims. The smallest of the above populations, the Manchus, were sometimes listed together with the Han Chinese as 'Manchurian', in which case Russians replaced the Han to be included among the five 'harmonious races'.[30] It was no coincidence that the Republic of China, created in 1911, had similarly advertised itself as consisting of five peoples: Han, Manchu, Muslim (Hui), Mongol and Tibetan. To these five, the Miao and the Yao were later added (the fifty-five national minorities, with which we are familiar today, are a creation of Maoist ethnic policy in 1954). Justly notorious for attempting to equate racial heterogeneity with interracial harmony (*minzu xiehe* 民族協和), the 'five nations' discourse in Manchukuo may have convinced only the Japanese, especially in Japan itself rather than on the ground in Manchuria. Among the 'five nations' in question, it could have had some limited appeal to the Manchus.[31]

In reality, however, on the eve of the Japanese occupation of Manchuria, Han Chinese made up almost 96 per cent of the region's population, while the Japanese amounted to less than 1 per cent. The Japanese vision of harmony among Asians (albeit under uncontested Japanese leadership) paid lip service to the idea, dominant since President Woodrow Wilson's Fourteen Points at the end of World War One, that plain old-style colonialism was no longer acceptable and state regimes should be determined by the free will of their populations. The image promoted in Manchukuo was also part of a larger pan-Asian vision. Japan proclaimed a 'new order in East Asia' in November 1938, and 'the Greater East Asia Co-Prosperity Sphere' was promulgated in 1943. It was outspokenly anti-Western and meant to replace the Versailles System, which Japan claimed had been imposed on the world after the Great War.

While the Manchu component of Manchukuo was often toned down, so as not to encourage restoration of the Qing, efforts were initially made to ensure the cooperation of the Mongols. The whole set of Japanese propaganda was presented in terms of *wangdao* 王道 (Japanese: *ōdō*), the 'kingly way', an ancient Chinese notion idealized in Confucian writing and advocated also by Sun Yat-sen and Chiang Kai-shek. The same slogan was later used in occupied China, once the collaborationist regime of Wang Jingwei 汪精衛 (1883–1944) was established in Nanking in March 1940. Wang was a former close associate of Sun Yat-sen, who had headed the left wing of the KMT in Guangzhou (Canton) after the split of the Nationalist Party in January 1927, but moved to the right so as to serve the Japanese. To promote the inculcation of these ideals in Manchukuo, the Kyowakai Association (Chinese: *Xiehe hui* 協和會), translated as Concordia, was founded on 1 April 1932. Initially called a 'party', it was reorganized as an 'association' on 25 July 1932. Four years later, it was fully integrated within the Manchukuo state apparatus. Kyowakai propaganda promoted Manchukuo as an 'ideal land'.[32] From April 1937, youths aged 16 to 19 were forced to join the movement, which counted over 1 million members by 1938, and from 1940 Kyowakai supervised the conscription of all males over 19 years old.

To lend credence to the illusion of Manchurian sovereignty, Japanese officers were required to learn Chinese, although Japanese was the official state language of Manchukuo. There was apparently some encouragement of intermarriage among the 'five nations', although this excluded the Japanese. The Japanese rulers presented themselves as patrons of Confucianism by building temples (both Confucian and Shinto) and by publicly rewarding dutiful sons and daughters-in-law and honouring the very old. The virtue of loyalty was celebrated by funeral ceremonies to soldiers of all nationalities, who served the Manchukuo regime.

In the villages, the Japanese enforced the ancient Chinese *baojia* 保甲 system of mutual responsibility, which also prevented contact between villagers and the Chinese resistance.[33] In China during the same period, Japan's rival Chiang Kai-shek launched his own Confucian revival, the New Life Movement (1934). The Japanese, for their part, established the New People's Society (*Xinmin hui* 新民會) in Manchukuo as a further ideological tool to justify their rule.

Religious indoctrination went hand in hand with denunciation of the atheist Communist state beyond the border. Like Russia, Zhang Xueliang (whose past regime was always referred to as a corrupt tyranny, *badao* 霸道) and the KMT were presented as the arch enemies of Manchukuo. In Japan, the press celebrated Japanese women settlers as future breeders of little 'Manchurian Japanese'. A recurrent slogan was *jianguo jingshen* 建國精神, state-building spirit, designed to evoke enthusiasm for the 'construction of the country'; both notions were taught at schools. In 1934 the Japanese opened a Judicial Law College, and in 1937 a Law University was founded in Changchun.[34] A National Foundation University (Kenkoku in Japanese, or Jianguo Daxue 建國大學 in Chinese) was also established in 1937 to train the state's future leaders from among all nationalities (including Russians). It devoted three years of the six-year course to indoctrination in *jianguo* (state-building) spirit, military training and the Japanese language. After this university closed down in 1945, its buildings continued to serve Chinese institutions of higher education in the PRC.

Emperor Puyi travelled to Japan with his wife in 1934 on a voyage that also included the US coast and Hawaii, and returned for an official audience with Emperor Hirohito (1901–89) in 1935.[35] After the Japanese forced Puyi to make another visit to Hirohito in June 1940 and accept the symbols of the Shinto religion from him, they introduced worship of the divine founder of Japan, the goddess Amaterasu, in Manchukuo (an attempt was even made to introduce this cult into Russian churches), and Shinto was declared the official religion of the state.[36] A copy of the Imperial Shrine of Yasukuni was built in Puyi's palace in Changchun.

The Manchukuo State

Figure 11a Emperor of Manchuria, Puyi, visits Yasukuni shrine. Japanese postcard, 1935. Lafayette College, East Asia Image Collection.

City-building and administration

The heavy Manchukuo propaganda campaign targeted the outside world and the inhabitants of Manchuria, but it was also needed to reaffirm Japan's self-image and ensure the support of the Japanese public opinion at home. A major component of Japanese imperialism in Manchuria was construction.[37] The Japanese imperial vision originally comprised a utopian programme of building fifty new cities and model villages for future Japanese settlers, who never arrived, but Changchun/Xinjing/Shinkyō is the place where this vision came closest to realization. When chosen for the role of capital in April 1932, Changchun was a small riverside town of about 130,000 people, serving as the northernmost terminus of the SMR and the southernmost of the CER.

Contrary to 'Russian' Harbin and the Manchu heritage in Shenyang, Changchun offered the new regime an opportunity to launch a new and ambitious project. The Japanese already possessed a base there in the form of their railway settlement, which had been much developed before 1931, along with the parallel settlement in Mukden. The architects of new Xinjing had formerly been associated with the SMR and, in particular, with its first president, Gotō Shinpei, who supervised building in the settlement near Changchun in the 1910s. Their affiliation was civilian rather than military. But after a long and bitter struggle, by 1934 the Kwantung Army managed to restrict the authority of the SMR to operating the railway, so it could no longer be involved in the management of Manchukuo. Instead, the creation of a Manchurian Affairs Bureau eliminated the remnants of 'informal empire' and effectively subordinated Manchukuo to the army.[38]

The first five-year plan (1932–7) aimed to enlarge Changchun considerably and bring its population to 300,000. Broad avenues and large squares were built in grand imperial style, supposedly modelled after Paris, as well as many parks and other green spaces. To these were added a new sanitary system, telephone and electricity, asphalt pavements and an efficient public transport system. The population rose to 172,000 in 1933, then to 335,000 (of whom 20 per cent were Japanese) in 1937, 415,000 in 1939 and over 500,000 in 1940; a new population target of 1 million was set in 1939. As modernization was equated with Westernization, construction in Changchun (apart from the Japanese temples) was carried out in an architectural style close to European Art Nouveau, with only the symbolic incorporation of Chinese tiled roofs.

The brilliant new capital was intended to demonstrate Japan's abilities to the world, as well as offer a future model for cities in Japan itself. Emperor Puyi, however, resided in the outskirts of the city in a complex of buildings that had previously housed the administration of the salt trade; this complex, where parts of the 1987 film *The Last Emperor* by Bernardo Bertolucci were filmed, is now a tourist attraction in Changchun as the Museum of the Imperial Palace of Manchukuo. Only in 1938 did Puyi's Japanese patrons consent to build him a palace in Chinese style, which was meant to face south in accordance with the emperor's place in the cosmic order, but construction stopped in 1943.

War crimes

The Japanese occupation in Manchuria is by now most infamously associated with the atrocities of Unit 731. At Pingfang 平房, 20 km south of Harbin city, Unit 731 made experiments in bacteriological warfare (BW) on Chinese and possibly also a number of Russian captives under the guise of an epidemic prevention centre and a water-purifying factory. BW experiments were also conducted in a suburb of Changchun, in another centre of bacteriological warfare called Unit 100. The biologist Ishii Shiro (1892–1959), commander of Unit 731 from 1933 to 1942 and again from March to August 1945, established his laboratory at Pingfang in 1938 with a staff of three thousand. His elder brother was in charge of the unit's underground prison, to which the victims, known as *maruta* (Japanese for wood logs) were brought by 'special delivery'. A railway connected the unit with the Pingfang railway station (no longer in use today), photographs of which bring to mind images of the Holocaust. The medical experiments on human subjects by Ishii and other Japanese doctors certainly recall those of Josef Mengele (1911–79), who also escaped justice and died of natural causes in Brazil.

The 'experiments' conducted in Manchuria included infection with plague, cholera and typhoid bacteria, and subjection to frostbite. Live dissection was practised and poison gas used against those who resisted. In a pioneering study of the Japanese war crimes in Manchuria, historian Sheldon Harris estimated the number of people killed by Unit 731 at between 10,000 and 12,000.[39] As of 2011, the memorial in Pingfang only indicated the figure of 'at least 3,000' people killed in the laboratories from 1939 to 1945.[40] According to the explanatory texts at the exhibition, the Japanese army used chemical weapons 'more than two thousand times' in nineteen provinces of China, affecting nearly 200,000 persons. Long after the end of the war, chemical weapons left behind by the Japanese and buried in the Manchurian ground continued to cause damage, as happened in Qiqihar in 2003 and in two cases in Jilin province in 2004 and 2005. Following exposure to mustard gas at a building site in Qiqihar in August 2003, the victims travelled to Tokyo to prepare a lawsuit against the Japanese government at the initiative of a group of volunteer Japanese lawyers.[41]

Unit 731 operated in strict secrecy: the dead were cremated and the last prisoners to remain alive were liquidated before Japan's capitulation, when the Japanese army also destroyed the site in Pingfang. After the war's end, the US occupation authorities in Japan made a deal with Ishii that he would not be prosecuted in return for some of the results of his biological warfare experiments on humans (of the kind that could not be conducted in the US). In 1948 Ishii and his staff were granted immunity on these conditions. When Ishii was still alive, a book under the pseudonym Akiyama Hiroshi, *Special Unit 731*, came out in Japan in 1956; a translation into Russian was published in 1958. The international breakthrough in research on the subject came only in 1993, as Sheldon Harris published his *Factories of Death: Japanese Biological Warfare, 1932–45, and the American Cover-up*; a revised second edition came out in 2002.

Japanese war criminals were tried by an international tribunal in Tokyo, from May 1946 to November 1948. Initially the US and the USSR intended to collaborate in this trial, but then the Americans, who in August 1946 had first informed the tribunal that the Japanese had carried out biological warfare, did not hand over their prisoners despite repeated Soviet requests to question Ishii.[42] The US had itself begun a BW programme at Fort Derrick, Maryland, in 1943, but lagged behind Japanese and Soviet research. Scientists from Fort Derrick interviewed Ishii while he was in US detention and obtained information from him, although a later allegation (spread by Communist China and initially supported by the Soviet Union) that the Americans used biological warfare in the Korean War (1950–3) was a pure propaganda hoax.[43]

Lacking access to Ishii and his staff, the Soviets did not raise the issue of bacteriological warfare in Tokyo and instead put their own Japanese prisoners on trial in Khabarovsk in December 1949. Under laws originally formulated for trying the Nazis, twelve men were convicted of using BW and experimenting on humans. After pleading guilty, they were sentenced to imprisonment in labour camps from two to twenty-five years. They were released and repatriated once the Soviet Union declared an amnesty for Japanese prisoners in December 1956. Harris suggests that these Japanese were released in return for BW information they had revealed. The Soviets had a similar research unit, 'the laboratory of death', running under Grigorii Mairanovskii (1899–1964), and poison gas was tested on Gulag prisoners. Also in 1956, the PRC staged in Shenyang a trial of thirty-six Chinese collaborators with the Manchukuo regime.[44]

In the PRC, papers related to Unit 731 were already discovered in Changchun in 1953, but they were filed away in the archives. At the time, Communist China had no interest in these Japanese atrocities, or in those perpetrated on a far larger scale in 'the rape of Nanjing', from December 1937 to January 1938, where over 100,000 civilians perished. When the Mao government re-established relations with Japan in 1972, China gave up reparations for the war in return for Japanese economic investments in the PRC (previously, Japan had established its relations with the Republic of China on Taiwan on the same basis, signing the Treaty of Taipei in 1952). This policy silenced the war's living victims until the 1980s, when the CCP began to base the legitimacy of its rule by portraying itself as the sole power able to defend China from foreign aggression.[45] Making people remember the Japanese atrocities was also useful in the context of the history textbook controversy with Japan, which began in 1982, over interpretation of the war, and it helped to repress the much more recent trauma of the Cultural Revolution.[46]

The memorial in Pingfang, now part of Harbin, was opened in 1985, also the year when the Nanjing Massacre Memorial Hall was created (later, in 1991, a September 18 History Museum opened in Shenyang to commemorate the 'Mukden incident' of 1931). Between 2014 and 2015, the Harbin memorial underwent a major expansion.[47] Among the exhibits are the US files related to Unit 731, which were declassified in 2007, including medical reports detailing the results of the unit's experiments: this supports the claim that the US had obtained the reports in exchange for guaranteeing the immunity of the Japanese perpetrators. As of 2011, there were also the photographs and names of the Japanese staff, such as the leader of the germ production squad (who killed himself while awaiting trial in Khabarovsk) and the anatomy squad, next to statements of repentance by former members of Unit 731. Images of vivisection were displayed using plaster models. The last hall of the exhibition was a corridor with name tablets covering both its walls; there were several hundred names and only a few among them had a small photograph attached, suggesting that only a small proportion of the victims have been identified. Beneath the tablets, there were scattered flowers, probably offerings brought by visitors.

Japanese wartime brutality towards Chinese and members of other nationalities in Manchuria had many other manifestations. First described in two well-known wartime publications in English (which can be safely assumed to have been embellished for effect),[48] since the 1980s they have been assiduously documented by historians in China.

Notes

1 Louise Young, 'Imagined Empire: The Cultural Construction of Manchukuo', in Duus et al., eds, *The Japanese Wartime Empire, 1931–1945*, pp. 73–9.

2   Zara Steiner, *The Lights That Failed: European International History, 1919–1933* (Oxford: Oxford University Press, 2005), ch. 13.
3   Ibid., pp. 739–40.
4   Ibid., quoting pp. 750–1, 741.
5   Thomas David DuBois, 'Inauthentic Sovereignty: Law and Legal Institutions in Manchukuo', *Journal of Asian Studies*, vol. 69, no. 3 (Aug. 2010), p. 766.
6   Aron Shai, *Zhang Xueliang: The General Who Never Fought* (Basingstoke: Palgrave Macmillan, 2012; original Hebrew edition in 2008).
7   The younger sister of Sun Yat-sen's wife, Song Qingling (1892–1981).
8   The First United Front had lasted from 1923 to the Shanghai coup of 12 April 1927; it had enabled the joint Northern Expedition of 1926, which aimed to unite China under Chiang's rule.
9   David Tucker, 'Labor Policy and the Construction Industry in Manchukuo: Systems of Recruitment, Management, and Control', in Paul H. Kratoska, ed., *Asian Labor in the Wartime Japanese Empire: Unknown Histories* (Armonk: M. E. Sharpe, 2005), pp. 36, 39, 42, gives the following data: from 630,000 in 1933, the numbers declined to 491,000 in 1935, but leapt to 1,123,663 in 1939 and 1,475,158 in 1940.
10 Cf. Ju Zhifen, 'Northern Chinese Laborers and Manchukuo', in Kratoska, ed., *Asian Labor in the Wartime Japanese Empire*, pp. 61–80.
11 This section mostly draws on Ann Waswo and Nishida Yoshiaki, eds, *Farmers and Village Life in Twentieth-Century Japan* (London: RoutledgeCurzon, 2003).
12 'In other words, only a few thousand Japanese have settled in Manchuria proper.' Simpich, 'Manchuria, Promised Land of Asia', p. 410.
13 The idea was to ensure that Japanese would make up 10 per cent of the whole Manchurian population (which was expected to reach 50 million in twenty years' time). See Young, 'Imagined Empire', pp. 88–94.
14 Louise Young, 'Colonizing Manchuria: The Making of an Imperial Myth', in Stephen Vlastos, ed., *Mirror of Modernity: Invented Traditions of Modern Japan* (Berkeley: University of California Press, 1998), pp. 100–1.
15 Mori Takemaro, 'Colonies and Countryside in Wartime Japan', in Waswo and Nishida, eds, *Farmers and Village Life*, at p. 183. The total number of Japanese in Manchuria in 1940 was 1 million, according to Mori, pp. 178–9 (which must include the majority of non-settlers).
16 On the arrival of Japanese women in Manchukuo, see Faye Yuan Kleeman, 'Inscribing Manchuria: Gender, Ideology and Popular Imagination', *East Asian History*, no. 30 (Dec. 2005), pp. 47–66.
17 See George Hicks, 'The "Comfort Women"', in Duus et al., eds, *The Japanese Wartime Empire, 1931–1945*, pp. 305–23. There have been a number of monographs especially devoted to this subject since 2000.
18 See Rana Mitter, *The Manchurian Myth: Nationalism, Resistance, and Collaboration in Modern China* (Berkeley: University of California Press, 2000).

19 Elizabeth McGuire, *Red at Heart: How Chinese Communists Fell in Love with the Russian Revolution* (Oxford: Oxford University Press, 2018), pp. 214–19.
20 See the two-volume biography by Carter J. Eckert, *Park Chung Hee and Modern Korea* (Cambridge MA: Belknap Press; vol. 1, 2016).
21 Hoo Nam Seelmann, 'Held oder Terrorist? Kontroverse um ein Museum in Harbin', *Neue Zürcher Zeitung* (NZZ), 24 Jan. 2014. On An as a celebrated hero and martyr in South Korea, see Guy Podoler, *Monuments, Memory, and Identity: Constructing the Colonial Past in South Korea* (Bern: Peter Lang, 2011), pp. 190–9.
22 On this, and more on the volunteer armies, see Anthony Coogan, 'Northeast China and the Origins of the Anti-Japanese United Front', *Modern China*, vol. 20, no. 3 (July 1994), pp. 282–314.
23 Thomas David DuBois, 'Manchukuo's Filial Sons: States, Sects and the Adaptation of Graveside Piety', *East Asian History*, vol. 36 (Dec. 2008), p. 15.
24 Y. Tak Matsusaka, 'Managing Occupied Manchuria, 1931–1934', in Duus et al., eds, *The Japanese Wartime Empire, 1931–1945*, p. 108, n. 29.
25 See David P. Barrett and Larry N. Shyu, eds, *Chinese Collaboration with Japan, 1932–1945: The Limits of Accommodation* (Stanford: Stanford University Press, 2001).
26 Takeshi Nakashima, 'Forming the Russian Fascist Party in Harbin 1925–1933', *The Journal of Social Sciences and Humanities* (Jinbun Gakuko, Tokyo), no. 505 (March 2015), pp. 1–19.
27 Mark Gamsa, 'The Many Faces of Hotel Moderne in Harbin', *East Asian History*, vol. 37 (Dec. 2011), pp. 27–38.
28 Avraham Altman, 'Controlling the Jews, Manchukuo Style', in Roman Malek, ed., *From Kaifeng . . . to Shanghai: Jews in China* (Sankt Augustin: Monumenta Serica Monograph Series, vol. 46, 2000), pp. 279–317.
29 Olga Bakich, 'Russian Émigrés in Harbin's Multinational Past: Censuses and Identity', in Dan Ben-Canaan et al., eds, *Entangled Histories: The Transcultural Past of Northeast China* (Heidelberg: Springer, 2014), p. 94.
30 Olga Bakich, 'Émigré Identity: The Case of Harbin', *The South Atlantic Quarterly*, vol. 99, no. 1 (Winter 2000), p. 62.
31 See Shao Dan, *Remote Homeland, Recovered Borderland*, ch. 4.
32 On Concordia and *baojia*, see esp. Xie Xueshi, 'The Organization and Grassroots Structure of the Manzhouguo Regime', in Stephen R. MacKinnon et al., eds, *China at War: Regions of China, 1937–45* (Stanford: Stanford University Press, 2007).
33 Mo Tian, 'The *Baojia* System as Institutional Control in Manchukuo under Japanese Rule (1932–45)', *Journal of the Economic and Social History of the Orient*, vol. 59, no. 4 (Oct. 2016), pp. 531–54.
34 DuBois, 'Inauthentic Sovereignty', pp. 752–3.
35 Gavan McCormack, 'Manchukuo: Constructing the Past', *East Asian History*, vol. 2 (Dec. 1991), here pp. 112–15.
36 Sergei I. Kuznetsov and Sergei V. Karasov, 'The Last Emperor of China: Internment in the Soviet Union', *Journal of Slavic Military Studies*, vol. 18 (June 2005), at pp. 223–6, reproduces Puyi's letter to the Soviet authorities on

his audience with Hirohito in 1940 and his forced acceptance of Shinto under Japanese pressure. On the uses of Shinto in Japanese wartime propaganda, see more in Helen Hardacre, *Shinto: A History* (Oxford: Oxford University Press, 2016).

37 See Edward Denison and Guangyu Ren, *Ultra-Modernism: Architecture and Modernity in Manchuria* (Hong Kong: Hong Kong University Press, 2017) and esp. Bill Sewell, *Constructing Empire: The Japanese in Changchun, 1905–45* (Vancouver and Toronto: UBC Press, 2019). Cf. David Tucker, 'City Planning without Cities: Order and Chaos in Utopian Manchukuo', in Mariko Asano Tamanoi, ed., *Crossed Histories: Manchuria in the Age of Empire* (Honolulu: University of Hawaii Press, 2005).
38 Matsusaka, 'Managing Occupied Manchuria, 1931–1934', pp. 112–35.
39 Sheldon Harris, *Factories of Death: Japanese Biological Warfare, 1932–45, and the American Cover-up*, revised 2nd edn (New York: Routledge, 2002).
40 Here and below I use my notes from visit to the War Crimes Museum in Harbin on 4 August 2011.
41 Yukiko Koga, 'Accounting for Silence: Inheritance, Debt, and the Moral Economy of Legal Redress in China and Japan', *American Ethnologist*, vol. 40, no. 3 (Aug. 2013), pp. 494–507.
42 V. V. Romanova, 'Ot Tokiiskogo suda k Khabarovskomu: iz istorii podgotovki sudenbogo protsessa nad iaponskimi voennymi prestupnikami-bakteriologami', *Istoriia meditsiny*, vol. 2, no. 1 (2015), pp. 72–82.
43 The fictional charges made against the USA by the PRC and North Korea were lent support by a British committee headed by the pro-Communist sinologist Joseph Needham; see Anne-Marie Brady, *Making the Foreign Serve China: Managing Foreigners in the People's Republic* (Lanham: Rowman & Littlefield, 2003), pp. 85–6. On there being a hoax, see current research by Anton Weiss-Wendt (Oslo).
44 See Adam Cathcart, 'Resurrecting Defeat: International Propaganda and the Shenyang Trials of 1956', in Kerstin von Lingen, ed., *War Crimes Trials in the Wake of Decolonization and Cold War in Asia, 1945–1956: Justice in Time of Turmoil* (New York: Palgrave Macmillan, 2016); and Yun Xia, *Down with Traitors: Justice and Nationalism in Wartime China* (Seattle: University of Washington Press, 2018).
45 Koga, 'Accounting for Silence', pp. 498–9. See also Isabel Hinton, 'China: At War with Its History', *Prospect Magazine*, no. 187 (21 Sept. 2011); Perry Link, 'Beijing's Dangerous Game', *New York Review of Books* blog (20 Sept. 2012).
46 Tony Brooks, 'Angry States: Chinese Views of Japan as Seen through the Unit 731 War Museum 1949–2013', in Mark R. Frost et al., eds, *Remembering Asia's World War Two* (London: Routledge, 2019), pp. 27–55.
47 Didi Kirsten Tatlow, 'A New Look at Japan's Unit 731 Wartime Atrocities and a U.S. Cover-Up', *The Asia-Pacific Journal*, vol. 13, 44:3 (16 Nov. 2015).
48 Amleto Vespa, *Secret Agent of Japan: A Handbook to Japanese Imperialism* (London: Victor Gollancz, 1938), and Alexandre Pernikoff, *'Bushido': The Anatomy of Terror* (New York: Liveright, 1943).

12

Soviet Occupation, Civil War and Communist Victory, 1945–9

On 6 August 1945 the United States dropped the atomic bomb on Hiroshima, and on 8 August Stalin, too, declared war on Japan. On 9 August the Soviet Union began its advance into Manchuria with an army of 1.5 million troops. The USSR had signed a neutrality pact with Japan in April 1941, which was supposed to last until April 1946. Days before the invasion of Manchuria, Japan's leaders still hoped to use Soviet Russia as an intermediary to negotiate a peace treaty with the United States. However, the Japanese, who did not know about the nuclear bomb, were also unaware that after conferring with Roosevelt and Winston Churchill in Yalta in February 1945 Stalin had obtained American and British permission to restore the tsarist positions of power in Manchuria as they had been before the Russo-Japanese War, including the unification of Sakhalin and continued influence in Mongolia, in return for his promise to fight Japan.

The Japanese army had occupied and run Manchukuo since 1932, but the Japanese forces which the Soviets had to fight in northern Manchuria consisted mainly of recent conscripts and the colonists called 'pioneer settlers'. After Emperor Hirohito announced Japan's surrender in a radio broadcast on 15 August 1945, the regular army filled the trains heading south to Korea, from which the soldiers sailed back to Japan. Civilians, however, were left to fend for themselves. Of the approximately 223,000 settlers, about 78,500 perished, whether by direct violence including collective suicides and lynching by the Chinese, or by starvation and disease. The survivors spent a year in Soviet refugee camps.[1] Some women settlers married Chinese peasants and remained in China.[2] About five thousand Japanese children were abandoned or sold to villagers in Manchuria. While acknowledging the differences, there is room for comparison here with the fate of Jewish children in Poland, who were raised by Christians during the war and also had to struggle with the subsequent discovery of their ethnicity and separation from their adoptive parents.[3]

The process of repatriating the Japanese children from China started after the war, but stopped with the end of Sino-Japanese cooperation in 1958. At that point the Japanese government began declaring the missing persons of the war as dead. Almost another decade after the normalization of Chinese–Japanese relations in 1972, the grown-up children, raised by Chinese foster parents, began arriving in Japan in thirty organized 'relative-seeking visits', from 1981 to 1999. It was a highly complex process, in which the Japanese state and society showed unwillingness to accept the repatriates, who usually spoke no Japanese and did not even know their original Japanese names, and who, by their unlikely return from the dead, revived buried shadows of the war. After protests by the so-called war orphans about the obstacles raised to their naturalization in Japan, a legal settlement guaranteeing them acceptable living conditions was reached only as late as 2007.[4] Some of the war orphans, however, preferred to remain in China.

Surprisingly, over 60,000 of the Japanese soldiers left behind were mobilized into the Chinese armies, both Nationalist and Communist.[5] Of 'more than a million and a half Japanese nationals' who were in Manchuria on the day of the Soviet attack in August 1945,[6] including about 100,000 Japanese in Harbin, a city where they had made up one sixth of the total population, over 600,000 were taken as prisoners to Siberia.[7] During the eight-day war, the Japanese placed Soviet citizens in Harbin in prisons or detention camps, and their families expected their execution. Those who survived these tense days were released once Emperor Puyi abdicated on 17 August 1945.

The historical events of that momentous month can be followed from day to day. On 18 August 1945, Soviet troops entered Harbin and were welcomed by the city's Russians, who did not anticipate the swift purge which was to follow. About 12,000 of Harbin's 'White Russians' were loaded on trucks and wagons, later to be executed or sentenced to years of imprisonment in Siberian labour camps. The operation was carried out by Smersh (short for *Smert' shpionam*, meaning 'Death to the spies'), the sinister military counter-intelligence unit of the Soviet army. Arrests also took place elsewhere in Manchuria, especially in Dairen where several former leaders of the White military had lived under Japanese protection. The Cossack ataman (military leader), Grigorii Semenov (born 1890), once the self-declared supreme commander of the White Army, was arrested by Smersh in Dairen in August 1945. The following year, he was tried and hanged in Moscow.

Among those arrested in Harbin for collaborating with the Japanese was the physician Abram Kaufman (1886–1971), who had lived in Harbin from 1912 and was the leader of the Jewish community. He was to spend sixteen years in Soviet camps and in Kazakhstan, after which he joined his family in Tel Aviv. He related his experiences in a memoir entitled *The Camp Doctor*, published in Israel in both Hebrew and Russian.⁸ The question of alleged Jewish collaboration with Manchukuo's regime continues to arouse debate. In place of the Bureau for the Affairs of Russian Emigrants, during the year of Soviet power in Manchuria a Society of Soviet Citizens was created in Harbin, which continued to administer the affairs of remaining Soviet subjects there in collaboration with the Soviet Consulate.

On 19 August 1945, former Emperor Puyi was arrested at the Mukden airport together with his entourage, including his brother Pujie 溥傑 (1907-94). Puyi was about to be evacuated to Japan, against his will as he later claimed. He then passed five years in comfortable confinement in the Soviet Far East, the first six weeks in Chita and the rest in Khabarovsk. During that time, Puyi wrote letters to Stalin, asking permission to remain in the USSR and even expressing a wish to join the Soviet Communist Party.⁹ In the trial of Japanese war criminals in Tokyo in August 1946, he performed to the satisfaction of his Soviet captors by placing all responsibility for Manchukuo on the Japanese.

Even the Soviets were surprised to hear Puyi declare himself an atheist at the Tokyo trial. In 1998 the USA declassified archival documents, in which American agents in Japan in 1948 had reported on a Soviet plan to 'reinstall' Puyi as president of a 'united Manchurian-Mongolian republic or a "Chinese Soviet District Government" with two branches for Manchuria and Mongolia'.¹⁰ Despite his entreaties, Puyi and his associates were extradited to the PRC in August 1950. They were sent for ten years of 're-education' in the War Criminals Management Centre in Fushun. The outcome was Puyi's famous autobiography, *From Emperor to Citizen*, translated into many languages.¹¹ The former emperor of China and Manchukuo was eventually allowed to marry, but not to have children. He died in Beijing of natural causes in October 1967.

Parallel to the arrests they conducted, some of the Soviet troops looted civilians and raped women in Manchuria, especially the defenceless Russian émigrés. Two days after Harbin, the Red Army captured Shenyang on 20 August. Under the definition of Japanese war booty, the Soviets dismantled and confiscated most of the infrastructure of the Manchurian industry, which had been set up in the Manchukuo period. Terrible inflation raged. Teddy Kaufman (1924–2012), who took over his father's past role in Harbin as the head of the Association of Former Jewish Residents from China in Israel, recalled that by the time the Soviets left Harbin on 30 April 1946 he was earning a monthly salary of 5 million *yuan*, the equivalent of only five American dollars.¹²

Figure 12 Soviet soldiers in process of removing industrial equipment from Manchurian factories. Photograph by US Army Signal Corps, 1946. Library of Congress.

Civil war renewed

The USSR and USA invaded the Far East at the same time, racing to establish facts on the ground.[13] The Soviets grabbed Manchuria and North Korea, while the Americans took South Korea and Japan. In Dalian, the Soviet forces were to stay from 1945 to 1955. Chinese Communist troops joined the fray in Manchuria in August 1945, acting to prevent the establishment of Soviet power. At the Seventh Congress of the CCP, held in April–June 1945, Mao had declared that it was now time for the Party to change its tactic of relying on the peasantry and take control of the cities. After Mao's negotiations with Chiang (which the Americans had set up in Chongqing between 28 August and 10 October) had failed to resolve their differences, the Communist army launched its offensive in the Northeast, which would prove decisive in winning the Civil War.

Stalin, true to his preference for the Nationalists, whom he still considered more likely to win, signed a treaty with the KMT regime in August 1945. In late November this treaty was followed by an agreement, according to which the KMT administration was to be restored in Manchuria and the Soviet army would retreat on 1 February, in return for joint Sino-Soviet control over the Northeast industry. Stalin also invited Chiang Kai-shek to the USSR and met his Moscow-educated, Russian-speaking son Chiang Ching-kuo in December.

From mid-November to mid-January, accordingly, the KMT was able to appoint its own administrators in Manchurian cities under limited Soviet protection. But rather than commit himself to the Soviet Union, Chiang Kai-shek preferred to play it off against the Americans. For its part, the USSR pursued a flexible and sometimes contradictory policy which left options open in case the balance of power changed in favour of the CCP. Failing to obtain the hoped-for economic concessions from Chiang, under growing American pressure and due to global Cold War considerations, the Red Army withdrew from Manchuria in a process lasting from 7 March to 3 May 1946. The slow Soviet withdrawal was accompanied by demonstrations organized by the KMT in the territories it controlled, in which imperialist Russia was urged to vacate Chinese territory. Despite pleas from the KMT, the Russians did not wait for their representatives to arrive in each evacuated location. As soon as the Soviets left, the ceasefire arranged in January by General George C. Marshall (1880–1959), head of the US mission in China, collapsed and battles broke out between Nationalist and Communist forces.[14]

On 18 April the CCP forces already moved into the power vacuum, occupying Changchun, and they took Harbin on 28 April 1946. It was not until 6 June that Marshall managed to secure a new truce. By that time the Communists had suffered several defeats at the hands of the Nationalist army, notably in Siping 四平, and they were about to evacuate Harbin; hence the American intervention probably saved them.[15] The USA was concerned by the impending fall of Northeast China to Communist China, and Marshall was entrusted with mediation to bring about coalition rule of Manchuria, and the whole of China, by the CCP and the KMT. When these efforts failed, the Americans did not go out of their way to save the faltering regime of Chiang Kai-shek, beyond arranging that in summer 1945 the Japanese would surrender to the Nationalist rather than the Communist army. Barely out of the World War and being preoccupied with Japan, the US was not yet ready for a preventive military campaign in China, although in 1950 America would go to war again in an attempt to block the spread of Communism into Korea.

Fighting between the Communists and the Nationalists resumed in autumn 1946 and, despite other victories by the KMT until summer 1947, by the end of that year the CCP had seized 586 cities, probably more than it had expected or was able to hold.[16] The KMT had suffered its worst defeats in Manchuria, where it lost 470,000 men out of a total force of 3.73 million. Chiang's army lost 1.5 million men from September 1948 to January 1949 alone.[17] The complete conquest of Manchuria was achieved by the Communist army under Lin Biao 林彪 (1907–71), later to become Mao Zedong's deputy, by 5 November 1948. In mid-November, thousands of KMT soldiers escaping from Manchuria looted Tianjin. That northern port, too, was soon conquered by the Communists on 15 January 1949; Beijing fell on 31 January and Nanjing on 24 April (forcing the escape of the KMT government first to Guangdong and thence, on 13 October, to Chongqing). Establishment of the PRC was proclaimed by Mao Zedong on Tiananmen Square on 1 October 1949, while the KMT retreated to Taiwan on 8 December.

After Communist victory

Harbin was the first city 'liberated' by the CCP, and the methods used there were a laboratory for later urban takeovers. Between seizing the city in the end of April 1946 and September that year, the CCP arrested 933 persons in the outskirts of Harbin. These included suspected Japanese war criminals, their Chinese collaborators, landlords, KMT agents and counter-revolutionaries; seventy persons were executed. The plan had been to 'cleanse' the outskirts before tackling the city itself, but this operation was already a second Communist purge after the one carried out by the Soviet army in summer 1945. The resulting chaos spread into Harbin, too, as random arrests and lack of security continued into 1947.

The Chinese Communists had been used to the living conditions in their mountain base of Yan'an 延安 in Shaanxi province and most of their cadres were villagers with no prior knowledge of city life. The early debacles in Harbin caused embarrassment to the Party, so it elaborated a policy of 'studying' cities before takeover, registering all the inhabitants to be able to monitor them,[18] and (although this was not the case in Harbin) co-opting the former KMT police while purging its more dangerous elements. As a part of this strategy, in February 1947 the CCP ordered the formation of internal security groups in every work unit, to uncover and register all potential enemies of the regime. Harbin, accordingly, was a testing ground for the systems of population control that would soon spread all over the PRC. But let us defer the further review of Manchuria under Communist power for a look at Northeastern literature.

Notes

1   Data from Robert Efird, 'Japan's "War Orphans": Identification and State Responsibility', *Journal of Japanese Studies*, vol. 34, no. 2 (Summer 2008),

pp. 367–8. The estimate of 5,000 Japanese children left in China follows Mayumi Itoh, *Japanese War Orphans in Manchuria: Forgotten Victims of World War II* (New York: Palgrave Macmillan, 2010). Meyer, *In Manchuria*, p. 183, gives the total number of Japanese settlers as 270,000, of whom 80,000 (mostly women and children) died by the end of the war. On the suicides and Soviet-run camps, see ibid., pp. 186–8.

2 Meyer, *In Manchuria*, pp. 188–90, describes a visit to Fangzheng County 方正縣 (under the jurisdiction of Harbin city) and its graveyard, a pilgrimage site for descendants of Japanese settlers. Yeeshan Chan, *Abandoned Japanese in Postwar Manchuria: The Lives of War Orphans and Wives in Two Countries* (London: Routledge, 2011), uses the figure of 13,000 for both categories of 'orphans and wives', based on a PRC government estimate of 1959.

3 See, for example, Nahum Bogner, trans. Ralph Mandel, *At the Mercy of Strangers: The Rescue of Jewish Children with Assumed Identities in Poland* (Jerusalem: Yad Vashem, 2009); and the memoir by Irene Eber, *The Choice: Poland, 1939–1945* (New York: Schocken Books, 2004).

4 Efird, 'Japan's "War Orphans"'. See on this also: Mariko Asano Tamanoi, *Memory Maps: The State and Manchuria in Postwar Japan* (Honolulu: University of Hawaii Press, 2008), esp. chs. 3 and 4.

5 Meyer, *In Manchuria*, p. 187. Cf. Donald G. Gillin and Charles Etter, 'Staying On: Japanese Soldiers and Civilians in China, 1945–1949', *Journal of Asian Studies*, vol. 42, no. 3 (May 1983), pp. 497–518.

6 Efird, 'Japan's "War Orphans"', p. 367. Meyer, *In Manchuria*, p. 183, also says there were 1.5 million Japanese living in Manchukuo at the time, of whom only 17 per cent were village settlers.

7 See Andrew E. Barshay, *The Gods Left First: The Captivity and Repatriation of Japanese POWs in Northeast Asia, 1945–1956* (Berkeley: University of California Press, 2013).

8 Dr A. I. Kaufman, *Lagernyi vrach. 16 let v Sovetskom Soiuze – vospominaniia sionista* (Tel Aviv: Am oved, 1973).

9 Kuznetsov and Karasov, 'The Last Emperor of China', pp. 212–13, 220–3.

10 Quoted in Giovanni Stary, 'Il mistero Pu Yi: da ultimo imperatore della Cina a presidente di un'ipotetica "Repubblica Sovietica della Manciuria"?', *Scritture di storia* (Naples), no. 4 (2005), p. 289.

11 Puyi, trans. W. J. F. Jenner, *From Emperor to Citizen: The Autobiography of Aisin-Gioro Pu Yi*, in 2 vols (Peking: Foreign Languages Press, 1964–5).

12 Theodore (Teddy) Kaufman, *The Jews of Harbin Live on in My Heart* (Tel Aviv: Association of Former Jewish Residents from China in Israel, 2006).

13 Much of the following draws on Steven I. Levine, *Anvil of Victory: The Communist Revolution in Manchuria, 1945–1948* (New York: Columbia University Press, 1987).

14 General Marshall was appointed as special representative of the US president in China. He replaced General Joseph Stilwell (1883–1946), commander of the American forces in China, Burma and India, who had been recalled in 1944. Marshall went on to serve as Secretary of State in 1947–9, launching

the Marshall plan for the post-war reconstruction of Europe. He became President Harry S. Truman's Secretary of Defense in 1950 and was awarded the Nobel Peace Prize in 1953. See Daniel Kurtz-Phelan, *The China Mission: George Marshall's Unfinished War, 1945–1947* (New York: W. W. Norton, 2018).

15 Harold M. Tanner, *The Battle for Manchuria and the Fate of China: Siping, 1946* (Bloomington: Indiana University Press, 2013).
16 Michael Dutton and Li Shaorong, 'Seizing the City: Policing in the Era of the City Takeover (1945–1949)', *Berliner China-Hefte*, no. 22 (May 2002), at p. 58, n. 18; p. 59, n. 19.
17 Hsü, *The Rise of Modern China*, pp. 632–3.
18 In November 1946, 568,948 inhabitants were counted in Harbin. The aim was to ensure what Dutton and Li, 'Seizing the City' call *stasis*; by 1958, any unauthorized movement of citizens became impossible through the implementation of the *hukou* 戶口 registration system.

13

The Northeast through Literature

Xiao Hong and others

The celebrated woman writer Xiao Hong 蕭紅 (1911–42) and the two men in her life, Xiao Jun 蕭軍 (1907–88) and Duanmu Hongliang 端木蕻良 (1912–96), together made up the famous trio of Northeast writers in the twentieth century.[1] Xiao Hong was born in Hulan, by now a district of Harbin. She lived in Harbin from 1926 to 1929, then went to Beijing with a lover who turned out to be married, and she returned penniless to Harbin in 1931. She published an appeal for help in a Harbin paper, and the writer Xiao Jun answered it. Their moving in together in 1932 became the subject of her book *Market Street*. The couple had a child, whom Xiao Hong gave away at the Harbin hospital. After the Japanese invasion, the Xiaos moved to Qingdao and later to Shanghai, where they met Lu Xun, and Xiao Hong published *The Field of Life and Death* in 1935: a novelistic depiction of life in the Manchurian countryside, suffused with an intensity of feeling for its landscape and people. In failing health, after separating from Xiao Jun, Xiao Hong moved from town to town during the war. She decided against joining friends who went to serve the Communist cause in Yan'an. Despite poverty and illness, in Hong Kong in 1940 she completed another work that brought her posthumous fame, *Tales of Hulan River*. She died in war-torn Hong Kong soon after it fell to the Japanese. Her tomb was transferred to Guangzhou in 1957 and a museum opened in her birth house in Hulan in 1986.

The Field of Life and Death (first published in English in 1979) was incidentally one of the first full-length translations by Howard Goldblatt, who wrote his doctoral dissertation on Xiao Hong and later a monograph about her.[2] Since then, Goldblatt became the main translator of modern Chinese literature into English. A major film on Xiao Hong's life by director Ann Hui, *Huangjin shidai* 黃金時代 (The Golden Era), released in 2014, describes her harsh life and stormy relationship with Xiao Jun, emphasizing her quest for independence as a writer.

Xiao Jun himself, who came from a village near Jinzhou, is best known for his novel *Village in August* (published in the summer of 1935, shortly before Xiao Hong's *Field of Life and Death*). This idealized tale of peasant guerrilla

Figure 13 Xiao Hong Museum ('old residence of Xiao Hong'), Hulan. Public domain.

resistance to the Japanese under the guidance of the Communist Party was indebted to Lu Xun's 1931 translation, via the Japanese, of *The Rout* (Razgrom, 1926) by Alexander Fadeev (1901–56). In the Soviet novel, Red Army partisans in the Far East flee from pursuing Cossacks and Japanese interventionist forces. Xiao Jun's novel is much the opposite of Xiao Hong's *Field of Life and Death*, as it is blatantly anti-Japanese and justifies violence in the name of patriotism and class struggle. During World War Two, *Village in August* became the first modern Chinese novel to be translated into English.

The literary capital of the Northeast up to 1935 was Harbin. After that, once the established writers had left Manchukuo, younger authors emerged in Xinjing (Changchun) and Fengtian (Shenyang).[3] The war in the Northeast first turned the eyes of the nation and the writers resident in Shanghai to the remote region, where literary fiction had been written (but little noticed) already before the Japanese invasion. The best hope a refugee writer from Manchuria had of achieving fame was to contribute to the literature of resistance against the Japanese. Emboldened by his success, when Xiao Jun returned to Harbin from Yan'an in 1946 he allowed himself to criticize the brutality of Chinese and Soviet Communists during the still raging civil war.

He was sentenced to hard labour in the Fushun coal mines. Upon his release, in 1954, he published a huge 1,100-page volume, the first of a projected historical trilogy on Manchuria (*The Past Generation*, on which he had been working since the early 1940s). In 1958, after publishing another novel, *Coal Mines in May* (1955), Xiao Jun was branded 'rightist' for neglecting to highlight the role of Mao in coal production. He was victimized in all subsequent political campaigns until the end of the Cultural Revolution.

Duanmu Hongliang from western Liaoning, who married Xiao Hong in 1938, wrote much on the Manchurian and Inner Mongolian landscape and rural life. Aged only 21, he completed his long autobiographical novel *The Korchin Banner Plains* (published in 1939). The regional focus of his writing is reminiscent of writer Shen Congwen 沈從文 (1902–88), who described the landscape and minorities (the Miao and the Tujia) of Hunan province, in central China. But in contrast to Shen, who stopped writing in the 1940s, Duanmu adapted his literary work to the demands of the War of Resistance and later participated in the political mobilization of literature by the CCP. Identifying with the great Qing writer Cao Xueqin 曹雪芹 (1715?–63), through a putative family connection and a shared background in the Plain White Banner, Duanmu also wrote a commentary on Cao's classical novel *Dream of the Red Chamber*.[4]

At the same time, paradoxically, writers who remained in occupied Manchuria enjoyed greater creative freedom: subjected to Japanese censorship, they could not discuss politics (there were at least two collective arrests of writers in Harbin: in June 1936 and on the last December day of 1941),[5] but they could write on relationships, love and separation as long as their treatment of such themes was not considered lewd by the puritanical and patriarchal regime. To give but one example of a particularly original figure, Jue Qing 爵青 (1917–62), born and died in Changchun, was a self-taught, voracious reader of foreign literature, who wrote modern urban prose. Chinese women writers in Manchukuo are the subject of a monograph by historian Norman Smith, which from its title onwards aims at exonerating them from any possible charge of collaborating with the Japanese occupation regime. The reality must have been much more complex. The writers who had not left Manchukuo were tried as traitors beginning from the early 1950s; in the anti-rightist campaign of 1957 they were labelled 'writers of the enemy occupation' and this tag was only officially removed after the Cultural Revolution in 1978. Their works remained unpublished in the PRC until the late 1980s,[6] as the regime left no alternative to its own narrative of 'resistance'.

Born in Mohe 漠河, in the extreme north of Heilongjiang, in 1964, writer Chi Zijian 迟子建 is among the best-known Chinese women authors of her generation, who by now has been widely translated. A novel, originally published in Chinese as *The Right Bank of the Argun* and available in English as *The Last Quarter of the Moon*, is about the decline of the Evenki people in Inner Mongolia: it traces their move into urban housing from the 1990s, with flashbacks to the earlier twentieth century. The novel *Goodnight, Rose*, is set in Harbin, centring on a Jewish émigré, who had stayed in the city after other foreigners left it.[7]

Russian literature in Manchuria

The emergence of a whole corpus of Russian literature written and published in China was not a self-evident development; indeed, there was no parallel to it in British or American Shanghai, other than novels and memoirs mostly written already after the authors' departure from China. Russian literature in Harbin developed thanks to demand that grew especially after the arrival of refugees from the Revolution. It was facilitated by the existence of a large daily and periodical press, served by many publishing firms. Until the 1920s, Harbin literature was closely related to the literature of the Russian Far East, with the main themes of natural wilderness, hunting and encounters with 'exotic' minorities. A Harbin counterpart of Vladimir Arsenyev in Khabarovsk (the author of *Dersu Uzala*, already mentioned in our discussion of the indigenous peoples of Manchuria) was Nikolai Baikov (1872–1958), who wrote hugely popular sketches of tiger hunting in the Manchurian 'taiga'.

Another strain in Harbin Russian literature reflected a growing nostalgia for Russia and resulted in the predominance of poetry over prose and the creation of works that, rather than exploiting the Far Eastern surroundings, did not reveal that they were written in China. Accordingly, these Russian writers were reluctant to acknowledge the daily presence of the Chinese around them (much as Chinese authors, with few exceptions, also refrained from describing Russians in their works).

The main exception to this rule was Valerii Pereleshin (1913–92), the only Harbin writer or poet who studied Chinese. He was also almost the only one to translate from the original classical Chinese poetry, which he began publishing in Harbin journals from 1935. As a homosexual, Pereleshin was an outsider in more ways than this: his example, therefore, only illustrates the rule.[8] Indeed, almost no translations of Chinese literature appeared in Harbin, and the few that did were publications by the local sinological circle. Most of the work of collecting émigré Russian poetry from obscure Harbin publications has been done over many years by the Harbin-born literary scholar Olga Bakich of Toronto University, who has co-edited the most extensive collection of what she called 'the Russian poetry of China'[9] and has written a superb biography of Pereleshin. Since the 2000s, Russian émigré poetry from Manchuria has also begun appearing in Chinese translations – for the first time since they were written during the first half of the previous century. Reflecting the change of political agenda, from denunciation of Russian imperialism and the 'White' emigration to celebration of China's generous hospitality towards foreigners, Russian émigré literature has thereby officially entered the history of Northeast literature.

Notes

1 See on them (but mostly on Duanmu Hongliang): Haili Kong, 'The Significance of the Northeastern Writers in Exile, 1931–1945', in Yingjin Zhang, ed., *A Companion to Modern Chinese Literature* (Malden MA: Wiley-Blackwell, 2016), pp. 312–25.
2 Howard Goldblatt, *Hsiao Hung* (Boston: Twayne, 1976). See esp. Xiao Hong, trans. Howard Goldblatt, *The Field of Life and Death & Tales of Hulan River* (Boston: Cheng & Tsui, 2002).
3 Norman Smith, *Resisting Manchukuo: Chinese Women Writers and the Japanese Occupation* (Vancouver and Toronto: UBC Press, 2007), pp. 42–3, 79.
4 Kong, 'The Significance of the Northeastern Writers in Exile', p. 317. See Duanmu Hongliang, *The Sorrows of Egret Lake: Selected Stories* (Chinese-English Bilingual Edition) (Hong Kong: The Chinese University Press, 2009).
5 Smith, *Resisting Manchukuo*, pp. 44, 54.
6 Ibid., respectively pp. 135, 12.
7 Chi Zijian, *The Last Quarter of the Moon* (London: Harvill Secker, 2013), trans. Bruce Humes; and *Goodnight, Rose* (Penguin Books China, 2019), trans. Poppy Toland. See also Chi Zijian, *Figments of the Supernatural* (Sydney: James Joyce Press, 2004), trans. Simon Patton.
8 See Olga Bakich, *Valerii Pereleshin: Life of a Silkworm* (Toronto: University of Toronto Press, 2015).
9 Vadim Kreid and Olga Bakich, eds, *Russkaia poeziia Kitaia* (The Russian Poetry of China) (Moscow: Vremia, 2001).

14

The Northeast under Mao

Industrialization achieved and a border war with the Soviet Union averted

During the Korean War, the Northeast was always in the headlines; much of the CCP propaganda 'to resist the United States and aid North Korea' was aimed at this frontier region.[1] The military conflict also closely affected the civilian population of the Northeast, mobilized to take part in patriotic campaigns and donate in support of the war; factories from Liaoning (as well as all enterprises and government facilities from the border city Andong) were relocated to Jilin and Heilongjiang along with their staff while intensive industrialization continued.[2] During the 1950s the Northeast was filled with Soviet experts, who soon spread all over the country before being pulled out abruptly in 1960. The memory of their presence is by now more vivid to people in Harbin or Dalian than that of the previous large Russian community of tsarist settlers and post-revolutionary émigrés, which had reached its peak well before the Japanese occupation. The senior Communist administrator of the Northeast, Gao Gang 高崗 (1905–54), appointed in 1946, seems to have maintained an especially close relationship with the Soviets. He was purged with the involvement of Deng Xiaoping 鄧小平 (1904–97) in March 1954 and committed suicide the same year.[3]

In the 1950s, Heilongjiang became the forced destination of urban Chinese people resettled by government fiat. Many of them were from Shanghai, sent to work in the swamp reclamation project known as the 'Great Northern Wilderness' (Beidahuang 北大荒, later the subject of many literary reminiscences).[4] Some intellectuals, purged in 1957, actually volunteered to work there so as to redeem themselves in the Party's eyes.[5] But the population group that ultimately contributed most to the changes in the Heilongjiang landscape and economy since the 1950s were the demobilized soldiers, who settled in Beidahuang after the Korean War. They began farming there and, unlike the intellectuals, never left, being succeeded by a second generation, their children. In PRC propaganda today, Beidahuang is lauded as China's main grain producer: the Party has renamed Heilongjiang 'Great Northern Granary' (beidacang 北大倉) in contradistinction to the tag of 'Great

Figure 14 Soldiers reassigned to agricultural work in Beidahuang. Public domain.

Northern Wilderness', which had been associated with the province in the Mao era. Since 1999, however, land reclamation was stopped and a nature reserve was created, in the effort to reintroduce some of the area's once rich wildlife.

The province suffered greatly during the Cultural Revolution because of the special class vigilance, which border regions were expected to manifest.

While neighbouring Inner Mongolia registered the highest number of casualties in any region or province in the course of the Cultural Revolution,[6] Heilongjiang had also paid a heavy economic price due to the withdrawal of Soviet capital in 1960 and the cessation of trade across the border until the early 1980s. From the early 1960s, young people began to be drafted into commune militias and trained to resist a future Soviet invasion. On 31 January 1967 Heilongjiang became the first province in the PRC to replace its government and CCP officials by a 'revolutionary committee'.

The Cultural Revolution in Harbin and in the Heilongjiang countryside was extensively documented by a photographer for *Heilongjiang Daily*, Li Zhensheng 李振盛, who was born in Dalian in 1940 and trained in Changchun. Decades later, he was able to show his photographs of that time to Western audiences in the exhibition and accompanying book *Red-color News Soldier*.[7] Li was present, for example, when the main symbol of Russian Harbin, the St Nicholas Cathedral, was demolished. His photographs and book, exhibited and published in Europe and the US, have provided the most detailed visual images of the Cultural Revolution anywhere in China, but they are still unpublished in the PRC.

The Party boss in Liaoning during the Cultural Revolution was Mao's ruthless nephew and would-be successor, Mao Yuanxin 毛遠新, who was a student at the Military Institute of Engineering in Harbin in 1964. Born in 1941, he was arrested with the Gang of Four, whom he had closely supported, in 1976, and was sentenced to seventeen years' imprisonment; released in 1993, he now lives in Shanghai.

The border tensions of 1969

In March 1969, Sino-Soviet border skirmishes at the small island of Zhenbao 珍寶, which Russians called Damansky, near the Chinese bank of the Ussuri River, led to serious fears of a total war between the PRC and the Soviet Union. The entire Northeast was then mobilized and trained for the coming war, and air-raid shelters were constructed in the cities. These underground shelters, tunnels and hospitals, a curious legacy of the conflict, have since become underground shopping centres.

The essence of the conflict lay in the Soviet reading of the 1860 Treaty of Peking: the USSR interpreted a map appended to the treaty to mean that China had no control over river waters in the Amur and the Ussuri, whereas the PRC considered the border to pass in the middle of both rivers. On 2 March the Chinese army attacked and killed over twenty soldiers of the

Soviet army in Damansky. The PRC probably initiated the military clash due to the inner dynamics of the Cultural Revolution, when anti-Soviet provocations were repeatedly staged; Mao apparently needed to generate an 'external threat'.[8] A conflict with the USSR may also have been useful for China in order to draw closer to the US.[9] On 15 March, the Soviets retaliated by expelling the Chinese soldiers from the island. At the end of the clashes, which continued along the borders of the two countries during 1969, Beijing scored a victory as Moscow balked at launching an all-out war and accepted the reoccupation of Damansky by the PLA in September. President Richard Nixon would make his historic trip to Mao's China in February 1972.

However, the border conflict lasted for almost two decades: only Mikhail Gorbachev, in a speech in Vladivostok in July 1986, was finally able to acknowledge that 'the official border could pass along the main stream' and thereby give up Soviet claims to Zhenbao as well as to most of the other river islands.[10] Sino-Soviet relations were normalized between 1989 and 1991.[11] An agreement on fixing the border in the mid-stream was accordingly signed in May 1991 and ratified by both sides in 1992. The demarcation process of the Amur and Ussuri then took the whole of the 1990s and was successfully concluded only in 2008. In July that year, China and Russia formally agreed 'to end a long-running dispute over the demarcation of their eastern border'.[12] Subsequently Russia returned Yinlong Island 銀龍島 (Russian: Tarabarov Island) and half of Heixiazi Island 黑瞎子島 (Bolshoi Ussuriiskii) to China. Heixiazi, at the confluence of the Amur and the Ussuri near Khabarovsk, was a concession that Qing China had been tricked into making in 1861, when a Russian boundary commissioner presented to the Chinese officials a map he claimed was an expression of the Treaty of Peking. Both islands were the last and thorniest issues in the long border negotiations.

Notes

1 The Soviet-trained army of North Korea attacked South Korea on 25 June 1950. China's intervention on behalf of the North greatly worsened its relations with the USA, which prevented unification under Communist rule by perpetuating the division between North and South in the Korean Armistice Agreement of July 1953.
2 Mo Tian, 'The Korean War and Manchuria: Economic and Human Effects', in Tessa Morris-Suzuki, ed., *The Korean War in Asia: A Hidden History* (Lanham: Rowman & Littlefield, 2018), pp. 39–54.
3 Michael Sheng, 'Mao and Chinese Elite Politics in the 1950s: The Gao Gang Affair Revisited', *Twentieth-Century China*, vol. 36, no. 1 (Jan. 2011), pp. 67–96.

4   On this, see Ning Wang, *Banished to the Great Northern Wilderness: Political Exile and Re-education in Mao's China* (Vancouver and Toronto: UBC Press, 2017).
5   Cf. *idem*, 'Border Banishment: Rightists in the Army Farms of Beidahuang', in Diana Lary, ed., *The Chinese State at the Borders* (Vancouver and Toronto: UBC Press, 2007), pp. 198–220.
6   Uradyn E. Bulag, 'Alter/native Mongolian Identity: From Nationality to Ethnic Group', in Elizabeth J. Perry and Mark Selden, eds, *Chinese Society: Change, Conflict and Resistance*, 3rd edn (London and New York: Routledge, 2013), p. 268.
7   Li Zhensheng, *Red-color News Soldier* (London: Phaidon Press, 2003). See also Sim Chi Yin, 'A Panoramic View of China's Cultural Revolution', *New York Times*, 10 Sept. 2012, and http://red-colornewssoldier.com, which have a selection of the photographs.
8   This is the conclusion of Lyle J. Goldstein, 'Return to Zhenbao Island: Who Started Shooting and Why It Matters', *China Quarterly*, no. 168 (Dec. 2001), pp. 985–97.
9   See the pro-Soviet perspective of Dmitri Ryabushkin, 'Origins and Consequences of the Soviet–Chinese Border Conflict of 1969', in Iwashita Akihiro, ed., *Eager Eyes Fixed on Eurasia*, vol. 2, pp. 73–91.
10 Cf. the optimistic (and consistently pro-Chinese) interpretation of Neville Maxwell, 'How the Sino-Russian Boundary Conflict was Finally Settled: From Nerchinsk 1689 to Vladivostok 2005 via Zhenbao Island 1969', *Critical Asian Studies*, vol. 39, no. 2 (2007), pp. 229–53.
11 See Sergey Radchenko, *Unwanted Visionaries: The Soviet Failure in Asia at the End of the Cold War* (Oxford: Oxford University Press, 2014), ch. 5.
12 'China and Russia Sign Agreement on Border Dispute', *New York Times*, 21 July 2008.

15

The Northeast after Mao

The 'rust belt' and Dongbei identity

China's modern Northeast has been neglected by historians, who are more interested in 'Manchuria' than in 'Dongbei'. A particularly large theme is the region's industrialization.[1] Because of the heavy state-owned industry carried over from the Mao era, the whole Northeast had difficulties adjusting to the open market economy from the 1990s.[2] The region has therefore been called China's 'rust belt'. As late as the 1990s, some voices coming out of the Northeast (as well as from Henan and Hebei provinces) proposed to return to a planned economy and to Maoist principles.

Corruption has certainly contributed to popular frustration. The governor of Heilongjiang from 1994 to 2000, Tian Fengshan 田鳳山, was sentenced to life imprisonment for bribery in 2005. In the early 2000s, parallel to rapid industrial growth and economic development, the city of Shenyang was also under a cloud of corruption scandals. In 2000 the so-called Mu/Ma affair exploded: the Shenyang mayor Mu Suixin 慕綏新 was arrested in October 2001 and sentenced to death, his execution was delayed, and he died in prison. Within the walls of his two villas, police found gold bars worth 6 million dollars as well as 150 Rolex watches. His deputy Ma Xiangdong 馬向東, who drove a red Ferrari and had embezzled 4 million dollars for gambling expenses in Macao and Las Vegas,[3] was executed in December 2001. Dozens of Shenyang's top officials fell along with the Mu/Ma clique.

In March 2002, serious labour unrest broke out in Daqing 大慶, Heilongjiang: the restructuring of inefficient state-owned enterprises (SOEs), a policy accepted in the 15th Congress of the Communist Party in 1997, had allowed a new company, PetroChina (which belongs to the China National Petroleum Corporation), to dismiss workers of the local oil industry. Protests against these mass dismissals expressed longing for the Mao era, when the Daqing oilfield had been the pride of the nation. In what became one of the largest protest movements in China since Tiananmen Square in 1989, representatives of Heilongjiang workers travelled to Beijing, both to petition the central government and to make a pilgrimage to Mao's mausoleum. In

March and April 2002, Mao posters were also carried in demonstrations by laid-off workers from state factories in Liaoyang.⁴

By the end of the same decade Daqing had become a booming capitalist town, which like many Chinese towns today displayed striking disparity between rich and poor. As the first region in which the CCP came to power, Heilongjiang used to be known as 'eldest son of the republic'. According to a recent study on the poor in Harbin, laid-off industrial workers still strongly associated the idea of 'Dongbei' with the past contribution of the working class to the building of the new China.⁵ In 2009, the representative of the private company which had taken over the SOE Tonghua Steel was beaten to death by workers; another company then took charge of the plant but it, too, had to dismiss a third of the workforce due to falling steel prices in 2015.⁶ Protests of laid-off steelworkers again erupted in Tonghua 通化, southern Jilin, in 2016, as the country continued to reduce its steel production.

In October 2003, the government of Hu Jintao 胡錦濤 (President of the PRC between 2002 and 2012) launched a plan to 'revitalize the Northeast'. This operated by analogy with the earlier programme 'to develop the West', launched in 1999 by President Jiang Zemin 江澤民 (in power, 1989–2002). While China's West (making up 71 per cent of the territory of the PRC) is supposed to continue developing until 2050, the completion of the programme for the Northeast (covering only 8 per cent of the country) is expected by 2020 or 2025.⁷ Beijing's idea was to let the three provinces attract

Figure 15 Anshan Steelworks, 2000. Photograph by Frühtau.

foreign direct investment, which had been very low in the Northeast. Transport between them was to be upgraded, e.g. by an express railway between Harbin and Dalian, and a new highway system in Heilongjiang. To fight corruption and Northeast 'conservatism', the government brought in officials from southern and central China.

Jilin province, the less developed of the three in the Northeast, has had its share of local political scandals, as in 2004 when Governor Hong Hu 洪虎 had to resign from office after a shop fire killed fifty-one people. In November 2005, a Jilin plant spilled oil and other poisonous substances into the Songhua River; the local authorities denied anything had gone wrong even while water supply was cut off in Harbin. They were only forced to acknowledge their responsibility after the pollution reached Khabarovsk on the Amur, provoking Russian protest. The industrialization of the Northeast had created some of the worst pollution in the world. In line with the general search for outside trade contacts, Jilin now maintains economic ties with neighbouring North Korea.

Like Shenyang, Harbin went through a major corruption scandal with the arrest of former vice-mayor Zhu Shengwen 朱胜文 in 1997; Zhu committed suicide in prison in 2004. Other top provincial officials indicted in the late 1990s were the Party secretary of Qiqihar and the mayor of oil-producing town Daqing. Unemployment because of the privatization policy of SOEs, and the growing anger at cadre corruption, led to mass protests by workers in several Heilongjiang towns in November 1997.

Figure 15a Harbin Grand Theatre, 2016. Photograph by Katushang.

In recent years Harbin has attempted to raise its international profile in various ways. One such area of activity was international sports. Harbin made a bid for the 2010 Winter Olympics but failed to make the shortlist; a later bid to host the 2012 winter Youth Olympics also did not succeed as Innsbruck, in the Austrian Tyrol, was chosen instead. Harbin did host the third 1996 Winter Asian Games and the 2009 Winter Universiade. The Alpine skiing events took place in the largest ski resort in China, Yabuli 亞布力 in Shangzhi 商志 County of greater Harbin, about 180 km to the southeast of the city.[8] Several impressive buildings have emerged in Harbin, adding new landmarks to its surviving and restored Russian churches. The most striking of these is surely the Harbin Grand Theatre, by Beijing architect Ma Yansong 馬岩松, which opened in 2015. Since 2010, Harbin has promoted itself as 'City of Music', claiming that China's first symphony orchestra was founded there (by Russians) in 1908 – a false narrative that Harbin Symphony Orchestra currently spreads at home and abroad. In point of fact, the orchestra was created by Russian musicians during the Japanese occupation in the 1930s. The purpose of this revision of history, harking back for support to the tsarist Russian era, is to promote Harbin as an important city with a cosmopolitan past.[9]

Policy-makers in the Russian Far East today fear Chinese migration much as Chinese in the early twentieth century feared the migration of Russians into Manchuria. Many local Russians blame the Chinese for all the region's problems, and political analysts often express alarmist positions as well.[10] By 2001 the Chinese economy had quadrupled as a result of Deng Xiaoping's reforms of 1978, while by the same point in time, a decade after the collapse of the USSR, the Russian economy had shrunk by half. Also in 2001 Vladimir Putin's Russia concluded a 'strategic partnership' with the PRC.

The population of the three provinces of the Chinese Northeast is rapidly growing, having passed the 122-million mark by 2010, whereas the Russian Far East, with a total population of about 6,300,000 in the Russian census of 2010, has consistently suffered from negative migration since 1991. The Russian Far East depends on China for much of its export (raw fabrics and wood) and for a half of its import trade (mainly Chinese textile, groceries and simple consumers' articles). Chinese migrant workers first began crossing the border into Russia, ostensibly as tourists, in large numbers in the late 1980s, establishing a 'shuttle trade' which peaked in the 1990s. Fearing illegal Chinese immigration, Russia now maintains a strict visa regime for persons entering across the Chinese border, while China allows a no-visa thirty-day stay for Russians arriving in Heihe (the permit is limited to residents of Blagoveshchensk and the border region). Russian shuttle-traders use these regulations and the permission to bring back up to 50 kg of goods at each border crossing to buy electrical appliances and alcohol in Heihe, later to sell them for a much higher price in Russia. Russians arriving in Heilongjiang today, therefore, include smugglers along with tourists, and in Harbin and other cities there are shops selling Russians souvenirs over the counter and other merchandise under it. In the 2000s, estimates of the numbers of illegal Chinese in the Russian Far East reached over 200,000 but they have gradually declined since, as Chinese migrant workers have been replaced by those coming from Central Asia.

The growing economic gap between the two sides of the Amur is evident in the contrast between development in Blagoveshchensk and newly booming Heihe. The increasingly close ties between Moscow and Beijing are seen by both sides as a coalition against the influence of the USA in world affairs. China also needs Russian oil and gas, as well as Russian military equipment. In October 2009 the two countries signed agreements to further expand cooperation between them, including the installation of new oil and gas pipelines to ensure their steady supply to China. Joint military exercises have already been conducted, while China has promised to double its investment in the Russian Far East. In May 2014, during a visit of President Putin in Shanghai, a major deal (the largest in the history of the Russian gas industry) was signed, to provide natural gas to China through the 'power of Siberia' pipeline.[11]

More than the three provinces of the Northeast collaborate with each other, they actually compete over border trade opportunities, as the governors and city mayors know that their future depends on prosperity or depression. At the same time, the central government in Beijing strives to promote regional development plans in the Northeast. The economic competition between the three provinces does not diminish the sense of common cultural identity, based on the shared origin of the great majority of the population of the Northeast. This sense of identity and the demographic reality in the region formerly called Manchuria have by now made it an integral part of China. In an age of separatist movements, when Scotland has nearly left the United Kingdom, Kurdistan voted to separate itself from Iraq, and Catalonia from Spain, no scenario of a revival of Manchuria as a political entity – which in modern history has only existed under Japanese occupation – is even remotely possible.

Notes

1 See on this Amy King, *China–Japan Relations after World War Two: Empire, Industry and War, 1949–1971* (Cambridge: Cambridge University Press, 2016), ch. 4.

2 As Alan P. L. Liu, 'Provincial Identities and Provincial Cultures: Modernism, Traditionalism, Parochialism, and Separatism', in Shiping Hua, ed., *Chinese Political Culture 1989–2000* (Armonk: M. E. Sharpe, 2001), p. 261, puts it: 'The Chinese identity of the Northeast has a certain Cinderella quality to it, and Mao was its prince. [...] In China, the Northeast is virtually synonymous with central planning and state-owned enterprises.'
3 Becker, *Dragon Rising*, pp. 84–5. See more in Philip P. Pan, *Out of Mao's Shadow: The Struggle for the Soul of a New China* (London: Picador, 2008).
4 Timothy B. Weston, 'The Iron Man Weeps: Joblessness and Political Legitimacy in the Chinese Rust Belt', in Peter Hays Gries and Stanley Rosen, eds, *State and Society in 21st-Century China: Crisis, Contention, and Legitimation* (New York and London: RoutledgeCurzon, 2004).
5 Mun Young Cho, *The Specter of 'The People': Urban Poverty in Northeast China* (Ithaca NY and London: Cornell University Press, 2013), pp. 25, 29, 33.
6 Note the title under which this news was reported: 'Death and Despair in China's Rustbelt', Bloomberg News, 2 March 2016.
7 Jae Ho Chung et al., 'Assessing the "Revive the Northeast" (*zhenxing dongbei*) Programme: Origins, Policies and Implementation', *China Quarterly*, no. 197 (March 2009), p. 115. According to Becker, *Dragon Rising*, pp. 89, 95–7, this plan has infused life into the old SOEs, which have become profitable again, hiring young migrants rather than the older employees who had been dismissed from the same factories.
8 Yabuli hosted the Winter Asian Games in 1996, which were held in Changchun later in 2007. In 2008 Yabuli hosted the National Winter Games.
9 Cities of Music are chosen by UNESCO, which has yet to include any Chinese city in that category (see https://citiesofmusic.net). The Harbin administration and the PRC press pretend that Harbin obtained such recognition from the United Nations on the strength of a private gesture by a UN Under-Secretary for Economic Affairs, the PRC diplomat Sha Zukang 沙祖康. 'UN Recognizes China's Northeastern Harbin as "Music City"', *The People's Daily*, 26 June 2010.
10 A recent expression of the alarmist view is Ivan Tselichtchev, 'Chinese in the Russian Far East: A Geopolitical Time Bomb?', *South China Morning Post*, 8 July 2017.
11 Jane Perlez, 'China and Russia Reach 30-Year Gas Deal', *New York Times*, 21 May 2014.

Part Two

16

History and Geography: Heilongjiang

Heilongjiang province measures about 463,000 sq km (179,000 sq miles). It is the largest province of the Northeast and sixth largest administrative unit of the PRC: among the twenty-two provinces, excluding the autonomous regions, it ranks third in size after Qinghai and Sichuan. In 2010, Heilongjiang had over 38 million inhabitants. The province has forty-nine minorities, which, however, make up only about 5 per cent of the total population (compare this with the forty-four minorities, making up 16 per cent of the population in Liaoning, and the forty-four minorities making up 9 per cent

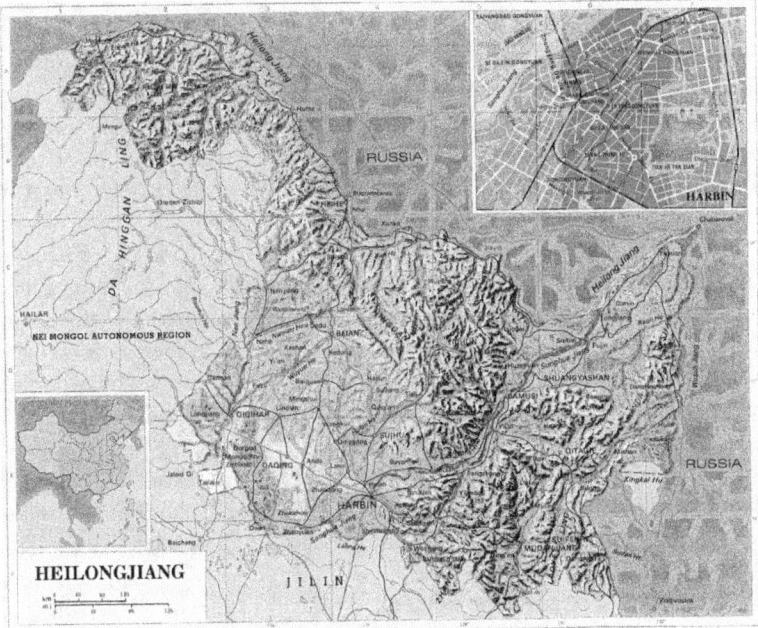

Figure 16 Heilongjiang. From Hsieh, *China Provincial Atlas*. © 1995 Gale, a part of Cengage, Inc. Reproduced by permission.www.cengage.com/permissions.

in Jilin). Almost all the recognized minority ethnicities in China are represented in the Northeast. The province takes its name from the river, meaning The Black Dragon in Chinese (a translation of the Manchu Sakhalian, which is also the origin of Sakhalin Island). The Russian and international name Amur comes from the Evenki language. At 2,824 km, it is the tenth longest river in the world. Its tributary the Songhua, or the Sungari, measuring 1,927 km, is in turn one of the longest rivers to pass entirely within Chinese territory.

The largest minority group in Heilongjiang are the Manchus, counting about 1.18 million. Most are concentrated in Shuangcheng 雙城, a town which became a district of Harbin in 2014. The next minorities in size order are: the Koreans (450,000), descendants of both post-1910 emigrants and forced labourers from the era of Japanese occupation, who chiefly inhabit the south-east of the province; and the Hui (Chinese Muslims; about 140,000) and Mongols (also 140,000) in the west of the province. About 120,000 Daurs are also recorded in Heilongjiang, mainly along the Nenjiang River. The capital city Harbin had by 2010 reached over 4 million in the city centre alone and over 9 million in the whole territory belonging to the city administration, making it the largest provincial capital in China (apart from the special municipalities Beijing, Shanghai, Tianjin and Chongqing).[1] In China, Harbin is today best known for the ice sculpture festival it hosts every winter, a huge attraction for domestic tourism. The city also presents a north-eastern variety of a cosmopolitan heritage most familiar from Shanghai: the image of a formerly multinational city with 'a foreign flavour'. The exotic Russian component is now part of the Harbin brand.

Most of the population in Heilongjiang is concentrated in the province's cities and towns, and it is one of the most industrialized provinces in China. A recent book, the first in English on Heilongjiang, by Patrick Fuliang Shan, looks closely at the history of Han Chinese settlement in the province: over 4 million settlers arrived there from 1900 to the Japanese invasion, with the result that by 1930 almost half of the Heilongjiang population consisted of post-1918 immigrants.[2] While most immigrants came from Shandong, there were also arrivals from Hebei and (in 1929–30) Henan. There was migration within Manchuria towards Heilongjiang from Liaoning and Jilin and some return migration of Chinese from the Russian Far East after the Russian Revolution.[3]

Three border towns on the Amur are especially important: Heihe, the city lying near Aigun, which was destroyed by the Russian military during the Boxer war in 1900, is the closest meeting point between Russia and China, as the Amur there is only 750 metres wide. From Heihe, one can therefore see Blagoveshchensk and vice versa. Since 2016, Russia and China have been busy constructing and publicizing the first road bridge across the Amur, between Heihe and Blagoveshchensk, which was agreed upon as long ago as 1995 and is presently scheduled to open for traffic in December 2019.[4] A ferry across the Amur takes ten minutes, many of the passengers being Russian citizens, whom Chinese traders in Heihe hire to sell their wares, especially vodka, in the Russian market. The Amur starts freezing in mid-October, becoming ice-bound by mid-November, when buses can cross the ice; the river becomes again ice-free in May. Apart from contrabandists, cross-border contact includes some cultural exchange through art: Russian painters come to work at Heihe and exhibit in a private local museum of Russian art, which was established to satisfy the Chinese taste for realist Russian painting. The Aihui History Museum fosters patriotic feelings by documenting China's losses in the Aigun treaty of 1858 and the drowning of the Chinese of Blagoveshchensk in 1900.

At Tongjiang 同江 (formerly called Lahasusu 拉哈蘇蘇 in the Hezhe language), as the Chinese place name, meaning 'joining rivers' suggests, the Sungari joins the Amur. The town still has a native Hezhe population. At the confluence of the Amur and the Ussuri, is the county-level city Fuyuan 撫遠,

Figure 16a View of Heihe from the Amur River, 2006. Photograph by Viktor Bakhmutov.

where, because of the single time zone in China, the summer sun rises at 2 o'clock in the 'morning', the earliest in the country. Fuyuan faces at some distance Russia's Khabarovsk. North of the Amur, between Blagoveshchensk and Khabarovsk, lies the Jewish Autonomous Region, a failed project created in the Soviet Union in 1924. Only a few Jews (less than 1 per cent of the population) remain in the Jewish Autonomous Region today. The construction of a bridge over the Amur to connect Tongjiang with the Russian village of Nizhneleninskoe is presently being completed.

Important locations in Heilongjiang include the Jingbo Lake 鏡泊湖 in the south-east of the province, close to the border with (and formerly part of) Jilin. Further to the east, the Ussuri spills into Lake Khanka (Chinese Xingkai 興凱湖), the biggest freshwater lake in East Asia, only a quarter of which belongs to China – the rest is Russian. In the same region, located along the Mudan River (Mudanjiang, a tributary of the Sungari), is the old town Ninguta (meaning 'the six' in Manchu, called after six brothers), now called Ning'an. The town Mudanjiang itself, at 115 km from the Russian border, had been overshadowed by Ning'an before being developed as a military and administrative centre by the Japanese; in 1935 a railway was built linking the town westward to Harbin and later eastward to Jiamusi 佳木斯.

A Japanese hydroelectric power plant at Mudanjiang was dismantled and taken home by the Soviet army in 1945, but rebuilt in the early 1950s. Today Mudanjiang has a population approaching 3 million and its industry mainly produces car tyres for the automobile industry in Changchun. Jiamusi, too, was developed by the Japanese, attracting many Japanese settlers in the Manchukuo period and becoming a military and air force base. Since 1956 it has been mainly known for producing paper and for its sugar refineries.

Railways have remained highly important in Heilongjiang and the total length of track there is larger than in any other province in the PRC (the densest concentration of railways in China is in Liaoning). A main symbol of industry in Heilongjiang, already mentioned above, is the Daqing oilfield and town by the same name, about halfway between Harbin and Qiqihar. The oil plant, which opened in 1959, became a model of worker heroism and China's self-reliance, as the crisis in Chinese–Soviet relations had brought an end to the supply of oil from the Soviet Union. Workers from all of north China came to settle in Daqing in the 1960s; and in 1964 Mao called on the entire PRC industry 'to learn from Daqing'. During the Cultural Revolution, Daqing was displayed as a model town to sympathetic foreign visitors. Daqing remains an oil city today even as most of its oil reserves have been exploited. Heilongjiang is also one of the leading producers of grain and timber, as well as of milk. The Chinese hardly consumed milk before the twentieth century, but after milk was redefined as beneficial for health in the early 2000s a number of large dairies were established in Heilongjiang.[5]

The old Manchu town Qiqihar (formerly Bukui 卜奎), founded in 1670, remains the second most populated city in the province with over 5 million residents as of 2010. Also in western Heilongjiang is Nenjiang (originally the Manchu town of Mergen) on the river of the same name, which is the main tributary of the Sungari. In the eighteenth century, those who fell out of favour with the emperor were exiled to these towns. Qiqihar was the Heilongjiang capital during most of the Qing and it grew rapidly again in the 1950s. To the north-east of Qiqihar lie the 'five big connected ponds', Wudalianchi 五大連池, where Chinese tourists come to see the craters created by the eruption of fourteen volcanoes in 1719–21. Thirty km to the south-east from Qiqihar is the Zhalong 扎龍 Nature Reserve, the main tourist attraction of this region and the home of numerous bird species.

Another old garrison town, the port of Sanxing (Chinese translation of the Manchu 'Yilan Hala', meaning 'three families/clans'), now known again as Yilan, at the confluence of the Songhuajiang and the Mudanjiang in central Heilongjiang, was, like Ninguta, a centre of the tribute system between natives and Manchus in Manchuria. According to legend, the baby Nurhaci, born at the source of the Sungari in the Changbai mountains, was carried to Sanxing by the stream. The 'three clans' of Sanxing then made him their lord. The central place of this river in Manchu lore as well as political and economic considerations made the Sungari a more important river for the Qing than the Amur: while the Manchu dynasty showed little opposition to Russia's exclusive shipping in the Amur, they always resisted Russian navigation on the Sungari. Similarly, Mongols attached many legends to the Argun River in the Amur basin, which they associated with the birth of their leader, Genghis Khan.[6]

The border town Suifenhe (former Russian name: Pogranichnaia station) in south-east Heilongjiang was the last station of the CER in Chinese territory. With the creation in 2013 of a visa-free trade zone between Suifenhe (whose population grew more than tenfold from 1991 to 2005) and the Russian town on the opposite side of the border, Pogranichnyi, this became the only location in China where the Russian rouble is used as legal currency next to the *renminbi*. Russians are allowed to enter Suifenhe for fifteen days without a visa, and the town now accounts for almost half the volume of Heilongjiang's trade with Russia.

Mohe is the most northern place in China and the only one where the northern lights occasionally appear. Tourists flock to the Polar Village, Beijicun 北極村, north of Mohe, every year in the spring, in hopes of seeing the red or green lights, though many years pass between their appearances, and even local people remember the spectacle as a special occasion in their lives. Here temperatures during the winter months average between minus 25 and minus 30 degrees Celsius (the lowest ever temperature in China, minus 52.3 Celsius, was recorded in Mohe). The annual average is minus 4 degrees. Together with the county capital Xilinji 西林吉, Mohe was devastated by the greatest forest fire in recorded Chinese history, which raged for twenty-eight days from 6 May 1987 and left over 200 people dead.[7] After the fire, Mohe was rebuilt. Until 2008, the only way to reach the town was by a twenty-hour train journey from Harbin. Since then, Mohe has an airport (flights from Harbin take two hours) and several hotels catering to the tourists. From Mohe, one can travel 18 km further by train, to reach Gulian 古蓮, the northernmost train stop in China.

Between 1883 and 1886 as many as 10,000 Russian and Chinese gold prospectors congregated on a small tributary river of the Amur, above present-day Mohe, which they called Zheltuga. Reports that the mining camp was regulated by some form of direct democracy led to much exaggerated press descriptions of a Zheltuga 'republic', which spread around the world.[8] The Qing forces expelled the illegal miners and established a Chinese mine in Mohe in 1887. A 'gold route' (*huangjin zhi lu* 黃金之路) opened between Mohe and Mergen. Gold-mining was practised on both sides of the Amur and the Argun Rivers later in the twentieth century, and the gold industry still operates in the region today.

The north of Heilongjiang province was once covered with dense forests, parts of which still survive. Originally timber was transported south by horses and mules; in the 1920s railway wagons were used, and today trucks. Fishing, too, has always been important in Heilongjiang as well as throughout Manchuria.

Notes

1 Data on the three provinces of the Northeast and on Inner Mongolia in this section of the book are drawn partly from Tara Boland-Crewe and David Lea, *The Territories of the People's Republic of China* (London: Europa Publications, 2002), from a number of Chinese atlases and, of course, from the Internet.
2 Shan, *Taming China's Wilderness*, pp. 17, 44.
3 Ibid., pp. 24–5.
4 See https://thediplomat.com/2018/11/china-russia-and-the-case-of-the-missing-bridge/
5 Cf. 'Agriculture and Industry: The Heart of Heilongjiang's Future', *China Daily*, 30 Nov. 2010.

6 Henry de Rosny, *Étude sur la Mandchourie* (Paris: J. Maisonneuve, 1891), pp. 24–5, 38.
7 Harrison E. Salisbury, *The Great Black Dragon Fire: A Chinese Inferno* (Boston: Little, Brown, 1989).
8 Mark Gamsa, 'California on the Amur, or the "Zheltuga Republic" in Manchuria (1883–86)', *Slavonic and East European Review*, vol. 81, no. 2 (April 2003), pp. 236–66.

17

History and Geography: Jilin

Jilin province measures 187,000 sq km (72,201 sq miles). Its population of over 27 million makes it the least populated province in the Northeast. The centre of the province is much more densely settled than other regions. The name Jilin means 'fortunate forest' in Chinese, but in fact it is a transcription from Manchu, in which *Jilin* means 'along'; the original full place name was *Jilin ula* ('along the river', a reference to the Sungari). The 9 per cent of minority population mostly consists of ethnic Koreans, followed by Manchus, Mongols and Hui.

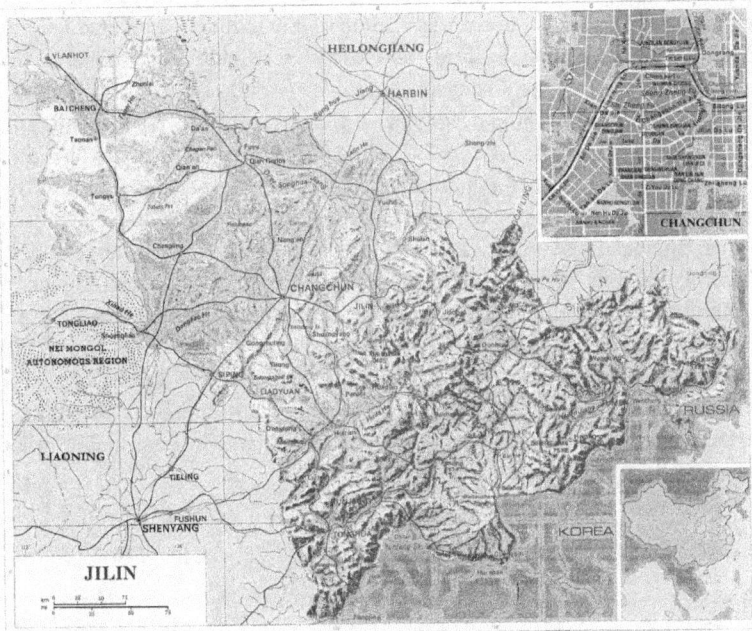

Figure 17 Jilin. From Hsieh, *China Provincial Atlas*. © 1995 Gale, a part of Cengage, Inc. Reproduced by permission.www.cengage.com/permissions.

Jilin province was formed by the Qing in August 1908. The Sungari formerly divided it from Heilongjiang. With the redrawing of provincial borders in 1954, however, northern Jilin became part of Heilongjiang and the border separating Heilongjiang from its much diminished neighbouring province was set along Lalin 拉林 River, a tributary of the Sungari. 'The three treasures' of Jilin (the 'sanbao' 三寶) are defined as ginseng, sable fur and *wula* grass ('the treasure of the poor', used for shoemaking). Deer antlers have also been harvested in Jilin for use in Chinese medicine as an aphrodisiac powder. These products were part of the tribute, which the Qing levied on the natives of Manchuria. The most important of them, known as 'ginseng' in English, is a transcription of the Chinese *renshen* 人参, so called because the shape of the plant's root resembles a human being. The Qing attached high importance to ginseng since the time of Nurhaci and they were the first dynasty to establish a monopoly, which lasted to the mid-nineteenth century, over its collection. It is a prized plant in Chinese medicine; Manchuria and especially Jilin have become identified with its 'natural' home and the origin of the best-quality specimens.[1]

Although it is also grown for profit, in China as in North America (the US already exported ginseng to China in the 1780s) and elsewhere in the world, wild ginseng has always been prized more highly than the cultivated variety. Connoisseurs examine the roots as closely as religious Jews observe the qualities of the *etrog* (yellow citron) and *lulav* (frond of the date palm tree), which they buy for the Sukkot festival. Ginseng is surrounded by legends and a rich anthropomorphic folklore, including popular sayings, and is a favoured subject of the local art of paper cuts.[2] In autumn, seekers initiated into the cult of ginseng-collecting went out to the forests in groups under a chosen leader. They claimed to be guided by the forest spirits, which appeared to them in dreams. Taboos involved in the search for ginseng included prohibition on digging out the plant with anything but wooden or bone instruments.[3] The ginseng cults are reminiscent of ceremonies connected with the European truffle, or with the mandrake, a Mediterranean plant used in both medicine and magic, the root of which is supposed to resemble a human form – hence the presence of 'man' in its name in English and other European languages.

The Changbaishan

The Great Xing'an range rises in Inner Mongolia, whereas the Little Xing'an range spreads in north-east Heilongjiang and across the Amur River border on the Russian side. The still deeply forested Changbaishan (The Long, or the

Figure 17a Tianchi, The Heavenly Pond in the Changbaishan. Photograph by Shaani Applebaum.

Ever White Mountains) is where the Sungari, the Yalu and the Tumen Rivers all have their source and the place to which Manchus attributed their origin. While the Sungari rises north to merge with the Amur at Tongjiang, the 521-km long Tumen flows to the north-east and the 790-km long Yalu flows south-west to the Yellow Sea. These last two rivers form the eastern (Tumen) and the western (Yalu) borders between China and Korea, a natural geographic boundary, recognized by both states as early as the fifteenth century. Jilin topography is sometimes described by the saying *yi shan san shui* 一山三水, 'one mountain, three waters', referring to the Changbaishan and the Sungari, Yalu and Tumen Rivers.

The highest peak of the Changbai mountain range reaches over 2,700 metres above sea level.[4] At the altitude of 2,194 metres, in the crater of the volcano, lies the famous Tianchi 天池 Lake, literally Heavenly Pond, the deepest in China. One of the first European explorers who climbed there in 1886, Sir Evan James (1846–1923), wrote an important travel book about Manchuria entitled *The Long White Mountain*.[5] Deng Xiaoping, the leader of the PRC, who visited Changbaishan in the summer of 1983, said on that occasion: 'Never to have ascended the Changbaishan in your lifetime is too bad!' The Kangxi emperor, who kowtowed to this sacred mountain, would have agreed with his latter-day successor. By performing the sacred rites at Changbaishan, Kangxi not only honoured his ancestor Nurhaci but incorporated this Manchu holy site into the cosmic geography of China, adding it to the 'five sacred peaks' (the Taoist notion of *wuyue* 五嶽) and 'four great peaks' (in the Buddhist view) of the Han Chinese tradition.[6]

Changbaishan has been a nature reserve (the largest in China) since 1960 and under UNESCO protection from 1979. It is home to cranes, deer and many other animals. Southern Jilin, on the Korean border, was formerly a tiger habitat, but they are now extinct there, and the Amur tigers that can still be seen in zoos around the world originate in the Russian Far East, where they are also seriously endangered.

The Korean connection in Jilin

Tourism to the Changbaishan attracts many visitors from South Korea. Until 2005, the Changbaishan region was part of the Yanbian Korean Autonomous Prefecture (created in 1952); since then, it has been managed directly by Jilin province. In the whole of China, as of 2010, there were about 2,300,000 ethnic Koreans, known as Joseonjok.[7] About 750,000 of them lived in Yanbian 延邊, which is referred to as 'the third Korea', though it has had a Han Chinese majority since the 1960s.[8] In the late Qing as well as during the Japanese occupation most of the territory of today's Yanbian was known as Jiandao 間島 (a term now avoided in the PRC in political grounds, although the equivalent name Kando is used in Korea). Koreans are the most significant minority in the Northeast; they have a high living and educational standard, and relations between them and Han Chinese are by now free from racial tension.[9]

After the PRC and South Korea established diplomatic relations in 1992, the financial opportunities in South Korea attracted many ethnic Koreans in China to emigrate to that country. More recently, Joseonjok have found work as intermediaries for South Korean businesses operating in the large cities in China. While such prospects have given some young Chinese Koreans an incentive to improve their command of Korean, many of them have given up using their native language in their pursuit of integration into Chinese society.[10]

The origins of most ethnic Koreans in China are in what today is North Korea. They began to move to China in the 1870s, once again after the annexation of Korea by Japan in 1910, and lastly during the Manchukuo period. After Japan's defeat in 1945, some Chinese Koreans repatriated to Korea for both economic and patriotic reasons. Those who remained in China were recognized as a national minority in 1948. During the Cultural Revolution, violence against Chinese Koreans drove some of them to South

Korea. The Joseonjok today conceptualize their relationship with Korea and China by calling the former *guguo* 故國 (motherland, literally 'the ancient country') and the latter *zuguo* 祖國 (the fatherland), or by viewing their community as a bride, who married into China.[11]

China currently rejects defectors from North Korea, sending them back to an uncertain fate in their country. Amnesty International has reported that PRC police conduct round-ups and forced repatriations. Nonetheless, the illegal presence of North Koreans in the PRC has been estimated at as high as 200,000. Among these refugees from the North, there have been many orphaned children. Through the friendship between children coming from both sides of the border, the feature film *Dooman River* (La Rivière Tumen), a South Korean–French co-production made in 2010 by the South Korean director Zhang Lu, captures the impossible moral dilemmas in which the ethnic Korean villagers in Yanbian are caught as they encounter desperate refugees from the North across the Tumen and the tragic situation of the refugees themselves. In December 2017, as conflict escalated between the North Korean regime and the United States, it was revealed that China had begun constructing refugee camps in Yanbian in preparation for the human tide that threatened to arrive from across the border.[12]

The 'history wars'

A source of disagreement between China and Korea has been the question of who owns the history of Koguryo kingdom (37 BC–AD 668), which covered the present-day border area between the two countries. Although 'Korea' is a name derived from Koguryo, in 2002 a PRC committee declared this to have been a Chinese vassal state.[13] The later kingdom of Bohai 渤海 existed from 698 to its defeat by the Khitan in 926 (we must distinguish between the ancient state of Bohai and the Bohai Sea 渤海, the inner gulf of the Yellow Sea, formerly called the Gulf of Zhili or Beizhili, which includes Liaodong Bay on the Liaoning coast). Nationalist Koreans consider the Bohai (Parhae, in Korean) an ancestral land; irredentists see the kingdom's territory in Manchuria as having been lost to the Qing along with the Changbai during demarcation of the Qing–Choson border in the late seventeenth and early eighteenth centuries.

A cultural continuity between Jilin and Korea exists in the ginseng lore, which the Korean side shares; the right to gather ginseng in the Changbai was a source of friction between the Manchus and Choson (1392–1910) Korea from the early seventeenth century.[14] The Changbai Mountain is also important for Koreans since (like the Manchu legend about Nurhaci) they regard it as the birthplace of the divine Tangun, the mythical progenitor of the Korean people who supposedly founded the nation in 2333 BC. This event is believed to have happened on 3 October in that year, and the date has accordingly been the National Foundation Day in South Korea since 1949. In 1993 the North Korean regime claimed that it discovered Tangun's tomb and built a mausoleum on the site. A section of the Changbai/Paektu mountain range lies in North Korea, where it is littered with monuments to the alleged birthplace of Kim Jung Il, ruler of the North until his death in 2011 (in reality, as has already been mentioned, Kim first saw the light of day in Khabarovsk in 1941). The Paektu figures in the national emblem of North Korea as well as in the national anthem of South Korea.[15] As South Koreans cannot visit the part of Paektu which belongs to North Korea, they travel to the Chinese Changbai instead.

The Jilin towns bordering on North Korea, especially the picturesque Ji'an 集安 (formerly 輯安) on the southern tip of Jilin, derive much of their income from Chinese tourists crossing over the border. Entry into North Korea from Jilin is possible through five border crossings near Yanji, the county seat of Yanbian. Occasionally, however, Jilin and the border areas are closed because of tensions having to do with North Korean nuclear activity: when the North Koreans detonated a nuclear bomb in the midst of the Chinese New Year celebrations in February 2013, the echoes were well felt in Yanji.[16]

Another important site in Yanbian, in the extreme east of Jilin province close to the border with Russia and not far from Vladivostok, is Hunchun: an old garrison town, which was also an important trade centre in the Qing.[17] Contrary to Liaoning, Jilin is landlocked, and the Tumen River presently offers its best prospects for economic development. A highly ambitious programme to develop trade in the Tumen River Area was launched in 1990, involving collaboration between the PRC (Yanbian District), Russia, both Koreas, Mongolia and Japan.[18] Later the 'Greater Tumen Initiative' was announced, sponsored by the United Nations, with a strategic plan from 2006 to 2015. Located only 15 km from the Sea of Japan, but without access to the sea, small Hunchun developed into a boom town after it was opened for foreign trade in 1992; in 2001, the Hunchun China–Russia Free Market and Trade Zone was created.[19] The nearby village of Fangchuan 防川 offers the attraction of 'seeing three countries at a glance': a viewing platform there allows glimpses of Russian and North Korean territory.

Changchun and other Jilin cities

Originally a small walled town, from the end of the Russo-Japanese War Changchun was on the borderline between the Russian and Japanese spheres of influence in Manchuria. Both empires established their railway towns near Changchun and travellers changed there from CER to SMR trains and vice versa. From 1909 Japan constructed large office buildings in European style in its settlement near Changchun, including the obligatory Yamato Hotel. As has already been mentioned here, Changchun (renamed Xinjing) was chosen by the Japanese as the capital of Manchukuo.

Changchun and Jilin town were plundered and damaged by the Soviet army in 1945, even as the formerly large Japanese population of Changchun fled from the city. Younger residents of Changchun today are unaware of the five-month siege by the People's Liberation Army in 1948, which caused over a hundred thousand deaths from starvation prior to the city's so-called liberation. Historian Frank Dikötter begins his book *The Tragedy of Liberation* with the Communist siege of Changchun, estimating its human toll on the civilian population from April to October 1948 as 'at least 160,000'; when a mass grave of the victims was discovered in Changchun in 2006, it was mistaken for a Japanese wartime atrocity.[20] The model of encircling cities under Nationalist control was used by the Communists repeatedly in the civil war: in the earlier siege of Shenyang, 4 million civilians endured a ten-month blockade from December 1947 along with the 200,000 soldiers of the KMT army, who were stationed in the city. In summer 1948, the refugees from Shenyang headed for Jinzhou, where they found their path blocked by Nationalist fire. Those who managed to overcome this last obstacle continued from Jinzhou by rail to a refugee centre at Shanhaiguan.[21]

Located on the banks of Yitong River 伊通河, a tributary of the Songhua, Changchun became the provincial seat of Jilin only in 1954. The Soviets, who had invaded Manchuria in 1945, did not leave Changchun until 1956. In the 2010 census, the city population reached approximately 7,675,000. Industrialized since the 1950s with the establishment of the first (initially Soviet-managed) car factory in the PRC, Changchun produced the famous 'Liberation' truck.[22] The car business still prospers and has been updated to fit the market age; over 200 Audi cars were being produced daily in Changchun under German supervision as of 2009.[23] Companies like Mazda, Toyota and Volkswagen also construct their cars there, and the city has been called the Detroit of China. The Changchun Film Studio, taken over from the Japanese-era Manchuria Film Production, made the city well known in China before the Cultural Revolution. It was restructured as the Changchun Film Group Corporation after 2000 and the first film theme park in China was opened there in 2005.

The second largest city in Jilin province, Jilin town (120 km east of Changchun) is the only one in China today bearing its province's name, although in the past Qiqihar was also known by the name Heilongjiang, whereas Fengtian was a name used both for today's Shenyang and for Liaoning province. Jilin is the oldest town in Jilin province, dating to 1674. With the exception of the Manchukuo period it served as the provincial capital from 1912 to 1953, when the PRC recognized Changchun as the more populated and important location despite its problematic heritage as capital of the puppet regime. A fire in 1930 destroyed most of the wooden buildings in Jilin, but there are still traces of the French Catholic Mission and church. The Songhua is dammed here, creating an artificial lake. Some rocks from outer space are exhibited in the Jilin City museum: in March 1976, a meteorite rain fell over Jilin, the first in a series of 'nature disasters' in that year, as on 28 July China's worst-ever earthquake in Tangshan 唐山 (Hebei) killed about a quarter of a million people; Mao Zedong died, aged 83, on 9 September.[24]

The third main city in Jilin in terms of population and historical importance is Siping, on the border with Liaoning in the south-west. It had emerged as a CER station, but came under Japanese management after 1905.[25] It is now an industrial town on the railway line and a large grain producer, Jilin being the fourth producer of corn in China. With extensive forests, Jilin is the second most important timber producer in China after Heilongjiang; both provinces are also important sources of China's sugar beet.

The most famous native of Jilin province today is probably the founder of the persecuted Falun Gong movement, Li Hongzhi 李洪志 (born 1951), who hails from Gongzhuling 公主岭, a town between Siping and Changchun. Having first taught the Falun Gong practice in Changchun in 1992, he has lived in exile in the US since 1998.

Notes

1 Carla Nappi, 'Surface Tension: Objectifying Ginseng in Chinese Early Modernity', in Paula Findlen, ed., *Early Modern Things: Objects and their Histories, 1500–1800* (London and New York: Routledge, 2013), at pp. 35–9, describes the process by which the identification of 'the best ginseng' moved from south-east Shanxi to Manchuria in the Ming dynasty.
2 Cf. Mareile Flitsch, 'Papercut Stories of the Manchu Woman Artist Hou Yumei', *Asian Folklore Studies*, vol. 58, no. 2 (1999), pp. 353–75.
3 Mareile Flitsch, 'The Suobo Staff in Custom and Tale: Ginseng Seekers' Material Culture in Jilin Han Folk Literature', *Techniques & Culture*, no. 29 (Jan.–June 1997), pp. 41–67; cf. also Mareile Flitsch, 'A Ginseng Tale from Jilin', in Victor Mair and Mark Bender, eds, *The Columbia Anthology of Chinese Folk & Popular Literature* (New York: Columbia University Press, 2011), pp. 16–19.

4   A recent introduction to the mountain and its exploration since the seventeenth century is Ruth Rogaski, 'Knowing a Sentient Mountain: Space, Science, and the Sacred in Ascents of Mount Paektu/Changbai', *Modern Asian Studies*, vol. 52, no. 2 (March 2018), pp. 716–52.
5   Henry E. M. James, *The Long White Mountain* (London: Longmans, 1888).
6   Stephen H. Whiteman, 'Kangxi's Auspicious Empire: Rhetorics of Geographic Integration in the Early Qing', in Du and Kyong-McClain, eds, *Chinese History in Geographical Perspective*. The five Taoist peaks are Taishan in Shandong (east), Hengshan [Bei] in Shanxi (north), another Hengshan [Nan] in Hunan (south), Huashan in Shaanxi (west) and Songshan in Henan (centre). The four main mountains in the Chinese Buddhist belief are Wutaishan in Shanxi (north), Emeishan in Sichuan (west), Jiuhuashan in Anhui (south) and Putuoshan in Zhejiang (east).
7   Cf. Jeongwon Bourdais Park, *Identity, Policy, and Prosperity: Border Nationality of the Korean Diaspora and Regional Development in Northeast China* (New York: Palgrave Macmillan, 2017).
8   Enze Han, *Contestation and Adaptation: The Politics of National Identity in China* (Oxford: Oxford University Press, 2013), p. 68.
9   Colin Mackerras, 'What is China? Who is Chinese? Han–Minority Relations, Legitimacy, and the State', in Gries and Rosen, eds, *State and Society in 21st-Century China*, p. 222; cf. p. 230 on the Koreans as 'a "model" ethnic minority'.
10 Han, *Contestation and Adaptation*, pp. 74–6, and Eduardo Baptista, 'Caught between Two Countries: Northeastern China's Ethnic Korean Minority', *Los Angeles Review of Books*, 9 October 2018.
11 Han, *Contestation and Adaptation*, pp. 85–6.
12 Jane Perlez, 'Fearing the Worst, China Plans Refugee Camps on North Korean Border', *New York Times*, 11 Dec. 2017.
13 On this controversy, see the epilogue in Rawski, *Early Modern China and Northeast Asia*. A new history of the Sino-Korean border, Yanbian and the Tumen River is Nianshen Song, *Making Borders in Modern East Asia: Tumen River Demarcation, 1881–1919* (Cambridge: Cambridge University Press, 2018).
14 Seonmin Kim, *Ginseng and Borderland: Territorial Boundaries and Political Relations between Qing China and Choson Korea, 1636–1912* (Berkeley: University of California Press, 2017), ch. 2.
15 Podoler, *Monuments, Memory, and Identity*, pp. 27–33, 38–41; ibid., p. 44, on Bohai/Parhae. Cf. Rogaski, 'Knowing a Sentient Mountain', pp. 751–2.
16 Jane Perlez, 'Some Chinese Are Souring on Being North Korea's Best Friend', *New York Times*, 16 Feb. 2013.
17 Song, 'Northeast Eurasia as Historical Center'.
18 Christopher W. Hughes, 'Tumen River Area Development Programme: Frustrated Micro-regionalism as a Microcosm of Political Rivalries', working paper of the Centre for the Study of Globalisation and Regionalisation, University of Warwick, Aug. 2000.

19 Cf. Xiangming Chen, 'Beyond the Reach of Globalization: China's Border Regions and Cities in Transition', in Fulong Wu, ed., *Globalization and the Chinese City* (London and New York: Routledge, 2006), pp. 29–33.
20 Frank Dikötter, *The Tragedy of Liberation: A History of the Chinese Revolution, 1945–57* (New York: Bloomsbury Press, 2013). See also Homare Endo, trans. Michael Brase, *Japanese Girl at the Siege of Changchun: How I Survived China's Wartime Atrocity* (Berkeley: Stone Bridge Press, 2016).
21 Dikötter, *The Tragedy of Liberation*, pp. 20–1.
22 See Yishi Liu, 'Changchun across 1949: Rebuilding a Colonial Capital City under Socialism in the Early 1950s', in Yannan Ding et al., eds, *China: A Historical Geography of the Urban* (New York: Palgrave Macmillan, 2018).
23 'Audi – made in China', NZZ, 1 Oct. 2009.
24 Cf. Meyer, *In Manchuria*, p. 146, on the museum; on the Catholic past in Jilin, ibid., pp. 98–101, 272.
25 See Yu Jiang, 'Land, City, State, Nation, and Empire in Sipinggai, Northeast China, 1900–1945', *Studies on Asia*, vol. 4, no. 1 (Spring 2007), pp. 33–49.

18

History and Geography: Liaoning

Liaoning has a territory of 147,400 sq km, making it the smallest of the three provinces in the Northeast and the fourth smallest in China. The province was formed by the Qing in April 1907. The meaning of the name is Peaceful [territories] of the Liao [river], and it also calls to mind the Liao state (916–1125). At the time of the establishment of the PRC, there were two provinces in this territory, Liaodong and Liaoxi (to the east and to the west of the Liao), which were merged as Liaoning in August 1954. The 44 million inhabitants of the province include forty-four minorities, making up about 16 per cent of the total population (more than in any

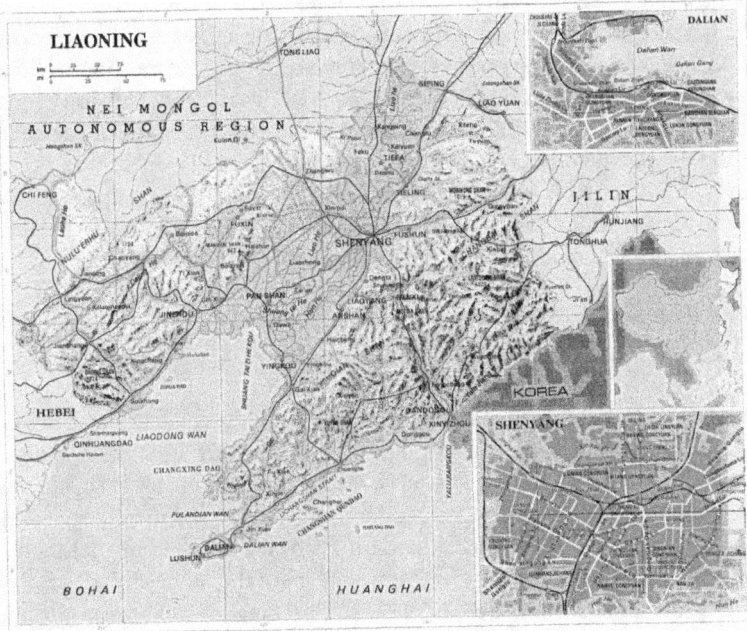

Figure 18 Liaoning. From Hsieh, *China Provincial Atlas*. © 1995 Gale, a part of Cengage, Inc. Reproduced by permission.www.cengage.com/permissions.

other Northeast province): as often is the case in the Northeast, the largest groups after the Han are Manchus, Mongols, Hui and Koreans. There are Manchu autonomous counties in Xinbin near Fushun and in Benxi 本溪, south-east of Shenyang.

The province is considered to have been settled by the Han Chinese since the Warring States (403–201 BC), although we know much more about the early Ming settlement, mentioned above. Liaoning has always been economically the most advanced of the three provinces (Jilin's former second place has by now been overtaken by Heilongjiang). Historically, Liaoning was alternatively known as Mukden, Shengjing or Fengtian; the province name Liaoning dates only from 1929. Because it was populated by the Han Chinese for the longest time, this is the only province in the Northeast where one can distinguish dialects within the mutually comprehensible spoken Mandarin. Partly because the local inhabitants of Dalian speak a Mandarin dialect, known as Jiao-Liao, they tend to refuse the collective 'Dongbei' identity, preferring instead to call themselves people of Dalian or Jiaodong 膠東, the peninsula across the Bohai Sea in Shandong.

Special importance is attached to the Liao 遼河, the main river in South Manchuria, which was still packed with junks carrying soybeans in the late 1920s.[1] Like the Sungari and the Yalu before the railway age, boats and barges plied the Liao, conveying grain as well as timber.[2] Situated at the mouth of the Liao, Yingkou 營口, formerly known as Newchwang (Niuzhuang) 牛莊, became a treaty port in 1858, but declined in the early twentieth century due to the development of Dalian by Japan after the Russo-Japanese War. From 1899, a British-built railway connected Yingkou to Peking, passing by Shanhaiguan, while the town was also connected to the Chinese Eastern Railway through another line at nearby Dashiqiao 大石橋.

Mukden / Shenyang

The province capital Shenyang 沈陽 had over 6 million residents in its urban area as of 2010. Its early history goes back to the Warring States and later rulers included Tang China (618–907), the Bohai kingdom, the Liao and the Jin. Among Northeast cities, it has the most serious claim for a place in Chinese history. At 10 km from modern Shenyang are the imperial tombs built by the founders of the Qing dynasty before they moved their capital from Mukden to Beijing: the Fuling 福陵 (or Dongling 東陵) mausoleum, where Nurhaci was buried, and the Zhaoling 昭陵 (or Beiling 北陵) mausoleum, the burial place of his son Hong Taiji. Both are tourist attractions today, as well as another Qing mausoleum of Nurhaci's ancestors, the Yongling

永陵, near Fushun. Since 2000 the whole burial complex has been a UNESCO World Heritage site.

The Yongling mausoleum lies near the first Manchu capital Hetu Ala (1603–21; named Xingjing 興京 in Chinese in 1634), where Nurhaci proclaimed himself emperor of the 'Later Jin' in 1616. The second capital of the Manchus (1621–5) was Liaoyang, south of present-day Shenyang. The name Mukden comes from the verb 'to arise' in Manchu, a meaning reflected in the parallel Chinese name Shengjing (Rising Capital; compare with the above Xingjing). Mukden became third capital of the Manchus (still called Nüzhen until Hong Taiji's decision to change his people's name in 1635) in 1625, four years after they had taken this city. In Mukden in 1636, Hong declared the founding of the Qing dynasty and the city kept the status of a secondary capital of the Qing after the move to Beijing in 1644.[3] The Manchus added their own symbolic structures to the city and also transferred buildings from the previous capital Liaoyang. The surviving palace of Hong Taiji (with its own 'little forbidden city', 小故宫) displays original Manchu architecture, which was later to be cast away in favour of a Chinese imperial building style. Other Qing palaces, official buildings and temples in Mukden have not survived.

After the fall of the Qing, the city was known as Fengtian 奉天 until the restoration of the Ming-dynasty name Shenyang (meaning the *yang* side of the river Shen, now called Hun 渾) in 1928. Westerners, however, continued using the name Mukden as did the Japanese authorities of Manchukuo. Apart from the old walled town, Mukden had a Japanese railway quarter (known as New Town), and – between these two – an International Settlement, where foreign consulates were located. We have already mentioned that Mukden/Fengtian was also the headquarters of Zhang Zuolin's regime, serving as an unofficial capital of Manchuria. Losing its prime administrative position in favour of Changchun (Xinjing or Hsinking) in the Manchukuo era, the city was heavily industrialized by the Japanese and later by the Maoist regime, which utilized and developed the Japanese infrastructure with Soviet assistance in the 1950s.

Contemporary Shenyang reached the headlines again along with much of the Northeast since the mid-1990s due to the crisis of industrial cities in the passage from state to market economy, when most state-owned enterprises closed down or were taken over by newly formed companies, leading to massive unemployment.[4] In 2003 the film director Wang Bing 王兵 made Shenyang the focus of an epic documentary on this human story, 'West of the Tracks'. At least the heavy pollution, with which Shenyang had struggled for years, has been reduced along with its industrial production. Much of the city's new-found prosperity is reflected in the construction of skyscrapers, which in recent years have altered its skyline.

Dalian and Lüshunkou

Dalian 大连 passed over to the Japanese at the end of the Russo-Japanese War after much construction work had already been done there by the Russians: in the harbour, for example, dredging had been carried out so the port could accommodate larger vessels. The original Chinese town Dalianwan 大連灣 was named after Dalian Bay; the Russians founded 'Dal'nii' as a new city by the tsar's decree, which also declared it an international open port. The centenary of Dalian was marked in the city in 1999. Under the Japanese, Dal'nii was renamed Dairen following the Japanese reading of the Chinese characters. It became headquarters of the SMR, which developed it into a 'model' city by introducing modern Western-style architecture. As the administrative capital of the Guandong Leased Territory, Dairen was the hub and centre of the Japanese colonial society in Manchuria until the creation of the Manchukuo state. By the 1930s Dairen had also become the centre of shipbuilding, as well as of locomotive construction.

The Japanese population was always larger proportionally in Dairen than anywhere else in Manchuria, including the 'capital' in Changchun: by the time of the Japanese defeat, it amounted to 225,000, nearing a third of Dairen's population total. A hierarchy was maintained, by which the Japanese residents ranked first whereas Chinese workers, in particular the migrants from Shandong, suffered discrimination.[5] In the Manchukuo era, when it was no

Figure 18a Dalian city hall in the Russian Period, subsequently a Yamato Hotel and the Dalian Natural History Museum (abandoned since 1998). Photograph by Qu Changliang, July 2016.

longer a leasehold capital of the SMR zone, the city evolved into the state's main border port. Dairen also underwent massive industrialization, particularly in the chemical sector, which supplied Japan's wartime needs.

Lüshunkou served as an entry port into southern Manchuria already by the Ming. Russia obtained a lease of Port Arthur, as the British called Lüshunkou, in 1898, but lost it to Japan along with Dalian after the Russo-Japanese War. The Soviet Union gained the permission to lease Port Arthur as a naval base for thirty years in the Yalta Conference of February 1945 (this was later acknowledged in the Treaty of Friendship and Alliance, which the USSR signed with Nationalist China on 14 August 1945), but the Soviets eventually stayed there for only another decade. In the first three years, until Soviet Russia finally committed itself to supporting the CCP in the Chinese civil war, Chinese Communists attempting to implement revolutionary 'class struggle' in Dalian were restrained by the Soviet military, whose main interests were in stability and increased production growth in the factories they had taken over from the Japanese.[6] While the Chinese Communist regime described Dalian as a model city (the ideal 'model' of an industrialized city now being Soviet), it did not acknowledge that its industry was a direct legacy of the Japanese era.[7] In 1950 the Lüshun Naval Base Area and the city of Dalian were formally reintegrated with China, although the Soviet Union kept its control of the Lüshun port until 1955. During this period, when 'friendship' with the Soviet Union was the order of the day in the whole of China, Dalian may have been the place where Soviet and Chinese citizens came into closest contact.[8]

The second boom of Lüshunkou and Dalian began in 1984, as 'LüDa' was given the status of a Special Economic Zone. Today the part of Lüshun which lies beyond the port (used by the Chinese navy) is an exclusive residential area. It also has an important museum, originally established under the Japanese in 1915, and the campuses of several universities, which have relocated from Dalian. A peculiar tourist attraction is the Russo-Japanese Prison, displaying prison cells and torture chambers.

Dalian ranks among the ten busiest container ports in China and is the largest one for oil shipment; in July 2010, 1.5 million litres of oil spilled into the sea here, creating an ecological disaster. Today's Dalian is a leading modern city in China, known both for its cleanliness and its nightclubs. Nowadays Russians are returning to Dalian as tourists and businessmen, and some shops in the city carry Russian signs. Bo Xilai 薄熙来 (born 1949), the former Politburo member who was disgraced in 2012 while serving as the Party Secretary in Chongqing and is now imprisoned, was mayor of Dalian in the 2000s. Bo had close connections with local billionaire Xu Ming 徐明, who was also found guilty of corruption in 2012 and died in prison in

2015.⁹ Dalian Wanda, founded in Dalian in 1988, is a huge property company and owner of a cinema chain, known across the country for supporting Chinese soccer.

Smaller cities in Liaoning

An important ancient city in Liaoning is Liaoyang, formerly one of the capital cities of the Liao dynasty in the tenth century and the Jin dynasty in the twelfth. It was then part of the territory included under Yuan and Ming rule and, as has been mentioned above, became the capital of the Manchus from 1621 until Nurhaci's move to Mukden in 1625. From 1653 to 1668 the Manchus briefly supported Chinese settlement in the Liaoyang area, which had lost much of its population during the war of conquest. Thereafter Han immigration continued illegally. The writer Cao Xueqin, whose 300th anniversary was celebrated in 2015, may have been born in Liaoyang; a memorial hall to him was created there in 1995.[10] In turn, Gao E 高鶚 (1758–1815), who edited Cao's novel *Dream of the Red Chamber* and first published it in 1792, came from Tieling 鐵嶺 (at about the same distance due north-east of Shenyang).

In Dandong (former Andong), the largest border city in China and the third most important port in the Northeast after Dalian and Yingkou, tourists look out on North Korea across the Yalu River from a bridge which was bombed by the US army in the Korean War and remains in ruins from the Korean side. It can be crossed up to the halfway point, affording a rare opportunity to gaze at a foreign country from within Chinese borders. The nostalgic allure of watching 'old Communism' from afar apparently beats the attraction of viewing Blagoveshchensk from Heihe, and the border town on the North Korean side of the Yalu, Sinuiju, is poorer still than the Russian one across the Amur. Dandong also has a museum and a monument celebrating the PRC contribution to the Korean War.[11] Oil pumped in Dandong is supplied to North Korea, which is dependent on PRC imports.

A major industrial centre in Liaoning is Anshan, where ironworks were established already by the Japanese in 1917 and industry was developed extensively with Soviet help during the first decade of Chinese Communist rule.[12] The Anshan-based Ansteel Group, a state-owned corporation, is presently one of the world's largest steel producers. Only 20 km to the southeast of industrialized Anshan, the Qianshan 千山 mountain range is dotted with ancient Buddhist and Daoist monasteries.[13] It has been a national park since 1982. South of Anshan, Haicheng 海城 (the birthplace of Zhang Zuolin) is now considered an example of the successful transformation of a county town to market economy, dominated by private business.

In Fushun, an industrial city east of Shenyang, coal was mined by the SMR from 1906 to 1945; besides coal, there was iron, steel and chemical production. Oil shale was also discovered there in 1926, making Fushun the largest oil producer in the areas under Japanese control; it was still a major source of oil for China in the 1950s. As a company town, Fushun also benefited from large Japanese investments, which funded construction of schools and hospitals, although the Japanese and Chinese populations were segregated in separate living areas of the city and paid differentiated wages, with the Japanese employees enjoying superior conditions.[14] Fushun today is a developed city, displaying a rather unusual monument of futuristic architecture, the 'big iron loop'. Prosperous as a whole, Liaoning province is also known as a producer of apples and it has the biggest fishing industry in north China. Heavy industry, especially steel and iron, continues to dominate, however.

Notes

1 Simpich, 'Manchuria, Promised Land of Asia', p. 394.
2 Rev. John Ross, 'Manchuria', *The Scottish Geographical Magazine*, vol. 11, no. 5 (1895), pp. 220–1.
3 Piero Corradini, 'The Manchu Capital Cities before the Conquest of China', *Ming Qing yanjiu*, vol. 13 (2005), pp. 67–91.
4 Antoine Kernen and Jean-Louis Rocca, 'Social Responses to Unemployment and the "New Urban Poor": Case Study in Shenyang City and Liaoning Province', *China Perspectives*, no. 27 (Feb. 2000), pp. 35–51.
5 Christian A. Hess, 'Gateway to Manchuria: The Port City of Dalian under Japanese, Russian and Chinese Control, 1898–1950', *Comparativ*, vol. 22, no. 5 (2012), pp. 50–2, 55.
6 Christian Hess, 'Big Brother Is Watching: Local Sino–Soviet Relations and the Building of New Dalian, 1945–1955', in Paul Pickowicz and Jeremy Brown, eds, *Dilemmas of Victory: The Early Years of the People's Republic of China* (Cambridge MA: Harvard University Press, 2007).
7 This is the argument of Christian Hess, 'From Colonial Port to Socialist Metropolis: Imperialist Legacies and the Making of New Dalian', *Urban History*, vol. 38, no. 3 (Dec. 2011), pp. 373–90.
8 Christian Hess, 'Sino-Soviet City: Dalian between Socialist Worlds, 1945–1955', *Journal of Urban History*, vol. 44, no. 1 (June 2017), pp. 9–25.
9 Edward Wong and Jonathan Ansfield, 'Fallen Leader is Indicted in China', *New York Times*, 24 July 2013.
10 An ancestor of Cao's was taken into Manchu slavery after the fall of Mukden in 1621 and conscripted into the Plain White Banner. Cao Xueqin's great-grandmother was the wet nurse of Emperor Kangxi. The poet and high official Cao Yin 曹寅 (1658–1712), either the grandfather or the great-uncle

of the writer, was the Imperial Textile commissioner in Nanjing. The Cao family in Nanjing became impoverished in 1728 and they probably moved to Peking in the 1730s.

11 John Cannon, 'Diary' (on the PRC–North Korea border), *London Review of Books*, vol. 22, no. 15 (10 Aug. 2000).
12 See e.g. the propaganda pamphlet *Builders of Anshan* (Peking: Foreign Languages Press, 1956).
13 See Yosano Akiko, trans. Joshua A. Fogel, *Travels in Manchuria and Mongolia: A Feminist Poet from Japan Encounters Prewar China* (New York: Columbia University Press, 2001), pp. 24–38, for an interesting description.
14 Limin Teh, 'From Colonial Company Town to Industrial City: The South Manchuria Railway Company in Fushun, China', in Marcelo J. Borges and Susana B. Torres, eds, *Company Towns: Labor, Space, and Power Relations across Time and Continents* (New York: Palgrave, 2012), esp. pp. 81–5.

19

The Mongol Component in Manchuria

Inner Mongolia needs to figure in this introduction to Manchuria because the north-eastern part of the present-day autonomous region belonged to Manchuria, and the Mongols were always an essential component of it.[1] By 2010 the Inner Mongolia Autonomous Region had a population of over 24 million, of whom only about 17 per cent were ethnic Mongols and the absolute majority were Han Chinese.[2] These proportions may be contrasted with Xinjiang, where at the same time the national 'minorities' still made up the demographic majority despite massive Han settlement. At

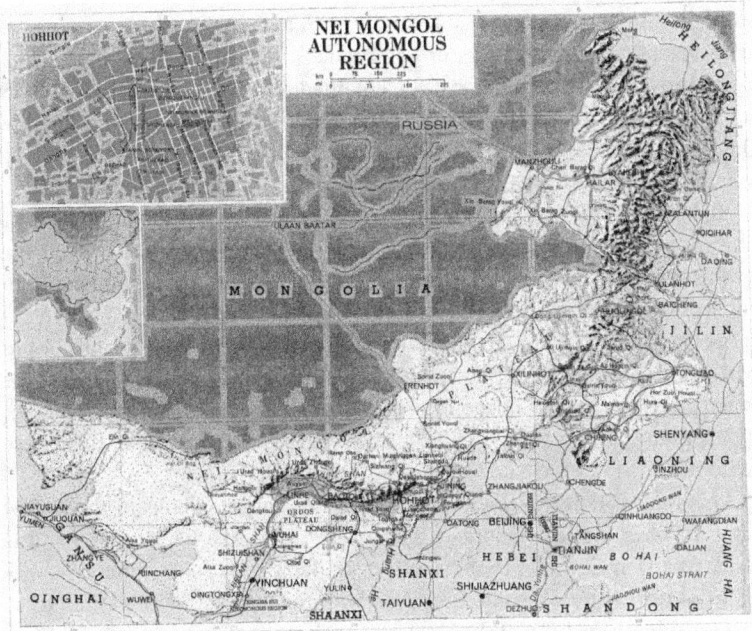

Figure 19 Inner Mongolia. From Hsieh, *China Provincial Atlas*. © 1995 Gale, a part of Cengage, Inc. Reproduced by permission.www.cengage.com/permissions.

1,177,500 sq km (454,520 sq miles), Inner Mongolia is the third-largest region of China after Xinjiang and Tibet; it is more than two and a half times the size of Heilongjiang, the largest province of the Northeast. While Inner Mongolia has one of the lowest density population ratios in the PRC, only 2,736,800 people lived in independent Outer Mongolia in 2009, making it the most sparsely populated country in the world. Inner and Outer Mongolia, though separated by the Gobi Desert, did not always belong to different states.

Hohhot and 'Xanadu'

The capital seat of the Autonomous Region is Huhehaote 呼和浩特 (Hohhot), close to the border with Shanxi province. Founded by the Mongol Altan Khan in 1557, it is a combination of the 'old' Chinese-Mongolian town Guihua 歸化 (as it was renamed in the Ming) and the 'new' Manchu garrison city of Suiyuan 綏遠 (founded in 1736, only 2 km to the north). Both Han and Hui Chinese settled in Hohhot from the 1720s. By the end of the nineteenth century, it was a huge centre of the transit trade between China, Mongolia, Eastern Turkestan and Russia, with at least ten Chinese transport firms operating a total number of 7,500 camels, mainly employed in carrying tea to those destinations.[3] A province named Suiyuan was created in 1928 with a capital in Guisui 歸綏 (as the twin towns had been known through the Qing), but in 1954 the Communist regime abolished it, adding the territory to Inner Mongolia and restoring the name Hohhot ('the blue town').[4]

The city had 790,000 inhabitants in 2000, reaching 1 million in 2006 (or 1.43 million including suburbs under the city's administration), when the local authorities announced their aspiration to bring the population to the 2-million mark so as to achieve the upgrade from the category of Very Large City to that of Super Large City. While Mongols made up only 14 per cent in Hohhot (2006 figures), redevelopment since the late 1990s has constructed the tourist image of a 'Mongolian' city with a 'Muslim' quarter, appropriating Mongolian steppe culture as part and parcel of Chinese civilization.

Less than 150 km to the west from Hohhot, on the banks of the Yellow River, is Inner Mongolia's largest industrial town Baotou. Like Hohhot, it is essentially Han Chinese. To the south from Baotou, Ordos (Chinese 鄂尔多斯, E'erduosi), is now mostly associated with the production of cashmere, as well as with the decision of the local authorities in 2003 to design and build a new city to accommodate population that never arrived. Ordos City has accordingly been called the world's biggest ghost town and an illustration of the Chinese property bubble.[5]

Close to the Hebei border due east, near the town of Duolun 多倫, lie the ruins of Shangdu 上都 (Upper Capital): Xanadu, the palace of Kubilai Khan (1215–94), the grandson of Genghis Khan and founder of the Yuan dynasty, which was described by Marco Polo, and then by the English romantic Samuel Taylor Coleridge (1772–1834) in his poem 'Kubla Khan: or A Vision in a Dream' (published 1816).[6] Shangdu was destroyed by the Chinese as the Yuan dynasty fell. It was left unattended until being turned into a meat-supply farm for the People's Liberation Army. Until recently a top-security military region, to which foreign travellers found it difficult to get access,[7] it was added to the UNESCO World Heritage list in 2012.

Most of the Mongol population in China has inevitably switched to agriculture from its original pastoralism. With high levels of sinicization and intermarriage with the Han Chinese, many ethnic Mongols no longer speak the Mongolian language.[8] Resistance against Han Chinese immigration and settlement in the region has characterized the entire twentieth century. Mongolian is more widely spoken in Hailar 海拉爾, a city in Hulunbuir District that borders on the grasslands in the north-east of Inner Mongolia between Heilongjiang and Russia. Like other cities in Inner Mongolia, Hailar has a monument to Genghis Khan in a square named after him. A symbol of Mongol identity, Genghis, however, has not escaped appropriation by the PRC.[9] Between Manzhouli and Hailar, the town of Zhalainor 扎賚諾爾, likewise a former station of the CER, has erected a copy of the facade of St Basil's Cathedral, a symbol of the Red Square near the Kremlin in Moscow – a reminder of the region's Russian past, which is now intended to attract domestic tourism.

The Mongols and the Qing

By the late Ming, the Mongols who had ruled over China during the preceding Yuan dynasty were divided into four groups: the Chahars of Inner Mongolia, the Khalkhas of Outer Mongolia, the Junghars in north-east Xinjiang and the smaller group of Buryats to the south and east of Lake Baikal (this region, conquered by Russia in the seventeenth century, is now the Buryat Republic, with its capital at Ulan-Ude).[10] In the last decades of the Qing and the early republic, many Buryats migrated from Russia to Mongolia and Manchuria.

The Mongols were early allies and then vassals of the Manchus, who already conquered Inner Mongolia in 1636. The Khalkha Mongols submitted to Emperor Kangxi in a ceremony in Duolun (Mongolian: Dolon Nor) in 1691, by which Outer Mongolia became a Qing protectorate. Kangxi set out to conquer Jungharia, but, although he defeated Galdan's army, he was unsuccessful. Emperor Qianlong, by using extreme violence, managed to complete the conquest in the 1750s. Later in 1768, Qianlong coined the new name of 'Xinjiang' for the region encompassing both Jungharia and Kashgaria.

The Mongolian aristocracy enjoyed a high status in the Qing, many of its members serving as senior military commanders. The Manchus, who did not intermarry with the Han Chinese until the last years of dynasty, did marry Mongols. The Manchu script was based on the Mongolian written language, which during the Qing era became third in importance after Manchu and Chinese. There were also close religious ties, as the Qing became patrons of Lamaism, i.e. Tibetan Buddhism, the Mongols' religion since Kubilai Khan; this dimension of the Manchu–Mongol relationship will be discussed below in connection with Chengde. In 1723, the Qing began allowing Han Chinese migration into Mongolia. Especially during the last decade of Qing rule, the court actively encouraged Han settlement in both Inner and Outer Mongolia; in July 1911 it formally incorporated the whole of Mongolia into China. Of all native populations faced by Han Chinese settlers, the Mongols alone resisted such encroachment: for a time, the Han colonization system, which was successful elsewhere in Manchuria, backfired in Mongolia as it drove Mongols to seek Russian protection.[11]

The Mongols and Russia

After Russia's defeat in the Russo-Japanese War, Mongolia was left as the only area of possible Russian expansion. The division of spheres of interest with Japan in the later 1900s assured Russia of Japanese neutrality in this arena. For their part, the Mongols resented Chinese rule and revolted six times between 1861 and 1901. In both Inner and Outer Mongolia almost half the men entered monasteries and, as these were tax-exempt, the Qing tax burden fell on the rest of the population. Han settlers and traders, to whom Mongols became indebted, were another major cause for anti-Chinese sentiment.

With the collapse of the Qing, Outer Mongolia relied on Russian support to declare its autonomy from Peking on 1 December 1911, claiming that it owed allegiance only to the Manchu dynasty. When Inner Mongolia joined the Outer Mongols in 1912, the troops of Yuan Shikai brutally put down the 'rebellion' there. Only Hulunbuir remained within the Outer Mongolian state from 1912 to 1915. Even after returning to full Chinese jurisdiction, this region was semi-autonomous and its sense of identification with Mongolia combined with a particular local identity.[12] Russia did not assist in the attempted secession of Inner Mongolia. After initially lending support to the Mongol revolt in Hulunbuir, it pressured for the return of Hulunbuir to China. Tsarist policy-makers were easily convinced to give up the prospects of Mongolian unity in return for trade privileges and de facto domination of Outer Mongolia. The Mongols thereby had to relinquish the dream of a united Mongolia, while China had to acknowledge the 'autonomy' of Outer Mongolia in a joint declaration with Russia in November 1913 and a tripartite treaty in June 1915.

However, two years later, when the tsarist regime collapsed and the Russian Far East became the arena of White Army opposition to the Bolsheviks, China attempted to regain Outer Mongolia. At the time, the Mongolian elite feared both the Reds and the Whites. Ataman Semenov, the White Army leader who was a Buryat on his mother's side, aspired to succeed the tsar as ruler of Mongolia. With Chinese backing, Mongolian forces fought Semenov and ejected his army from Mongolia in September 1919. In a petition signed in November by most of the nobles in Urga, Outer Mongolia renounced its autonomy and rejoined China. However, the Khutuktu, also known as 'living Buddha' or Eighth Bogd Gegeen (1869–1924), the third most important figure in Lamaism after the Dalai Lama and Panchen Lama of Tibet and the main religious authority in Mongolia, who had ruled it since independence in 1911, did not sign the petition calling the Chinese to return.[13] Warlord Xu Shuzheng 徐樹錚 (1880–1925) then went to Urga at the head of his Northwest Frontier Defense Army, putting the Khutuktu under house arrest.

Urga (Ulan Bator, now Romanized as Ulaanbaatar, capital of Mongolia) had a strong Russian connection as a centre of Russian–Chinese trade since the eighteenth century. In October 1920 the White Army officer, the Baltic German Baron Roman von Ungern-Sternberg (1886–1921), who had been a deputy of Semenov's until summer that year, entered Outer Mongolia at the head of his 'Asiatic Division'. By February 1921 he had conquered Urga from the Chinese. Ungern concocted an ideology combining Monarchism and mystical Orientalism with ruthless anti-Semitism. As he freed and restored the Khutuktu in his Urga palace, he proclaimed the independence of Outer Mongolia on 24 March 1921. Ungern then attacked the Red Army by crossing the Russian border at Kiakhta. In September, he was captured, tried and executed by the Bolsheviks before he could realize his aim of restoring the three toppled monarchies: Russian, Mongolian and Manchu.[14]

With the civil war still going on in Siberia and the Russian Far East, the Bolsheviks had created the buffer state of The Far Eastern Republic (April 1920 to November 1922). In June 1921 Mongolia was occupied by the Reds and a new declaration of Mongolian independence was issued, now by its People's Government, on 14 September. After the death of the Khutuktu in 1924 the Mongolian People's Republic was created under Soviet protection and China lost any influence on this country, which remained under Russian patronage until the 1990s, although a failed pan-Mongolian insurrection took place in 1928.[15] Nationalist China only very reluctantly recognized

Outer Mongolia's independence in the Sino-Soviet treaty of 1945. Mao Zedong subsequently had to accept this as a fact in his negotiations in Moscow in 1949–50. Even before their rise to power in Beijing, the Chinese Communists established the Autonomous Region of Inner Mongolia, under the sinicized Mongolian Communist Ulanhu (1906–88), on 1 May 1947. Some Mongols had been attracted by Mao's promise to restore Inner Mongolia, which had disappeared from the maps under the KMT. The first such autonomous region in China, it controlled only a limited territory at first, but expanded to reach its present borders by 1956.[16]

Two border towns played an important role in Russian–Chinese relations in and via Mongolia; one is long gone, but the other has grown into a large city and continues to function as the gateway from Russia into China and vice versa. The vanished town was called Maimaicheng 買賣城 (Shopping Town) in Chinese and Maimachen in Russian. We have already seen how the Treaty of Kiakhta fixed the borders of Outer Mongolia in 1727; this treaty also remained the frame of Russian–Chinese relations until the mid-nineteenth century. Between 1825 and 1850 tea constituted 90 to 95 per cent of all Russian imports from China, allowing the Russian millionaires in Kiakhta to live in opulent luxury. Maimaicheng was a town of Chinese merchants, mostly from Shanxi, which emerged opposite Kiakhta on the side of the Chinese (Outer Mongolian) border.

A historian has called such 'shopping towns', which were common in Mongolia, 'the Northern Asian version of Chinatowns'. As Muping Bao demonstrates, these settlements changed the appearance of towns like Kalgan, Hohhot and Urga.[17] Yet nothing remains of the Maimaicheng formerly located opposite Kiakhta, and the place is now an open field near the Mongolian town Altanbulag. As newly developed steamships started visiting the new ports opened in China for Western merchants from 1842, the overland route from China through Russia, which has been called the longest trade route in the world, became too expensive to be profitable. The *raison d'être* of the Kiakhta trade was further questioned by the opening of the Suez Canal in 1869, which enabled Chinese merchandise to reach the West through the East China Sea, passing by the South China Sea into the Indian Ocean and then sailing through the Red Sea into the Mediterranean.

Until as late as 1854 the Kiakhta trade was conducted in barter form, with tea traded for Russian furs, and only then were Russian merchants permitted to pay for Chinese goods in gold and silver. Kiakhta received a last boost in the Treaty of St Petersburg in 1881, which included a 62 per cent tariff reduction for the overland tea shipments. It has been in steep decline since the early twentieth century, but remains an interesting border town with a unique place in the history of Russian–Chinese relations.

Figure 19a Matryoshka Square in Manzhouli, 2009. Photograph by Niklaus Berger.

Manzhouli, formerly called Manchuria Station, was the small border town where the CER trains entered China. It now has the standing that Kiakhta had once possessed. Russian oil and timber arrive in China through Manzhouli, while Chinese cars and electronic appliances are exported into Russia. Since 2005, an airport has connected the city to Beijing by a two-hour flight, while the population has by now surpassed 300,000. The town that Manzhouli faces on the Russian side, Zabaikal'sk (with a current population of 13,000), is badly underdeveloped in comparison.[18] Russians from as far to the west as Chita cross the border here to shop in Manzhouli and are allowed to bring up to 30 kg with them to Russian territory. Chinese tourists visit the Manzhouli Russian Doll theme park, which has the world's largest *matryoshka*, almost 30 metres tall with a restaurant inside. A 'museum of Russian art' opened in Manzhouli in 2006, joining that in Heihe. Like Harbin, Manzhouli hosts an annual ice sculpture festival.

The Mongols and Japan

In the 1930s, to further its designs on the territory jointly referred to as Manmō (Manchuria and Mongolia), the Japanese Guandong army supported the anti-Chinese independence struggle of Inner Mongolia under the pan-

Mongolist leader De Wang 德王 (Prince De; short for Demchugdongrub, 1902–66). But despite Japanese assistance his army lost in battle against the KMT forces in November 1936 when it attempted an invasion of Suiyuan province.[19]

There is a detailed study of the process by which the idea of 'Manmō', not extant in Chinese geographical terminology, had formed in the Japanese geopolitical imagination after the end of the Russo-Japanese War, when Russia and Japan divided their spheres of 'special interest'.[20] In 1937, the Japanese created in Inner Mongolia a Mongolian Border Region United Autonomous Government, which was expanded under the name Mengjiang 蒙疆 in 1939, with Prince De among the leadership. The analogy with the Puyi regime in Changchun is evident. The Border Region's capital was in Zhangjiakou in present-day Hebei, an old trade town which the Mongols (and Russians) called Kalgan. Its authority stretched over the cities Datong 大同, Hohhot and Baotou, southern Chahar 察哈爾 and northern Shanxi prefectures.[21] This regime collapsed when Japan was defeated in August 1945.

A Japanese incursion from Manchukuo into the Soviet Maritime District led to the battle of Lake Khasan (near China's Fangchuan County; in Chinese, this is known as the Zhanggufeng 張鼓峰 incident) between July and August 1938, which the Red Army won. A year later Japan also attempted to invade Outer Mongolia, but was again defeated by the Soviet Union in the battle of Khalkhin-Gol (Japanese: Nomonhan).[22] After World War Two, Stalin tried to snatch Hulunbuir by establishing an 'autonomous' government there in January 1946 (in January 1945 a similarly 'independent' East Turkestan Republic was proclaimed in Xinjiang, only to be abolished after a year's existence through negotiations between the Soviet Union and the KMT). The district would have announced its 'wish' to join the Soviet protectorate of Outer Mongolia, had CCP forces not established their control over Hulunbuir in summer 1947. Prince De, captured in 1949, was imprisoned in the PRC until, like Puyi, he was released after re-education and wrote his memoirs in 1963. He worked in a Hohhot museum shortly before his death.

The Mongols and the PRC

The basic paradox of an autonomous ethnic region, in which Han Chinese have become the majority, has been analysed in a series of publications by the Cambridge University historian Uradyn Bulag. He has written on the Mongolian language becoming useless for ethnic Mongolians due to lack of demand for it in a Chinese-dominated society; moreover, even in the 'autonomous region', a perception of every minority language as being 'backward' in comparison to Chinese has become influential, while the Han have posed as rescuing the Mongols from a primitive feudalism. The most sinicized Mongols, according to Bulag, joined the Communists and then attempted to protect the Mongolian heritage in the Autonomous Region. The Han majority was meanwhile established with the help of a massive immigration during the 1950s, a trend encouraged by the great famine in 1958–60. At present, Han Chinese efforts to bolster the legitimacy of their presence in Inner Mongolia include replacing the traditional administrative division into 'leagues' by 'cities' and Mongolian place names by Chinese ones.[23]

Owen Lattimore

This is the appropriate occasion to briefly present the work of a pioneering scholar of Manchuria, who was as closely engaged in research on Mongolia. Owen Lattimore (1900–89) was born in the USA, but was raised in Tianjin, where his parents taught at the university. He began by travelling and writing on Xinjiang, following up with ethnographic work among the native peoples in Manchuria. His first famous book on Manchuria, *Cradle of Conflict*, appeared in 1932; an expanded edition in 1935 included two new chapters on the Mukden incident and on the creation of Manchukuo.[24] Lattimore had spent the year 1930 in Manchuria and the next seven years in Peking; after learning Mongolian and becoming concerned with the Mongolian cause, he published *The Mongols of Manchuria* (1934).[25] During his long time in China, he came to know Mao Zedong and Zhou Enlai, and to serve as US adviser to Chiang Kai-shek in the Nationalist wartime capital Chongqing.

Lattimore's most fully developed historical thesis was on the role of the north-east frontier in Chinese history and the impact of migration on Manchuria. He was among the first to question the established perception of China as an isolated empire, and of Chinese culture as radiating from the centre to the periphery and cultivating neighbouring peoples beyond the borders. Rather, Lattimore showed that northern peoples repeatedly entered China and influenced it. His conceptual language, stressing historical cycles and conflicts between 'rising and declining' ('young and old') cultures and civilizations, was inspired by a philosophy of history such as that of Oswald Spengler (1880–1936) and has aged less well than his contributions to world and comparative history.[26] Lattimore summed up his view of the historical dynamic between the Chinese and nomad worlds in his most ambitious book, *Inner Asian Frontiers of China* (1940).[27]

Notes

1. In a review of Shao Dan's *Remote Homeland, Recovered Borderland*, in *American Historical Review*, vol. 118, no. 1 (Feb. 2013), pp. 168-9, Uradyn E. Bulag criticized Shao's neglect of the Mongols. Although his claim that 'half of Manchuria was and remains Mongolian territory' is exaggerated, the Mongols were important.
2. A useful introduction as of 2007 is Li Narangoa, 'Nationalism and Globalization on the Inner Mongolia Frontier: The Commercialization of a Tamed Ethnicity', *Japan Focus*, no. 2575 (Nov. 2007).
3. Bao, 'Trade Centres (*Maimaicheng*) in Mongolia', pp. 219-21.
4. See Justin Tighe, *Constructing Suiyuan: The Politics of Northwestern Territory and Development in Early Twentieth-Century China* (Leiden: Brill, 2005).
5. See more in Alastair Bonnett, *Off the Map: Lost Spaces, Forgotten Islands, Feral Places, and What They Tell Us About the World* (London: Aurum Press, 2014), pp. 125-9, and the feature documentary film 'The Land of Many Palaces' (2015) by Adam J. Smith and Song Ting.
6. 'Kubla Khan or, A Vision in a Dream', in *The Portable Coleridge*, ed. I. A. Richards (1950; Harmondsworth: Penguin Books, 1978), pp. 156-8. In 1797, Coleridge had dreamt up the poem in his opium-induced sleep, in a farmhouse in the south-west of England, but writing it down as he awoke he was disturbed by 'a person on business from Porlock'. Hence, the story goes, he was only able to remember and write fifty-four lines.
7. Ch. 1, 'In Xanadu', in Becker, *City of Heavenly Tranquility*. See also William Dalrymple, *In Xanadu: A Quest* (1989; New York: Vintage Books, 2012) and John Man, *Xanadu: Marco Polo and Europe's Discovery of the East* (London: Bantam Books, 2010).
8. At the same time, many Han Chinese have registered as Mongolian in order to benefit from the social conditions that minorities enjoy, especially not being limited to having a single child and getting into university on 'ethnic minority' quotas.
9. Michal Biran, 'The Incarnations of Genghis Khan: Between Myth and Reality' (in Hebrew), *Zmanim*, no. 100 (Autumn 2007), pp. 56-71.
10. The 450,000 Buryats form the largest ethnic group in Siberia; there are also 42,000 Buryats in Mongolia and about 7,000 in Inner Mongolia. Another group are the Oirat Mongols, which include the population of the Kalmyk Republic. See more in Ivan Sablin, *Governing Post-Imperial Siberia and Mongolia, 1911-1924: Buddhism, Socialism and Nationalism in State and Autonomy Building* (London and New York: Routledge, 2016).
11. For more on this, see Owen Lattimore, *The Mongols of Manchuria: Their Tribal Divisions, Geographical Distribution, Historical Relations with Manchus and Chinese, and Present Political Problems* (New York: John Day, 1934).
12. Christopher P. Atwood, 'State Service, Lineage and Locality in Hulun Buir', *East Asian History*, no. 30 (Dec. 2005), pp. 5-22; and more recently, Sören

Urbansky, 'Tokhtogo's Mission Impossible: Russia, China, and the Quasi-independence of Hulunbeir', *Inner Asia*, vol. 16, no. 1 (2014), pp. 64–94.
13 The title (Dalai meaning Ocean in Mongolian) was created when Sonam Gyatso was recognized as the third Dalai Lama by the Mongol ruler Altan Khan in 1578. It was the fifth Dalai Lama (1617–82) who became king of Tibet and built the Potala palace. The thirteenth Dalai Lama (1876–1933) first escaped Lhasa to Mongolia during the British invasion in 1903. Returning in 1909, he soon fled to British India, because of Chinese military threat. After the fall of the Qing in 1911, however, 'central Tibet established a de facto independent regime which would last until 1950'. Esherick, 'How the Qing Became China', p. 242.
14 See Willard Sunderland, *The Baron's Cloak: A History of the Russian Empire in War and Revolution* (Ithaca NY and London: Cornell University Press, 2014).
15 Atwood, 'State Service, Lineage and Locality in Hulun Buir', pp. 16–17.
16 Uradyn E. Bulag, 'Inner Mongolia: The Dialectics of Colonization and Ethnicity Building', in Moris Rossabi, ed., *Governing China's Multiethnic Frontiers* (Seattle and London: University of Washington Press, 2004), pp. 90–3.
17 Bao, 'Trade Centres (*Maimaicheng*) in Mongolia', p. 217.
18 On Manzhouli and Zabaikal'sk, see Sören Urbansky, 'A Very Orderly Friendship: The Sino-Soviet Border under the Alliance Regime, 1950–1960', *Eurasia Border Review*, vol. 3 (2012), pp. 35–52.
19 According to James Boyd, 'In Pursuit of an Obsession: Japan in Inner Mongolia in the 1930s', *Japanese Studies*, vol. 22, no. 3 (2002), pp. 289–303, this incursion ended peace negotiations between China and Japan and prompted Zhang Xueliang to kidnap Chiang Kai-shek in Xi'an in Dec. 1936.
20 See Yoshihisa Tak Matsusaka, 'Imagining Manmō: Mapping the Russo-Japanese Boundary Agreements in Manchuria and Inner Mongolia, 1907–1915', *Cross-Currents: East Asian History and Culture Review*, no. 2 (March 2012), pp. 1–30.
21 Lu Minghui, 'The Inner Mongolian "United Autonomous Government"', in MacKinnon et al., *China at War*, at pp. 162–3 (also on Prince De's alleged ambition of 'becoming emperor of [a united] Mongolia').
22 Amnon Sella, 'Khalkhin-Gol: The Forgotten War', *Journal of Contemporary History*, vol. 18, no. 4 (Oct. 1983), pp. 651–87, and more in Stuart D. Goldman, *Nomonhan, 1939: The Red Army's Victory That Shaped World War II* (Annapolis: Naval Institute Press, 2013).
23 The chapters by Bulag, 'Inner Mongolia', and 'Alter/native Mongolian Identity', in Perry and Selden, eds, *Chinese Society*, voice Mongolian resentment against Chinese rule in a way not normally expected in an academic volume in English.
24 Owen Lattimore, *Manchuria: Cradle of Conflict*, rev. edn (New York: Macmillan, 1935). This edition was reprinted with a new introduction by the author in 1975 (New York: AMS Press).

25 *Idem, The Mongols of Manchuria.*
26 Spengler was author of *The Decline of the West* (1918–22), a hugely influential work at its time, which argued that all civilizations were subject to a cycle of growth and degeneration.
27 Owen Lattimore, *Inner Asian Frontiers of China* (New York: American Geographical Society, 1940). Arif Dirlik, 'Timespace, Social Space, and the Question of Chinese Culture', *boundary 2*, vol. 35, no. 1 (Spring 2008), pp. 10, 13, places Lattimore's work next to such pioneering studies as Wolfram Eberhard, *Conquerors and Rulers: Social Forces in Medieval China* (Leiden: Brill, 1952; 2nd rev. edn, 1965) and Edward H. Schafer, *The Golden Peaches of Samarkand: A Study of T'ang Exotics* (Berkeley: University of California Press, 1963). He sees this school being continued today by Victor H. Mair and other scholars of Chinese–Indian contact. See also William T. Rowe, 'Owen Lattimore, Asia, and Comparative History', *Journal of Asian Studies*, vol. 66, no. 3 (Aug. 2007), pp. 759–86.

20

Jehol / Rehe / Chengde: The Perspective of 'New Qing History'

The District of Rehe 熱河 was created as one of the three 'special administrative regions' of Inner Mongolia (next to Suiyuan and Chahar) in 1914, as Yuan Shikai's regime in Peking became bent on efficiently colonizing Inner Mongolia following the secession of Outer Mongolia. After Zhang Xueliang allied himself with the National government in late 1928, he created the 'Four North-eastern provinces', adding Rehe to Heilongjiang, Jilin and Fengtian. From 1929 to 1955 Rehe was a province with a capital originally established in Chengde, which the KMT moved to Hailar in 1945; the gateway to the province was Shanhaiguan. After dissolution, the territory of Rehe province was incorporated into Hebei, Liaoning and Inner Mongolia. Another administrative unit of Manchuria under Japanese rule, the large Xing'an (Hsingan) province, with its capital in Hailar, was created in 1932 and dissolved in 1949 to become part of Inner Mongolia.

The Japanese occupation of Rehe in January 1933 caused fears for the imminent invasion of Peking, which were to come true in 1937. After military clashes with the Japanese forces and their Chinese collaborators over Rehe in February–March 1933, Chiang Kai-shek blamed Zhang Xueliang for the loss of the city.[1] In May, Chiang acknowledged the addition of Rehe to Japanese-controlled Manchukuo as he signed the Tanggu Truce, which defined the territory between the Great Wall and Peking as a demilitarized zone. The struggle over Manchuria between China and Japan was not without colourful protagonists, such as the spy, adventurer and celebrity Kawashima Yoshiko. Born around 1906 as a Manchu princess of the Qing ruling house under the name Aisin Gioro Xianyu, she was given up for adoption by her father to a prominent political figure in Japan. As an adult she reached Manchuria and became part of the entourage of Emperor Puyi. She then volunteered for the Manchukuo military and secret services.[2] When in October 1947 she was brought before the KMT court, she tried in vain to present herself as Japanese, and she also claimed that, as a bannerwoman and a Manchu, she could not be considered a 'traitor to the Han' (*Hanjian* 漢奸). Because the Manchus were retrospectively counted as 'Chinese' (*Zhongguo ren* 中國人), the court referred to her throughout by her Chinese name and executed her for treason in the following March.[3]

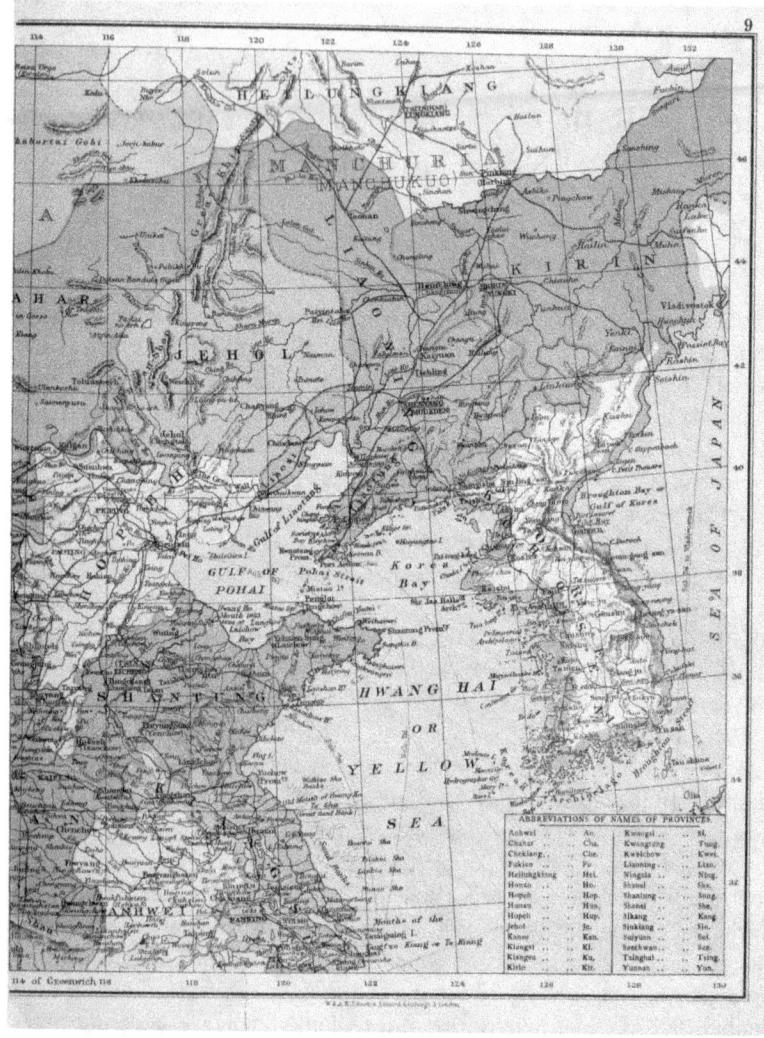

Figure 20 Northeast China, including Jehol (Rehe) province. Atlas for China, ed. G. S. Foster Kemp (London: Macmillan & Co., 1934).

Chengde and 'New Qing History'

The beginnings of the approach that became known as 'New Qing History' date to the 1990s, when North American scholars started studying Manchu, a development which corresponded with the opening of previously inaccessible Qing archives in China (German and Russian scholars of Qing history and literature had of course already been learning and using Manchu in the nineteenth century). The resulting monographs all underlined ethnic diversity and synergy within the Qing Empire, and the reaching out of the Manchu dynasty to encompass neighbouring peoples within their realm. By discovering the complexities of Manchu identity as rulers of China, historians have contested the previously widely held assumption of Manchu 'sinicization' and its underlying narrative of Han Chinese universalism: the claim that China's superior culture had transformed all alien intruders into Chinese.[4]

Chengde has been used as the best illustration for the Qing's newly found complexity and sophistication, as well as its continued adherence to non-Chinese cultural practices. The summer capital of the Qing in what is now northern Hebei, Chengde has traditionally been considered part of Manchuria. The town lies in a valley, about 180 km north-east of Beijing. It is famous for its eighteenth-century summer palace and temple complex, built by the Manchu emperors, which has been on the UNESCO World Heritage list since 1995. The second Qing emperor Kangxi began construction of the Rehe travelling palace on the site of a hunting camp in 1703; his grandson Qianlong completed the project in 1792 and is still the emperor most identified with it. Besides the political functions to be discussed below, Qing rulers used Chengde as a retreat from the summer heat and the perceived danger of smallpox in Beijing.

Research on Chengde by Stephen H. Whiteman has shown that the functions as well as the physical features of the complex differed under the two great emperors. The Buddhist elements acquired far greater prominence under Qianlong, who also appropriated his grandfather's heritage with the aim of boosting his own legitimacy.[5] From Kangxi onwards, with the exception of the intervening Yongzheng period (1723–35), the Qing court had spent every late summer and autumn in Chengde until 1820.

At Chengde there were artificial lakes and islands, as well as replicas of seventy-two scenic spots from all around China. The idea of copying and 'archiving' famous sites by the emperor's authority is comparable with the Yuanming Yuan 圓明園 (Old Summer Palace) in Beijing, another great architectural project begun by Kangxi, which was expanded and designed by Qianlong in the mid-eighteenth century.[6] So the replicas of Suzhou gardens, which were placed at Yuanming Yuan, were also reproduced at Chengde, the

Figure 20a Panoramic view of the Rehe Imperial Palace, late nineteenth century. Library of Congress.

largest of the Qing park-palaces at nearly 1,400 acres.[7] In 1712 Kangxi published his *Imperial Poems on the Mountain Estate for Escaping the Heat* in celebration of his newly built summer palace. Around the same time, the Italian missionary painter Matteo Ripa (1682–1746) made a series of copperplate engravings, commissioned by the emperor: the 'Views of Jehol' (which was the name for Rehe in Jesuit usage). The arrival of these engravings in Europe has been connected in recent research with the emergence of intense English interest in Chinese landscape gardening.[8] Even the great romantic poet William Wordsworth (1770–1850), in his most celebrated autobiographical poem, dedicated to Coleridge, wrote about 'that famed paradise of ten thousand trees, / Or Gehol's matchless gardens'. Wordsworth would have read a description of Jehol in *Travels in China* (1804) by Sir John Barrow (1764–1848).[9]

The eight outer temples beyond the wall of the imperial residence reflected Qing patronage of Tibetan Buddhism (or Lamaism) and included a reproduction of the Dalai Lama's Potala palace in Lhasa. Qianlong presented himself to the Tibetans as the reincarnation of Manjusri, the Bodhisattva of Wisdom. The Mongols, too, were susceptible to such religious imagery as believers in Tibetan Buddhism. High Lamas and Mongol dignitaries, accompanied by Qing officials, were received at Chengde; the 'Ten Thousand Trees Park' (*wanshu yuan* 萬樹園), alluded to by Wordsworth and a tourist attraction in Chengde today, featured a round Mongol tent.

Qianlong's eightieth-birthday celebrations in 1790 drew to Chengde delegates from Vietnam, Korea, the Ryukyu Islands, Burma, Mongolia and other peoples, for whom this was also a special opportunity to meet and communicate. The reception at Chengde was then followed by a second at Yuanming Yuan and a third at the court in Peking.[10] Qianlong celebrated his birthdays here every September and in 1793 he granted an audience in Chengde to Lord Macartney, the envoy of King George III, who had travelled there after first arriving in China's capital. In his deft manipulation of religious symbolism the Qianlong emperor can be seen as following the Russian tsars (Peter the Great became Supreme Head of the Russian Orthodox Church by creating the Holy Synod in 1721) and being followed by such European monarchs as Queen Victoria (ruled 1838–1901), who among her other titles acted as Supreme Head of the Anglican Church and Empress of India.[11]

The Chengde palace complex accordingly represented a different approach on the part of the Qing to its foreign relations from the more familiar expressions of the tribute system in Peking, although the two systems were not antithetical and could be combined. The question emerging from such evidence is to what extent the Manchu emperors really believed in the religious symbolism they performed, or played out, in front of Mongols and Tibetans. Did they pretend, or did Manchu identity have room for Lamaism as well as for Confucianism? The historian of Mongolia Johan Elverskog takes up this enquiry from the Mongol side: were Mongols convinced enough by the Manchu performance so as to identify with 'Our Great Qing'?[12] But these are probably the wrong questions to ask considering that the religious ceremony was part and parcel of a political arrangement, which suited all sides.

The summer palace was little used after Emperor Jiaqing died there in 1820; the last emperor to stay at Chengde was Xianfeng 咸豐 (ruled 1850–61), who took refuge there after the Arrow War in 1860 and died at Chengde in the following year. Visitors can still see the writing desk on which, shortly before his death, he signed the Treaty of Peking ceding vast territory to Russia. Xianfeng's concubine Cixi is said to have plotted her rise to power in Chengde.[13] But emperors also died in the Forbidden City and we can speculate that the more important reason for the end of imperial visits to Chengde was a weakening of the Lamaist symbolism by the latter half of the nineteenth century. The entire Chengde complex had fallen into disrepair by the 1930s.[14]

Restoration of the Chengde palaces since the 1980s has made use of the Tibetan theme to justify PRC rule over Tibet, emphasizing the union of the Han Chinese (perceived as natural successors of the Qing Empire) and Tibetan peoples. More recently Chengde has been successfully transformed into an ethnic theme park, although next to the tourists who pay to sit on the emperor's throne one also sees Buddhist pilgrims for whom the site retains its religious meaning.

North of Chengde, the mountainous imperial resort of Mulan 木蘭 was formerly covered with forests. The Mulan hunting preserve was established in 1683, before the creation of the imperial residence. Until 1820 the emperors staying at Chengde passed about forty days there in deer hunting every summer, accompanied by a retinue of up to 30,000 men. Kangxi himself is said to have shot 135 tigers, twenty bears, twenty-five leopards, ninety-six wolves and hundreds of deer and hares with his bow and arrow.[15] Qianlong and his son the Jiaqing emperor similarly enjoyed their sport at Mulan. Hunting was a symbol of the emperor's military prowess and loyalty to his ancestors. For members of the banners it was training in the eroding martial arts of the Manchu tradition. At the end of a hunt, Mongol notables were hosted at banquets, further strengthening the court's special relationship with them.[16] Even at Mulan, the travelling government was not on holiday, but in 'a summer capital', and officials went on working in tents, writing edicts while placing paper on top of wooden crates or on the ground. Kangxi signed there the Treaty of Nerchinsk after the conclusion of negotiations with Russia in 1689.

Today the Mulan hunting grounds are part of the Saihanba 賽罕坝 National Park, created in 1962 to counteract severe deforestation in this area; since the 1990s, this park has been part of a large project of environmental renovation. It is administered by the Weichang 圍場 Manchu and Mongol Autonomous County (itself a reminder of the historical contacts between Manchu and Mongols, which have been highlighted in this section) in northern Hebei province.

While the interpretations of New Qing History have engendered controversy,[17] this approach has certainly contributed to the revival of interest in the home region of the Manchu dynasty. On this note, it is fitting to end this introduction to Manchuria, which has presented the fascinating and turbulent history of the vast and largely unknown region while pointing out its cross-national and multi-ethnic connections from the rise of the Qing to our time.

Notes

1 On the Rehe campaign, see Richard T. Phillips, '"A Picturesque but Hopeless Resistance": Rehe in 1933', *Modern Asian Studies*, vol. 42, no. 4 (July 2008), pp. 733–50.
2 On Kawashima Naniwa and Prince Su, Yoshiko's father, see the chapter in Paula S. Harrell, *Asia for the Asians: China in the Lives of Five Meiji Japanese* (Portland: Merwin Asia Press, 2012).
3 Shao Dan, 'Princess, Traitor, Solder, Spy: Aisin Gioro Xianyu and the Dilemma of Manchu Identity', in Tamanoi, ed., *Crossed Histories*, pp. 82–119.

See now Phyllis Birnbaum, *Manchu Princess, Japanese Spy: The Story of Kawashima Yoshiko, the Cross-Dressing Spy Who Commanded Her Own Army* (New York: Columbia University Press, 2015). A chapter on her in Louise Edwards, *Women Warriors and Wartime Spies of China* (Cambridge: Cambridge University Press, 2016), mentions sensationalist but fictional rumours in the PRC that Xiangyu was not executed, but lived on to a ripe old age in Northeast China.

4   The most influential monographs have been Pamela Kyle Crossley, *Orphan Warriors: Three Manchu Generations and the End of the Qing World* (Princeton: Princeton University Press, 1990) and eadem, *A Translucent Mirror: History and Identity in Qing Imperial Ideology* (Berkeley: University of California Press, 1999); Evelyn S. Rawski, *The Last Emperors: A Social History of Qing Imperial Institutions* (Berkeley: University of California Press, 1998); Mark Elliott, *The Manchu Way: The Eight Banners and Ethnic Identity in Late Imperial China* (Stanford: Stanford University Press, 2001), and Rhoads, *Manchus & Han* (which, however, did not use Manchu-language sources).

5   Stephen H. Whiteman, 'From Upper Camp to Mountain Estate: Recovering Historical Narratives in Qing Imperial Landscapes', *Studies in the History of Gardens & Designed Landscapes*, vol. 33, no. 4 (2013), pp. 249–79.

6   See Cary Y. Liu, 'Archive of Power: The Qing Dynasty Imperial Garden-Palace at Rehe', *Guoli Taiwan daxue meishushi yanjiu jikan*, vol. 28 (2010), pp. 43–82.

7   Whiteman, 'From Upper Camp to Mountain Estate', p. 254.

8   Yue Zhuang, 'Hatchings in the Void: Ritual and Order in *Bishu Shanzhuang Shi* and Matteo Ripa's *Views of Jehol*', in Petra ten-Doesschate Chu and Ning Ding, eds, *Qing Encounters: Artistic Exchanges between China and the West* (Los Angeles: Getty Research Institute, 2015), pp. 142–57.

9   William Wordsworth, *The Prelude, 1799, 1805, 1850: Authoritative Texts, Context and Reception, Recent Critical Essays*, eds Jonathan Wordsworth et al. (New York and London: W. W. Norton, 1979), pp. 274–5.

10 Zhaoguang Ge, 'Costume, Ceremonial and the East Asian Order: What the Annamese King Wore when Congratulating the Emperor Qianlong in Jehol in 1790', *Frontiers of History in China*, vol. 7, no. 1 (March 2012), pp. 136–51.

11 Cf. C. A. Bayly, *The Birth of the Modern World, 1780–1914: Global Connections and Comparisons* (Oxford: Blackwell, 2004), p. 429, and the comparative commentary on imperial integration in Osterhammel, *The Transformation of the World*, p. 426.

12 Johan Elverskog, *Our Great Qing: The Mongols, Buddhism and the State in Late Imperial China* (Honolulu: University of Hawaii Press, 2006), pp. 4–6.

13 The short-lived Tongzhi 同治 emperor (1856–74) succeeded his father Xianfeng, to reign from 1861 to his death. In practice, until 1873 China was ruled by eight regents and two empresses dowager (Tongzhi's mother Cixi and Xianfeng's principal widow, the childless Ci'an 慈安, who died in 1881). Tongzhi then ruled for about a year before dying without male issue. The

next emperor Guangxu 光緒, Tongzhi's 3-year-old cousin, was the son of Cixi's favourite sister.
14 Geremie Barmé, 'Hedda Morrison's Jehol: A Photographic Survey', *East Asian History*, no. 22 (Dec. 2001), pp. 1–128. See also the description of Jehol in Fleming, *One's Company*, part 1, chs. 13–15.
15 Mark Elliott and Ning Chia, 'The Qing Hunt at Mulan', in James A. Millward et al., eds, *New Qing Imperial History: The Making of Inner Asian Empire at Qing Chengde* (London: Routledge, 2004), p. 72.
16 See more in Chia Ning, 'The Lifanyuan and the Inner Asian Rituals in the Early Qing (1644–1795)', *Late Imperial China*, vol. 14, no. 1 (June 1993), pp. 60–92.
17 See, for example, Guo Wu, 'New Qing History: Dispute, Dialog, and Influence', *The Chinese Historical Review*, vol. 23, no. 1 (2016), pp. 47–69.

Select Bibliography

Afinogenov, Gregory, *The Eye of the Tsar: Intelligence-Gathering and Geopolitics in Eighteenth-Century Eurasia*. PhD dissertation at Harvard University, 2015.
Altman, Avraham, 'Controlling the Jews, Manchukuo Style', in Roman Malek, ed., *From Kaifeng ... to Shanghai: Jews in China*. Sankt Augustin: Monumenta Serica Monograph Series, vol. 46, 2000, pp. 279–317.
Arsenyev, Vladimir K., trans. Malcolm Burr, *Dersu the Trapper*. Kingston NY: McPherson, 1996.
Arsenyev, Vladimir K., trans. Jonathan C. Slaght, *Across the Ussuri Kray: Travels in the Sikhote-Alin Mountains*. Bloomington: University of Indiana Press, 2016.
Artemyev, A. R., 'The Gantimurov Princes in Russian Service', *Journal de la Société Finno-Ougrienne*, vol. 84 (1992), pp. 7–20.
Atwood, Christopher P., 'State Service, Lineage and Locality in Hulun Buir', *East Asian History*, no. 30 (Dec. 2005), pp. 5–22.
Avery, Martha, *The Tea Road: China and Russia Meet across the Steppe*. Beijing: China Intercontinental Press, 2003.
Bakich, Olga, 'Émigré Identity: The Case of Harbin', *The South Atlantic Quarterly*, vol. 99, no. 1 (Winter 2000), pp. 51–73.
Bakich, Olga, 'Did You Speak Harbin Sino-Russian?', *Itinerario*, vol. 35, no. 3 (Dec. 2011), pp. 23–36.
Bakich, Olga, 'Russian Émigrés in Harbin's Multinational Past: Censuses and Identity', in Dan Ben-Canaan et al., eds, *Entangled Histories: The Transcultural Past of Northeast China*. Heidelberg: Springer, 2014, pp. 83–99.
Bakich, Olga, *Valerii Pereleshin: Life of a Silkworm*. Toronto: University of Toronto Press, 2015.
Banister, Judith, 'An Analysis of Recent Data on the Population of China', *Population and Development Review*, vol. 10, no. 2 (June 1984), pp. 214–71.
Bao, Muping, trans. Gaynor Sekimori, 'Trade Centres (*Maimaicheng*) in Mongolia, and their Function in Sino-Russian Trade Networks', *International Journal of Asian Studies*, vol. 3, no. 2 (2006), pp. 211–37.
Baptista, Eduardo, 'Caught between Two Countries: Northeastern China's Ethnic Korean Minority', *Los Angeles Review of Books*, 9 Oct. 2018.
Barmé, Geremie, 'Hedda Morrison's Jehol: A Photographic Survey', *East Asian History*, no. 22 (Dec. 2001), pp. 1–128.
Barrett, David P., and Larry N. Shyu, eds, *Chinese Collaboration with Japan, 1932–1945: The Limits of Accommodation*. Stanford: Stanford University Press, 2001.
Barshay, Andrew E., *The Gods Left First: The Captivity and Repatriation of Japanese POWs in Northeast Asia, 1945–1956*. Berkeley: University of California Press, 2013.

Bassin, Mark, *Imperial Visions: Nationalist Imagination and Geographical Expansion in the Russian Far East, 1840–1865*. Cambridge: Cambridge University Press, 1999.
Bayly, C. A., *The Birth of the Modern World, 1780–1914: Global Connections and Comparisons*. Oxford: Blackwell, 2004.
Becker, Jasper, *Dragon Rising: An Inside Look at China Today*. Washington DC: National Geographic, 2006.
Becker, Jasper, *City of Heavenly Tranquility: Beijing in the History of China*. London: Allen Lane, 2008.
Berton, Peter, *Russo-Japanese Relations, 1905–17: From Enemies to Allies*. Abingdon and New York: Routledge, 2011.
Bickers, Robert, *The Scramble for China: Strangers in the Middle Kingdom, 1832–1914*. London: Allen Lane, 2011.
Biran, Michal, 'The Incarnations of Genghis Khan: Between Myth and Reality' (in Hebrew), *Zmanim*, no. 100 (Autumn 2007), pp. 56–71.
Biran, Michal, 'The Mongols and Nomadic Identity: The Case of the Kitans in China', in Reuven Amitai and Michal Biran, eds, *Nomads as Agents of Cultural Change: The Mongols and their Eurasian Predecessors*. Honolulu: University of Hawaii Press, 2015, pp. 152–81.
Birnbaum, Phyllis, *Manchu Princess, Japanese Spy: The Story of Kawashima Yoshiko, the Cross-Dressing Spy Who Commanded Her Own Army*. New York: Columbia University Press, 2015.
Boland-Crewe, Tara, and David Lea, *The Territories of the People's Republic of China*. London: Europa Publications, 2002.
Borm, Jan, 'The French of the Tundra: Early Modern European Views of the Tungus in Translation', *Études mongoles et sibériennes, centrasiatiques et tibétaines*, vol. 49 (2018), pp. 1–14.
Boyd, James, 'In Pursuit of an Obsession: Japan in Inner Mongolia in the 1930s', *Japanese Studies*, vol. 22, no. 3 (2002), pp. 289–303.
Brady, Anne-Marie, *Making the Foreign Serve China: Managing Foreigners in the People's Republic*. Lanham: Rowman & Littlefield, 2003.
Brooks, Tony, 'Angry States: Chinese Views of Japan as Seen through the Unit 731 War Museum 1949–2013', in Mark R. Frost et al., eds, *Remembering Asia's World War Two*. London: Routledge, 2019, pp. 27–55.
Buck, David D., 'Railway City and National Capital: Two Faces of the Modern in Changchun', in Joseph W. Esherick, ed., *Remaking the Chinese City: Modernity and National Identity, 1900–1950*. Honolulu: University of Hawaii Press, 2000, pp. 65–89.
Builders of Anshan. Peking: Foreign Languages Press, 1956.
Bulag, Uradyn E., 'Inner Mongolia: The Dialectics of Colonization and Ethnicity Building', in Moris Rossabi, ed., *Governing China's Multiethnic Frontiers* (Seattle and London: University of Washington Press, 2004), pp. 84–116.
Bulag, Uradyn E., 'Rethinking Borders in Empire and Nation at the Foot of the Willow Palisade', in Franck Billé et al., eds, *Frontier Encounters: Knowledge*

and Practice at the Russian, Chinese and Mongolian Border. Cambridge: Open Book Publishers, 2012, pp. 33–53.

Bulag, Uradyn E., 'Inner Mongolia', and 'Alter/native Mongolian Identity: From Nationality to Ethnic Group', in Elizabeth J. Perry and Mark Selden, eds, *Chinese Society: Change, Conflict and Resistance*, 3rd ed. London and New York: Routledge, 2013, pp. 261–87.

Cannon, John, 'Diary' (on the PRC–North Korea border), *London Review of Books*, vol. 22, no. 15 (10 Aug. 2000).

Cathcart, Adam, 'Resurrecting Defeat: International Propaganda and the Shenyang Trials of 1956', in Kerstin von Lingen, ed., *War Crimes Trials in the Wake of Decolonization and Cold War in Asia, 1945–1956: Justice in Time of Turmoil*. New York: Palgrave Macmillan, 2016, pp. 261–78.

Chan, Yeeshan, *Abandoned Japanese in Postwar Manchuria: The Lives of War Orphans and Wives in Two Countries*. London: Routledge, 2011.

Chang, Che-Chia, trans. Penelope Barrett, 'Origins of a Misunderstanding: The Qianlong Emperor's Embargo on Rhubarb Exports to Russia, the Scenario and Its Consequences', *Asian Medicine*, vol. 1, no. 2 (2005), pp. 335–54.

Chekhov, Anton, trans. Brian Reeve, *Sakhalin Island*. Richmond: Alma Classics, 2013.

Chen Kaike 陳開科, *Jiaqing shi nian: Shibai de Eguo shituan yu shibai de Zhongguo waijiao* 嘉慶十年：失敗的俄國使團與失敗的中國外交 (The 10th Year of Jiaqing: The Failed Russian Embassy and the Failure of Chinese Foreign Relations). Beijing: Shehui kexue wenxian chubanshe, 2014.

Chen, Ping, 'China', in Andrew Simpson, ed., *Language and National Identity in Asia*. Oxford: Oxford University Press, 2007, pp. 140–67.

Chen, Xiangming, 'Beyond the Reach of Globalization: China's Border Regions and Cities in Transition', in Fulong Wu, ed., *Globalization and the Chinese City*. London and New York: Routledge, 2006, pp. 21–46.

Chi Zijian, trans. Simon Patton, *Figments of the Supernatural*. Sydney: James Joyce Press, 2004.

Chi Zijian, trans. Bruce Humes, *The Last Quarter of the Moon*. London: Harvill Secker, 2013.

Chi Zijian, trans. Poppy Toland, *Goodnight, Rose*. Penguin Books China, 2019.

Cho, Mun Young, *The Specter of 'The People': Urban Poverty in Northeast China*. Ithaca NY and London: Cornell University Press, 2013.

Christie, Dugald, *Thirty Years in Moukden, 1883–1913*. London: Constable, 1914.

Chung, Jae Ho, et al., 'Assessing the "Revive the Northeast" (*zhenxing dongbei*) Programme: Origins, Policies and Implementation', *China Quarterly*, no. 197 (March 2009), pp. 108–25.

Coogan, Anthony, 'Northeast China and the Origins of the Anti-Japanese United Front', *Modern China*, vol. 20, no. 3 (July 1994), pp. 282–314.

Corradini, Piero, 'The Manchu Capital Cities before the Conquest of China', *Ming Qing yanjiu*, vol. 13 (2005), pp. 67–91.

Crossley, Pamela Kyle, *Orphan Warriors: Three Manchu Generations and the End of the Qing World*. Princeton: Princeton University Press, 1990.

Crossley, Pamela Kyle, 'Manchu Education', in Benjamin A. Elman and Alexander Woodside, eds, *Education and Society in Late Imperial China*. Berkeley: University of California Press, 1994, pp. 340–78.

Crossley, Pamela Kyle, *A Translucent Mirror: History and Identity in Qing Imperial Ideology*. Berkeley: University of California Press, 1999.

Day, Jenny Huangfu, *Qing Travelers to the Far West: Diplomacy and the Information Order in Late Imperial China*. Cambridge: Cambridge University Press, 2018.

Denison, Edward, and Guangyu Ren, *Ultra-Modernism: Architecture and Modernity in Manchuria*. Hong Kong: Hong Kong University Press, 2017.

Di Cosmo, Nicola, 'Nurhaci's Gambit: Sovereignty as Concept and Praxis in the Rise of the Manchus', in Zvi Ben-Dor Benite et al., eds, *The Scaffolding of Sovereignty: Global and Aesthetic Perspectives on the History of a Concept*. New York: Columbia University Press, 2017, pp. 102–23.

Dikötter, Frank, *The Age of Openness: China Before Mao*. Berkeley: University of California Press, 2008.

Dirlik, Arif, 'Timespace, Social Space, and the Question of Chinese Culture', *boundary 2*, vol. 35, no. 1 (Spring 2008), pp. 1–22.

Di Toro, Anna, *La percezione della Russia in Cina tra XVII e XVIII sec.* (The Perception of Russia in China between the 17th and 18th Centuries). Rome: La Sapienza Orientale, 2012.

Du, Yongtao, and Jeff Kyong-McClain, eds, *Chinese History in Geographical Perspective*. Lanham: Lexington Books, 2013.

Duanmu Hongliang, *The Sorrows of Egret Lake: Selected Stories* (Chinese-English Bilingual Edition). Hong Kong: The Chinese University Press, 2009.

DuBois, Thomas David, 'Manchukuo's Filial Sons: States, Sects and the Adaptation of Graveside Piety', *East Asian History*, vol. 36 (Dec. 2008), pp. 3–27.

DuBois, Thomas David, 'Inauthentic Sovereignty: Law and Legal Institutions in Manchukuo', *Journal of Asian Studies*, vol. 69, no. 3 (Aug. 2010), pp. 749–70.

Dumont, Aurore, 'Declining Evenki "Identities": Playing with Loyalty in Modern and Contemporary China', *History and Anthropology*, vol. 28, no. 4 (2017), pp. 515–30.

Dutton, Michael, and Li Shaorong, 'Seizing the City: Policing in the Era of the City Takeover (1945–1949)', *Berliner China-Hefte*, no. 22 (May 2002), pp. 48–67.

Duus, Peter, et al., eds, *The Japanese Wartime Empire, 1931–1945*. Princeton: Princeton University Press, 1996.

Eckert, Carter J., *Park Chung Hee and Modern Korea*, in 2 vols. Cambridge MA: Belknap Press; vol. 1, 2016.

Edgerton-Tarpley, Kathryn, *Tears from Iron: Cultural Responses to Famine in Nineteenth-Century China*. Berkeley: University of California Press, 2008.

Edmonds, Richard L., *Northern Frontiers of Qing China and Tokugawa Japan: A Comparative Study of Frontier Policy*. University of Chicago, Department of Geography; Research Paper No. 213 (1985).

Edwards, Louise, *Women Warriors and Wartime Spies of China*. Cambridge: Cambridge University Press, 2016.
Efird, Robert, 'Japan's "War Orphans": Identification and State Responsibility', *Journal of Japanese Studies*, vol. 34, no. 2 (Summer 2008), pp. 363–88.
Elliott, Mark, 'The Limits of Tartary: Manchuria in Imperial and National Geographies', *Journal of Asian Studies*, vol. 59, no. 3 (Aug. 2000), pp. 603–46.
Elliott, Mark, *The Manchu Way: The Eight Banners and Ethnic Identity in Late Imperial China*. Stanford: Stanford University Press, 2001.
Elliott, Mark, 'Ethnicity in the Qing Eight Banners', in Pamela Kyle Crossley et al., eds, *Empire at the Margins: Culture, Ethnicity, and Frontier in Early Modern China*. Berkeley: University of California Press, 2006, pp. 27–57.
Elliott, Mark, and Ning Chia, 'The Qing Hunt at Mulan', in James A. Millward et al., eds, *New Qing Imperial History: The Making of Inner Asian Empire at Qing Chengde*. London: Routledge, 2004, pp. 66–83.
Elman, Benjamin A., 'Optical and Cognitive Illusions: The MIT Visualizing Cultures Controversy in Spring 2006', *Positions: East Asia Cultures Critique*, vol. 23, no. 1 (Feb. 2015), pp. 15–39.
Elverskog, Johan, *Our Great Qing: The Mongols, Buddhism and the State in Late Imperial China*. Honolulu: University of Hawaii Press, 2006.
Endo, Homare, trans. Michael Brase, *Japanese Girl at the Siege of Changchun: How I Survived China's Wartime Atrocity*. Berkeley: Stone Bridge Press, 2016.
Esherick, Joseph W., 'How the Qing Became China', in Esherick et al., eds, *Empire to Nation: Historical Perspectives on the Making of the Modern World*. Lanham: Rowman & Littlefield, 2006, pp. 228–59.
Etkind, Alexander, *Internal Colonization: Russia's Imperial Experience*. Cambridge: Polity, 2011.
Fan Lijun 范立君, *Chuang guandong: lishi yu wenhua yanjiu* 闖關東：歷史與文化研究 (Breakthrough to the East of the Pass: Historical and Cultural Research). Beijing: Shehui kexue wenxian chubanshe, 2016.
Fleming, Peter, *One's Company: A Journey to China in 1933*. Harmondsworth: Penguin Books, 1956 (originally published in 1934).
Flitsch, Mareile, 'The Suobo Staff in Custom and Tale: Ginseng Seekers' Material Culture in Jilin Han Folk Literature', *Techniques & Culture*, no. 29 (Jan.–June 1997), pp. 41–67.
Flitsch, Mareile, 'Papercut Stories of the Manchu Woman Artist Hou Yumei', *Asian Folklore Studies*, vol. 58, no. 2 (1999), pp. 353–75.
Flitsch, Mareile, 'A Ginseng Tale from Jilin', in Victor Mair and Mark Bender, eds, *The Columbia Anthology of Chinese Folk & Popular Literature*. New York: Columbia University Press, 2011, pp. 16–19.
Frank, V. S., 'The Territorial Terms of the Sino–Russian Treaty of Nerchinsk, 1689', *Pacific Historical Review*, vol. 16, no. 3 (Aug. 1947), pp. 265–70.
Gamsa, Mark, 'How a Republic of Chinese Red Beards was Invented in Paris', *Modern Asian Studies*, vol. 36, no. 4 (October 2002), pp. 993–1010.

Gamsa, Mark, 'California on the Amur, or the "Zheltuga Republic" in Manchuria (1883–86)', *Slavonic and East European Review*, vol. 81, no. 2 (April 2003), pp. 236–66.
Gamsa, Mark, 'The Epidemic of Pneumonic Plague in Manchuria 1910–1911', *Past and Present*, no. 190 (Feb. 2006), pp. 147–83.
Gamsa, Mark, 'The Many Faces of Hotel Moderne in Harbin', *East Asian History*, vol. 37 (Dec. 2011), pp. 27–38.
Gamsa, Mark, *Harbin, City between Russia and China: A Cross-cultural Biography*, forthcoming at University of Toronto Press, 2020.
Ge, Zhaoguang, 'Costume, Ceremonial and the East Asian Order: What the Annamese King Wore when Congratulating the Emperor Qianlong in Jehol in 1790', *Frontiers of History in China*, vol. 7, no. 1 (March 2012), pp. 136–51.
Gillin, Donald G. and Charles Etter, 'Staying On: Japanese Soldiers and Civilians in China, 1945–1949', *Journal of Asian Studies*, vol. 42, no. 3 (May 1983), pp. 497–518.
Goldblatt, Howard, *Hsiao Hung*. Boston: Twayne, 1976.
Goldman, Stuart D., *Nomonhan, 1939: The Red Army's Victory That Shaped World War II*. Annapolis: Naval Institute Press, 2013.
Goldstein, Lyle J., 'Return to Zhenbao Island: Who Started Shooting and Why It Matters', *China Quarterly*, no. 168 (Dec. 2001), pp. 985–97.
Golovachev, V. Ts., et al., *Tyrskie stely XV veka. Perevod, kommentarii, issledovanie kitaiskikh, mongol'skogo i chzhurchen'skogo tekstov* (Tyr Steles of the 15th Century: Translation, Commentary and Study of the Chinese, Mongol and Jurchen Texts). St Petersburg: Nauka, 2011.
Gottschang, Thomas R., and Diana Lary, *Swallows and Settlers: The Great Migration from North China to Manchuria*. Ann Arbor: Michigan Monographs in Chinese Studies, 2000.
Guo Junsheng 郭俊胜, ed., *Zhongdonglu yu Zhongdonglu shijian* 中東路與中東事件 (The CER and the CER Incident). Shenyang: Liaoning renmin chubanshe, 2010.
Han, Enze, *Contestation and Adaptation: The Politics of National Identity in China*. Oxford: Oxford University Press, 2013.
Hardacre, Helen, *Shinto: A History*. Oxford: Oxford University Press, 2016.
Harris, Sheldon, *Factories of Death: Japanese Biological Warfare, 1932–45, and the American Cover-up*, revised 2nd ed. New York: Routledge, 2002.
Hauer, Erich, 'Why the Sinologue Should Study Manchu', *Journal of the North China Branch of the Royal Asiatic Society*, vol. 61 (1930), pp. 156–64.
Hess, Christian A., 'Big Brother Is Watching: Local Sino–Soviet Relations and the Building of New Dalian, 1945–1955', in Paul Pickowicz and Jeremy Brown, eds, *Dilemmas of Victory: The Early Years of the People's Republic of China*. Cambridge MA: Harvard University Press, 2007, pp. 160–83.
Hess, Christian A., 'From Colonial Port to Socialist Metropolis: Imperialist Legacies and the Making of New Dalian', *Urban History*, vol. 38, no. 3 (Dec. 2011), pp. 373–90.

Hess, Christian A., 'Gateway to Manchuria: The Port City of Dalian under Japanese, Russian and Chinese Control, 1898-1950', *Comparativ*, vol. 22, no. 5 (2012), pp. 47-59.

Hess, Christian A., 'Sino-Soviet City: Dalian between Socialist Worlds, 1945-1955', *Journal of Urban History*, vol. 44, no. 1 (June 2017), pp. 9-25.

Hicks, George, 'The "Comfort Women"', in Duus et al., eds, *The Japanese Wartime Empire, 1931-1945*, pp. 305-23.

Hinton, Isabel, 'China: At War with Its History', *Prospect Magazine*, no. 187 (21 Sept. 2011).

Hoodie, Matthew, 'Ethnic Identity Change in the People's Republic of China', *Nationalism and Ethnic Politics*, vol. 4, nos. 1-2 (1998), pp. 119-41.

Hosie, Alexander, *Manchuria: Its People, Resources and Recent History*. Boston: J. B. Millet, 1910.

Hostetler, Laura, 'Imperial Competition in Eurasia: Russia and China', in *The Cambridge World History*, chief ed. Merry E. Wiesner-Hanks, in 7 vols. Cambridge: Cambridge University Press, 2014-15, vol. 6, part 1, eds Jerry H. Bentley et al., pp. 297-322.

Howard, Harvey J., *Ten Weeks with Chinese Bandits*. London: John Lane at the Bodley Head, 1927.

Hsieh, Chiao-min, and Jean Kan Hsieh, *China: A Provincial Atlas*. London and New York: Macmillan and Prentice Hall, 1995.

Hsu, Chia Yin, 'A Tale of Two Railroads: "Yellow Labor," Agrarian Colonization, and the Making of Russianness at the Far Eastern Frontier, 1890s-1910', *Ab Imperio*, no. 3 (2006), pp. 217-53.

Hsü, Immanuel C. Y., 'Russia's Special Position in China during the Early Ch'ing Period', *Slavic Review*, vol. 23, no. 4 (Dec. 1964), pp. 688-700.

Hsü, Immanuel C. Y., *The Rise of Modern China*, 6th ed. Oxford: Oxford University Press, 2000.

Hughes, Christopher W., 'Tumen River Area Development Programme: Frustrated Micro-regionalism as a Microcosm of Political Rivalries', working paper of the Centre for the Study of Globalisation and Regionalisation, University of Warwick, Aug. 2000.

Isett, Christopher M., 'Village Regulation of Property and the Social Basis for the Transformation of Qing Manchuria', *Late Imperial China*, vol. 25, no. 1 (June 2004), pp. 124-86.

Itō Takeo, trans. Joshua Fogel, *Life along the South Manchurian Railway*. Armonk: M. E. Sharpe, 1988.

Itoh, Mayumi, *Japanese War Orphans in Manchuria: Forgotten Victims of World War II*. New York: Palgrave Macmillan, 2010.

Ivanov, Andrey V., 'Conflicting Loyalties: Fugitives and "Traitors" in the Russo-Manchurian Frontier, 1651-1689', *Journal of Early Modern History*, vol. 13, no. 5 (2009), pp. 333-58.

Jackson, W. A. Douglas, *Russo-Chinese Borderlands: Zone of Peaceful Contact or Potential Conflict?* Princeton: D. Van Nostrand, 1962.

Jacobs, Andrew, 'Manchu, Former Empire's Language, Hangs On at China's Edge', *New York Times* (11 Jan. 2016).
James, Henry E. M., *The Long White Mountain*. London: Longmans, 1888.
Janhunen, Juha, *Manchuria: An Ethnic History*. Helsinki: The Finno-Ugrian Society, 1996.
Jiang, Yu, 'Land, City, State, Nation, and Empire in Sipinggai, Northeast China, 1900-1945', *Studies on Asia*, vol. 4, no. 1 (Spring 2007), pp. 33-49.
Ju Zhifen, 'Northern Chinese Laborers and Manchukuo', in Paul H. Kratoska, ed., *Asian Labor in the Wartime Japanese Empire: Unknown Histories*. Armonk: M. E. Sharpe, 2005, pp. 61-80.
Kaufman, Abram I., *Lagernyi vrach. 16 let v Sovetskom Soiuze - vospominaniia sionista* (The Camp Doctor: Sixteen Years in the Soviet Union. Memoirs of a Zionist). Tel Aviv: Am oved, 1973.
Kaufman, Theodore (Teddy), *The Jews of Harbin Live on in My Heart*. Tel Aviv: Association of Former Jewish Residents from China in Israel, 2006.
Keevak, Michael, *Embassies to China: Diplomacy and Cultural Encounters Before the Opium Wars*. Singapore: Palgrave Macmillan, 2017.
Kernen, Antoine, and Jean-Louis Rocca, 'Social Responses to Unemployment and the "New Urban Poor": Case Study in Shenyang City and Liaoning Province', *China Perspectives*, no. 27 (Feb. 2000), pp. 35-51.
Kim, Loretta E., *Ethnic Chrysalis: China's Orochen People and the Legacy of Qing Borderland Administration*. Cambridge MA: Harvard University Asia Center, 2019.
Kim, Seonmin, *Ginseng and Borderland: Territorial Boundaries and Political Relations between Qing China and Choson Korea, 1636-1912*. Berkeley: University of California Press, 2017.
King, Amy, *China-Japan Relations after World War Two: Empire, Industry and War, 1949-1971*. Cambridge: Cambridge University Press, 2016.
Kirsten Tatlow, Didi, 'A New Look at Japan's Unit 731 Wartime Atrocities and a U.S. Cover-Up', *The Asia-Pacific Journal*, vol. 13, 44:3 (16 Nov. 2015).
Kobzev, A. I., 'Kitaistika i summa sinologiae', in *Arkhiv rossiiskoi kitaistiki* (Archive of Russian Sinology), vol. 1. Moscow: Nauka - Vostochnaia literatura, 2013, pp. 8-50.
Koga, Yukiko, 'Accounting for Silence: Inheritance, Debt, and the Moral Economy of Legal Redress in China and Japan', *American Ethnologist*, vol. 40, no. 3 (Aug. 2013), pp. 494-507.
Köll, Elisabeth, *Railroads and the Transformation of China*. Cambridge MA: Harvard University Press, 2019.
Kong, Haili, 'The Significance of the Northeastern Writers in Exile, 1931-1945', in Yingjin Zhang, ed., *A Companion to Modern Chinese Literature*. Malden: Wiley-Blackwell, 2016, pp. 312-25.
Kowner, Rotem, *Historical Dictionary of the Russo-Japanese War*, 2nd revised and enlarged ed. Lanham: Rowman & Littlefield, 2017.
Kurtz-Phelan, Daniel, *The China Mission: George Marshall's Unfinished War, 1945-1947*. New York: W. W. Norton, 2018.

Kuznetsov, Sergei I., and Sergei V. Karasov, 'The Last Emperor of China: Internment in the Soviet Union', *Journal of Slavic Military Studies*, vol. 18 (June 2005), pp. 207-26.

Lach, Donald F., and Edwin J. van Kley, *Asia in the Making of Europe*, vol. 3, book 4. Chicago: University of Chicago Press, 1993.

Lague, David, 'China's Manchu Speakers Struggle to Save Language', *New York Times* (16 March 2007).

Lapin, P. A., *Pervaia shkola russkogo iazyka v Kitae* (The First School of Russian in China). Moscow: Vostochnaia literatura RAN, 2009.

Lattimore, Owen, 'Byroads and Backwoods of Manchuria', *National Geographic Magazine*, vol. 61, no. 1 (Jan. 1932), pp. 100-30.

Lattimore, Owen, *The Mongols of Manchuria: Their Tribal Divisions, Geographical Distribution, Historical Relations with Manchus and Chinese, and Present Political Problems*. New York: John Day, 1934.

Lattimore, Owen, *Manchuria: Cradle of Conflict*, revised ed. New York: Macmillan, 1935.

Lattimore, Owen, *Inner Asian Frontiers of China*. New York: American Geographical Society, 1940.

Lavrillier, Alexandra, et al., 'Human–Nature Relationships in the Tungus Societies of Siberia and Northeast China', *Études mongoles et sibériennes, centrasiatiques et tibétaines*, vol. 49 (2018), pp. 1-26.

LeDonne, John P., 'Proconsular Ambitions on the Chinese Border: Governor General Iakobi's Proposal of War on China', *Cahiers du monde russe*, vol. 45, nos. 1-2 (Jan.-June 2004), pp. 31-60.

Lee, Chong-Sik, *Revolutionary Struggle in Manchuria: Chinese Communism and Soviet Interest, 1922-1945*. Berkeley and Los Angeles: University of California Press, 1983.

Legerton, Colin, and Jacob Rawson, *Invisible China: A Journey Through Ethnic Borderlands*. Chicago: Chicago Review Press, 2009.

Levine, Steven I., *Anvil of Victory: The Communist Revolution in Manchuria, 1945-1948*. New York: Columbia University Press, 1987.

Li Zhensheng, *Red-color News Soldier*. London: Phaidon Press, 2003.

Liaozuo sanren 遼左散人 [Liu Jingyan 劉靜嚴], *Binjiang chenxiao lu* 濱江塵囂錄 (A Record of Binjiang Hubbub, 1929). Beijing: Zhongguo qingnian chubanshe, 2012.

Lim, Susanna Soojung, *China and Japan in the Russian Imagination, 1685-1922: To the Ends of the Orient*. London and New York: Routledge, 2013.

Lin, T. C., 'The Amur Frontier Question between China and Russia, 1850-1860', *Pacific Historical Review*, vol. 3, no. 1 (March 1934), pp. 1-27.

Link, Perry, 'Beijing's Dangerous Game', *New York Review of Books* blog, 20 Sept. 2012.

Liu, Alan P. L., 'Provincial Identities and Provincial Cultures: Modernism, Traditionalism, Parochialism, and Separatism', in Shiping Hua, ed., *Chinese Political Culture 1989-2000*. Armonk: M. E. Sharpe, 2001, pp. 246-75.

Liu, Cary Y., 'Archive of Power: The Qing Dynasty Imperial Garden-Palace at Rehe', *Guoli Taiwan daxue meishushi yanjiu jikan*, vol. 28 (2010), pp. 43–82.

Liu Dezeng 劉德增, *Chuang guandong: 2500 wan Shandong yimin de lishi yu chuanshuo* 闖關東: 2500 萬山東移民的歷史與傳說 (Breakthrough to the East of the Pass: The History and Legend of Twenty-Five Million Shandong Immigrants). Jinan: Shandong renmin chubanshe, 2008.

Liu, Yishi, 'Changchun across 1949: Rebuilding a Colonial Capital City under Socialism in the Early 1950s', in Yannan Ding et al., eds, *China: A Historical Geography of the Urban*. New York: Palgrave Macmillan, 2018, pp. 67–88.

Lu Minghui, 'The Inner Mongolian "United Autonomous Government"', in Stephen R. MacKinnon et al., eds, *China at War: Regions of China, 1937–45*. Stanford: Stanford University Press, 2007, pp. 148–71.

Lu Xun, trans. Julia Lovell, *The Real Story of Ah-Q and Other Tales of China: The Complete Fiction of Lu Xun*. London: Penguin Books, 2009.

Lukoianov, Igor V., 'Russian Imperialism in the Far East at the Turn of the Twentieth Century: The Collapse of S. Ju. Vitte's Program of Economic Expansion', in Kimitaka Matsuzato, ed., *Imperiology: From Empirical Knowledge to Discussing the Russian Empire*. Sapporo: Slavic Research Center, Hokkaido University, 2007, pp. 225–44.

Mackerras, Colin, 'What is China? Who is Chinese? Han–Minority Relations, Legitimacy, and the State', in Peter Hays Gries and Stanley Rosen, eds, *State and Society in 21st-Century China: Crisis, Contention, and Legitimation*. New York and London: RoutledgeCurzon, 2004, pp. 216–34.

McCormack, Gavan, *Chang Tso-lin in Northeast China, 1911–1928: China, Japan, and the Manchurian Idea*. Stanford: Stanford University Press, 1977.

McCormack, Gavan, 'Manchukuo: Constructing the Past', *East Asian History*, vol. 2 (Dec. 1991), pp. 105–24.

McDonald, Kate, 'Asymmetrical Integration: Lessons from a Railway Empire', *Technology and Culture*, vol. 56, no. 1 (Jan. 2015), pp. 115–49.

McKeown, Adam, 'Global Migration, 1846–1940', *Journal of World History*, vol. 15, no. 2 (June 2004), pp. 155–89.

McKeown, Adam, 'Chinese Emigration in Global Context, 1850–1940', *Journal of Global History*, vol. 5, no. 1 (March 2010), pp. 95–124.

Mancall, Mark, *Russia and China: Their Diplomatic Relations to 1728*. Cambridge MA: Harvard University Press, 1971.

'Manchuria in Dongbei', photo-essay by Cyrus Chen, *Cross-Currents*, no. 11 (June 2014), https://cross-currents.berkeley.edu/e-journal/issue-11/manchuria-dongbei/photo/manchuria-dongbei

Matsusaka, Y. Tak, 'Managing Occupied Manchuria, 1931–1934', in Duus et al., eds, *The Japanese Wartime Empire, 1931–1945*, pp. 97–135.

Matsusaka, Y. Tak, 'Japan's South Manchuria Railway Company in Northeast China', in Bruce A. Elleman and Stephen Kotkin, eds, *Manchurian Railways and the Opening of China: An International History*. Armonk: M. E. Sharpe, 2010, pp. 37–58.

Matsusaka, Y. Tak, 'Imagining Manmō: Mapping the Russo-Japanese Boundary Agreements in Manchuria and Inner Mongolia, 1907–1915', *Cross-Currents: East Asian History and Culture Review*, no. 2 (March 2012), pp. 1–30.
Maxwell, Neville, 'How the Sino-Russian Boundary Conflict was Finally Settled: From Nerchinsk 1689 to Vladivostok 2005 via Zhenbao Island 1969', *Critical Asian Studies*, vol. 39, no. 2 (2007), pp. 229–53.
Mervart, David, 'The Many Lives of Father Gerbillion's Sino-Russian Treaty: An Attempt at a "Global" Intellectual History', paper presented at the East Asian Seminar, University of Zurich, 26 Sept. 2014.
Meyer, Michael, *In Manchuria: A Village Called Wasteland and the Transformation of Rural China*. London and New York: Bloomsbury Press, 2015.
Millward, James A., 'Qing Inner Asian Empire and the Return of the Torghuts', in Millward et al., eds, *New Qing Imperial History: The Making of Inner Asian Empire at Qing Chengde*. London: Routledge, 2004, pp. 91–105.
Mitter, Rana, *The Manchurian Myth: Nationalism, Resistance, and Collaboration in Modern China*. Berkeley: University of California Press, 2000.
Monahan, Erika, 'Locating Rhubarb: Early Modernity's Relevant Obscurity', in Paula Findlen, ed., *Early Modern Things: Objects and their Histories, 1500–1800*. London and New York: Routledge, 2013, pp. 227–51.
Morris-Suzuki, Tessa, 'The Telescope and the Tinderbox: Rediscovering La Pérouse in the North Pacific', *East Asian History*, no. 39 (Dec. 2014), pp. 33–52.
Mosca, Matthew W., 'The Qing State and Its Awareness of Eurasian Interconnections, 1789–1806', *Eighteenth-Century Studies*, vol. 47, no. 2 (Winter 2014), pp. 103–16.
Moseley, Christopher, ed., *Atlas of the World's Languages in Danger*, 3rd ed. Paris: UNESCO Publishing, 2010.
Müller-Saini, Gotelind, 'Chinesische Perspektiven auf den Russisch-Japanischen Krieg', in Maik Hendrik Sprotte et al., eds, *Der Russisch-Japanische Krieg 1904/05 – Anbruch einer neuen Zeit?* Wiesbaden: Harrassowitz, 2007, pp. 203–39.
Myers, Ramon H., 'Japanese Imperialism in Manchuria: The South Manchuria Railway Company, 1906–1933', in Peter Duus et al., eds, *The Japanese Informal Empire in China, 1895–1937*. Princeton: Princeton University Press, 1989, pp. 101–32.
Nakashima, Takeshi, 'Forming the Russian Fascist Party in Harbin 1925–1933', *The Journal of Social Sciences and Humanities* (Jinbun Gakuko, Tokyo), no. 505 (March 2015), pp. 1–19.
Nappi, Carla, 'Surface Tension: Objectifying Ginseng in Chinese Early Modernity', in Paula Findlen, ed., *Early Modern Things: Objects and their Histories, 1500–1800*. London and New York: Routledge, 2013, pp. 31–52.
Narangoa, Li, 'Nationalism and Globalization on the Inner Mongolia Frontier: The Commercialization of a Tamed Ethnicity', *Japan Focus*, no. 2575 (Nov. 2007).

Nevel'skoi, G. I., *Podvigi russkikh morskikh ofitserov na krainem vostoke Rossii* (Heroic Deeds of Russian Navy Officers in the Extreme East of Russia). Moscow: Drofa, 2008.
Ning, Chia, 'The Lifanyuan and the Inner Asian Rituals in the Early Qing (1644–1795)', *Late Imperial China*, vol. 14, no. 1 (June 1993), pp. 60–92.
Ning, Chia, 'Manchu Language Resources in the People's Republic of China: A Comprehensive Review', *China Review International*, vol. 16, no. 3 (2009), pp. 308–22.
Nish, Ian, *The History of Manchuria, 1840–1948*, in 2 vols. Folkestone: Renaissance Books, 2016.
O'Dwyer, Emer, 'Mantetsu Democracy', *Modern Asian Studies*, vol. 47, no. 6 (Nov. 2013), pp. 1812–44.
O'Dwyer, Emer, 'Heroes and Villains: Manchukuo in Yasuhiko Yoshikazu's *Rainbow Trotsky*', in Roman Rosenbaum, ed., *Manga and the Representation of Japanese History*. London: Routledge, 2013, pp. 121–45.
Orbach, Danny, *Curse on This Country: The Rebellious Army of Imperial Japan*. Ithaca NY and London: Cornell University Press, 2017.
Orbach, Danny, 'The Military-Adventurous Complex: Officers, Adventurers, and Japanese Expansion in East Asia, 1884–1937', *Modern Asian Studies*, vol. 53, no. 2 (March 2019), pp. 339–76.
Osterhammel, Jürgen, trans. Patrick Camiller, *The Transformation of the World: A Global History of the Nineteenth Century*. Princeton: Princeton University Press, 2014.
Osterhammel, Jürgen, trans. Robert Savage, *Unfabling the East: The Enlightenment's Encounter with Asia*. Princeton: Princeton University Press, 2018.
Paine, S. C. M., *Imperial Rivals: China, Russia, and Their Disputed Frontier*. Armonk: M. E. Sharpe, 1996.
Paine, S. C. M., *The Sino-Japanese War of 1894–1895: Perception, Power, and Primacy*. Cambridge: Cambridge University Press, 2003.
Pan, Philip P., *Out of Mao's Shadow: The Struggle for the Soul of a New China*. London: Picador, 2008.
Pan, Quentin, 'Early Chinese Colonization in Manchuria', *The China Critic*, 7 Nov. 1929, pp. 889–92.
Papastratigakis, Nicholas, *Russian Imperialism and Naval Power: Military Strategy and the Build-up to the Russo-Japanese War*. London: I. B. Tauris, 2011.
Parham, Steven, *China's Borderlands: The Faultline of Central Asia*. London and New York: I. B. Tauris, 2017.
Park, Jeongwon Bourdais, *Identity, Policy, and Prosperity: Border Nationality of the Korean Diaspora and Regional Development in Northeast China*. New York: Palgrave Macmillan, 2017.
Perdue, Peter C., *China Marches West: The Qing Conquest of Central Eurasia*. Cambridge MA: Harvard University Press, 2005.
Perdue, Peter C., 'Boundaries and Trade in the Early Modern World: Negotiations at Nerchinsk and Beijing', *Eighteenth-Century Studies*, vol. 43, no. 3 (Spring 2010), pp. 341–56.

'Perepiska o podkupe kitaiskikh sanovnikov Li-Khun-chzhana i Chzhan-in-Khuana' (Correspondence on the Bribing of Chinese High Officials Li Hongzhang and Zhang Yinhuan), *Krasnyi arkhiv*, vol. 2 (1922), pp. 287–93.

Perlez, Jane, 'Some Chinese Are Souring on Being North Korea's Best Friend', *New York Times*, 16 Feb. 2013.

Perlez, Jane, 'China and Russia Reach 30-Year Gas Deal', *New York Times*, 21 May 2014.

Perlez, Jane, 'Fearing the Worst, China Plans Refugee Camps on North Korean Border', *New York Times*, 11 Dec. 2017.

Pernikoff, Alexandre, *'Bushido': The Anatomy of Terror*. New York: Liveright, 1943.

Phillips, Richard T., '"A Picturesque but Hopeless Resistance": Rehe in 1933', *Modern Asian Studies*, vol. 42, no. 4 (July 2008), pp. 733–50.

Pleshakov, Constantine, *The Tsar's Last Armada: The Epic Journey to the Battle of Tsushima*. New York: Basic Books, 2002.

Podoler, Guy, *Monuments, Memory, and Identity: Constructing the Colonial Past in South Korea*. Bern: Peter Lang, 2011.

Price, Willard, 'Japan Faces Russia in Manchuria', *National Geographic Magazine*, vol. 82, no. 5 (Nov. 1942), pp. 603–34.

Prodöhl, Ines, '"A Miracle Bean": How Soy Conquered the West, 1909–1950', *Bulletin of the German Historical Institute*, no. 46 (Spring 2010), pp. 111–29.

Pulford, Ed, 'The Nanai, Hezhe and Mobilized Loyalties along the Amur', *History and Anthropology*, vol. 28, no. 4 (2017), pp. 531–52.

Puyi, trans. W. J. F. Jenner, *From Emperor to Citizen: The Autobiography of Aisin-Gioro Pu Yi*, in 2 vols. Peking: Foreign Languages Press, 1964–5.

Quested, R. K. I., *Sino-Russian Relations: A Short History*, 2nd ed. London and New York: Routledge, 2005.

Radchenko, Sergey, *Unwanted Visionaries: The Soviet Failure in Asia at the End of the Cold War*. Oxford: Oxford University Press, 2014.

Rawski, Evelyn S., *The Last Emperors: A Social History of Qing Imperial Institutions*. Berkeley: University of California Press, 1998.

Rawski, Evelyn S., *Early Modern China and Northeast Asia: Cross-Border Perspectives*. Cambridge: Cambridge University Press, 2015.

Reardon-Anderson, James, *Reluctant Pioneers: China's Expansion Northward, 1644–1937*. Stanford: Stanford University Press, 2005.

Rhoads, Edward J. M., *Manchus & Han: Ethnic Relations and Political Power in Late Qing and Early Republican China, 1861–1928*. Seattle and London: University of Washington Press, 2000.

Richards, John F., *The Unending Frontier: An Environmental History of the Early Modern World*. Berkeley: University of California Press, 2003.

Robertson, Daniel T., *The Story of Our Mission: Manchuria*. Edinburgh: United Free Church of Scotland, 1913.

Rogaski, Ruth, 'Knowing a Sentient Mountain: Space, Science, and the Sacred in Ascents of Mount Paektu/Changbai', *Modern Asian Studies*, vol. 52, no. 2 (March 2018), pp. 716–52.

Romanova, V. V., 'Ot Tokiiskogo suda k Khabarovskomu: iz istorii podgotovki sudenbogo protsessa nad iaponskimi voennymi prestupnikami-bakteriologami' (From the Tokyo Trial to the Khabarovsk Trial: From the History of Preparing the Court Process of Japanese Bacteriologists, Military Criminals), *Istoriia meditsiny*, vol. 2, no. 1 (2015), pp. 72–82.

Rosny, Henry de, *Étude sur la Mandchourie*. Paris: J. Maisonneuve, 1891.

Ross, John, Rev. 'Manchuria', *The Scottish Geographical Magazine*, vol. 11, no. 5 (1895), pp. 217–31.

Rowe, William T., 'Owen Lattimore, Asia, and Comparative History', *Journal of Asian Studies*, vol. 66, no. 3 (Aug. 2007), pp. 759–86.

Ryabushkin, Dmitri, 'Origins and Consequences of the Soviet–Chinese Border Conflict of 1969', in Iwashita Akihiro, ed., *Eager Eyes Fixed on Eurasia*, in 2 vols. Sapporo: Slavic Research Center, Hokkaido University, 2007, vol. 2, pp. 73–91.

Saaler, Sven, 'The Kokuryūkai (Black Dragon Society) and the Rise of Nationalism, Pan-Asianism, and Militarism in Japan, 1901–1925', *International Journal of Asian Studies*, vol. 11, no. 2 (2014), pp. 125–60.

Sablin, Ivan, *Governing Post-Imperial Siberia and Mongolia, 1911–1924: Buddhism, Socialism and Nationalism in State and Autonomy Building*. London and New York: Routledge, 2016.

Salisbury, Harrison E., *The Great Black Dragon Fire: A Chinese Inferno*. Boston: Little, Brown, 1989.

Samoilov, N. A., *Rossiia i Kitai v XVII – nachale XX veka. Tendentsii, formy i stadii sotsiokul'turnogo vzaimodeistviia* (Russia and China in the 17th–Early 20th Centuries: Trends, Forms and Stages of Sociocultural Interaction). St Petersburg: Izdatel'stvo SPGU, 2014.

Scharping, Thomas, 'The Integration of Manchuria: Political Change, Demographic Development and Ethnic Structure from the Early Qing Period to Present Times (1610–1993)', in Lutz Bieg et al., eds, *Ad Seres et Tungusos: Festschrift für Martin Grimm*. Wiesbaden: Harrassowitz, 2000, pp. 343–75.

Schlesinger, Jonathan, *A World Trimmed with Fur: Wild Things, Pristine Places, and the Natural Fringes of Qing Rule*. Stanford: Stanford University Press, 2017.

Schorkowitz, Dittmar, and Chia Ning, eds, *Managing Frontiers in Qing China: The Lifanyuan and Libu Revisited*. Leiden: Brill, 2016.

Sella, Amnon, 'Khalkhin-Gol: The Forgotten War', *Journal of Contemporary History*, vol. 18, no. 4 (Oct. 1983), pp. 651–87.

Sergeev, Evgeny, *Russian Military Intelligence in the War with Japan, 1904–05: Secret Operations on Land and at Sea*. London and New York: Routledge, 2007.

Sewell, Bill, *Constructing Empire: The Japanese in Changchun, 1905–45*. Vancouver and Toronto: UBC Press, 2019.

Shai, Aron, *Zhang Xueliang: The General Who Never Fought*. Basingstoke: Palgrave Macmillan, 2012.

Shan, Patrick Fuliang, *Taming China's Wilderness: Immigration, Settlement and the Shaping of the Heilongjiang Frontier*. Farnham and Burlington: Ashgate, 2014.
Shao Dan, 'Princess, Traitor, Solder, Spy: Aisin Gioro Xianyu and the Dilemma of Manchu Identity', in Mariko Asano Tamanoi, ed., *Crossed Histories: Manchuria in the Age of Empire*. Honolulu: University of Hawaii Press, 2005, pp. 82–119.
Shao Dan, *Remote Homeland, Recovered Borderland: Manchus, Manchoukuo, and Manchuria, 1907–1985*. Honolulu: University of Hawaii Press, 2011.
Sheng, Michael, 'Mao and Chinese Elite Politics in the 1950s: The Gao Gang Affair Revisited', *Twentieth-Century China*, vol. 36, no. 1 (Jan. 2011), pp. 67–96.
Shi, Kun, and Richard Noll, 'Chuonnasuan (Meng Jin Fu): The Last Shaman of the Oroqen of Northeast China', *Journal of Korean Religions*, vol. 6 (2004), pp. 135–62.
Simpich, Frederick, 'Manchuria, Promised Land of Asia', *National Geographic Magazine*, vol. 56, no. 4 (Oct. 1929), pp. 379–428.
Smith, Norman, *Resisting Manchukuo: Chinese Women Writers and the Japanese Occupation*. Vancouver and Toronto: UBC Press, 2007.
Solovieva, Olga V., 'The Erased Grave of Dersu Uzala: Kurosawa's Cinema of Memory and Mourning', *Journal of Japanese and Korean Cinema*, vol. 2, no. 1 (2010), pp. 63–79.
Song, Nianshen, 'Northeast Eurasia as Historical Center: Exploration of a Joint Frontier', *The Asia-Pacific Journal*, vol. 13, 43:1 (2 Nov. 2015).
Song, Nianshen, *Making Borders in Modern East Asia: Tumen River Demarcation, 1881–1919*. Cambridge: Cambridge University Press, 2018.
Stary, Giovanni, 'Il mistero Pu Yi: da ultimo imperatore della Cina a presidente di un'ipotetica "Repubblica Sovietica della Manciuria"?' (The Mystery of Puyi: From the Last Emperor to the President of a Projected 'Manchurian Soviet Republic'?), *Scritture di storia* (Naples), no. 4 (2005), pp. 283–93.
Steinberg, John W., et al., eds, *The Russo-Japanese War in Global Perspective: World War Zero*, in 2 vols. Leiden: Brill, 2005–7.
Steiner, Zara, *The Lights That Failed: European International History, 1919–1933*. Oxford: Oxford University Press, 2005.
Stephan, John J., *The Russian Far East: A History*. Stanford: Stanford University Press, 1994.
Su Fenglin, 'Questions Regarding Past and Present Sino–Russian Cultural Exchange', in Iwashita Akihiro, ed., *Eager Eyes Fixed on Eurasia*, vol. 2, pp. 93–109.
Suleski, Ronald, *Civil Government in Warlord China: Tradition, Modernization and Manchuria*. New York: Peter Lang, 2002.
Sunderland, Willard, *The Baron's Cloak: A History of the Russian Empire in War and Revolution*. Ithaca NY and London: Cornell University Press, 2014.
Sutton, F. A., *One-Arm Sutton*. New York: The Viking Press, 1933.

Tamanoi, Mariko Asano, *Memory Maps: The State and Manchuria in Postwar Japan*. Honolulu: University of Hawaii Press, 2008.
Tanner, Harold M., *The Battle for Manchuria and the Fate of China: Siping, 1946*. Bloomington: Indiana University Press, 2013.
Teh, Limin, 'From Colonial Company Town to Industrial City: The South Manchuria Railway Company in Fushun, China', in Marcelo J. Borges and Susana B. Torres, eds, *Company Towns: Labor, Space, and Power Relations across Time and Continents*. New York: Palgrave, 2012, pp. 69–90.
Tian, Mo, 'The *Baojia* System as Institutional Control in Manchukuo under Japanese Rule (1932–45)', *Journal of the Economic and Social History of the Orient*, vol. 59, no. 4 (Oct. 2016), pp. 531–54.
Tian, Mo, 'The Korean War and Manchuria: Economic and Human Effects', in Tessa Morris-Suzuki, ed., *The Korean War in Asia: A Hidden History*. Lanham: Rowman & Littlefield, 2018, pp. 39–54.
Tighe, Justin, *Constructing Suiyuan: The Politics of Northwestern Territory and Development in Early Twentieth-Century China*. Leiden: Brill, 2005.
Tsao Lien-en, *The Chinese Migration to the Three Eastern Provinces*. Shanghai: Bureau of Industrial and Commercial Information, Ministry of Industry, Commerce and Labor, National Government of the Republic of China, 1930.
Tselichtchev, Ivan, 'Chinese in the Russian Far East: A Geopolitical Time Bomb?', *South China Morning Post*, 8 July 2017.
Tucker, David, 'Labor Policy and the Construction Industry in Manchukuo: Systems of Recruitment, Management, and Control', in Kratoska, ed., *Asian Labor in the Wartime Japanese Empire*, pp. 25–60.
Tucker, David, 'City Planning without Cities: Order and Chaos in Utopian Manchukuo', in Tamanoi, ed., *Crossed Histories*, pp. 53–81.
Urbansky, Sören, 'A Very Orderly Friendship: The Sino-Soviet Border under the Alliance Regime, 1950–1960', *Eurasia Border Review*, vol. 3 (2012), pp. 35–52.
Urbansky, Sören, 'Tokhtogo's Mission Impossible: Russia, China, and the Quasi-independence of Hulunbeir', *Inner Asia*, vol. 16, no. 1 (2014), pp. 64–94.
VanderVen, Elizabeth R., *A School in Every Village: Educational Reform in a Northeast China County, 1904–31*. Vancouver and Toronto: UBC Press, 2012.
Vespa, Amleto, *Secret Agent of Japan: A Handbook to Japanese Imperialism*. London: Victor Gollancz, 1938.
Wagner, Rudolf G., 'China "Asleep" and "Awakening." A Study in Conceptualizing Asymmetry and Coping with It', *Transcultural Studies*, no. 1 (2011), pp. 4–139.
Waldron, Arthur, 'The Warlord: Twentieth Century Chinese Understandings of Violence, Militarism, and Imperialism', *American Historical Review*, vol. 96, no. 4 (Oct. 1991), pp. 1073–1100.
Waley-Cohen, Joanna, *Exile in Mid-Qing China: Banishment to Xinjiang, 1758–1820*. New Haven and London: Yale University Press, 1991.
Walker, Michael, *The 1929 Sino-Soviet War: The War Nobody Knew*. Lawrence: University Press of Kansas, 2017.

Wang, Ning, 'Border Banishment: Rightists in the Army Farms of Beidahuang', in Diana Lary, ed., *The Chinese State at the Borders*. Vancouver and Toronto: UBC Press, 2007, pp. 198–220.
Wang, Ning, *Banished to the Great Northern Wilderness: Political Exile and Re-education in Mao's China*. Vancouver and Toronto: UBC Press, 2017.
Wang, Yuanchong, 'Claiming Centrality in the Chinese World: Manchu–Chosŏn Relations and the Making of the Qing's "Zhongguo" Identity, 1616–1643', *The Chinese Historical Review*, vol. 22, no. 2 (2015), pp. 95–119.
Waswo, Ann, and Nishida Yoshiaki, eds, *Farmers and Village Life in Twentieth-Century Japan*. London: RoutledgeCurzon, 2003.
Wei, Shuge, 'Beyond the Front Line: China's Rivalry with Japan in the English-language Press over the Jinan Incident, 1928', *Modern Asian Studies*, vol. 48, no. 1 (Jan. 2014), pp. 188–224.
Weston, Timothy B., 'The Iron Man Weeps: Joblessness and Political Legitimacy in the Chinese Rust Belt', in Gries and Rosen, eds, *State and Society in 21st-Century China*, pp. 67–86.
Whiteman, Stephen H., 'Kangxi's Auspicious Empire: Rhetorics of Geographic Integration in the Early Qing', in Du and Kyong-McClain, eds, *Chinese History in Geographical Perspective*, pp. 33–54.
Whiteman, Stephen H., 'From Upper Camp to Mountain Estate: Recovering Historical Narratives in Qing Imperial Landscapes', *Studies in the History of Gardens & Designed Landscapes*, vol. 33, no. 4 (2013), pp. 249–79.
Wong, Edward, and Jonathan Ansfield, 'Fallen Leader is Indicted in China', *New York Times*, 24 July 2013.
Wright, Tim, 'The Manchurian Economy and the 1930s World Depression', *Modern Asian Studies*, vol. 41, no. 5 (Sept. 2007), pp. 1073–1112.
Wu, Guo, 'New Qing History: Dispute, Dialog, and Influence', *The Chinese Historical Review*, vol. 23, no. 1 (2016), pp. 47–69.
Xia, Yun, *Down with Traitors: Justice and Nationalism in Wartime China*. Seattle: University of Washington Press, 2018.
Xiao Hong, trans. Howard Goldblatt, *The Field of Life and Death & Tales of Hulan River*. Boston: Cheng & Tsui, 2002.
Xie Xueshi, 'The Organization and Grassroots Structure of the Manzhouguo Regime', in MacKinnon et al., eds, *China at War*, pp. 134–47.
Yin, Sim Chi, 'A Panoramic View of China's Cultural Revolution', *New York Times*, 10 Sept. 2012.
Yosano Akiko, trans. Joshua A. Fogel, *Travels in Manchuria and Mongolia: A Feminist Poet from Japan Encounters Prewar China*. New York: Columbia University Press, 2001.
Young, Louise, 'Imagined Empire: The Cultural Construction of Manchukuo', in Duus et al., eds, *The Japanese Wartime Empire, 1931–1945*, pp. 71–96.
Young, Louise, 'Colonizing Manchuria: The Making of an Imperial Myth', in Stephen Vlastos, ed., *Mirror of Modernity: Invented Traditions of Modern Japan*. Berkeley: University of California Press, 1998, pp. 95–109.

Yuan Kleeman, Faye, 'Inscribing Manchuria: Gender, Ideology and Popular Imagination', *East Asian History*, no. 30 (Dec. 2005), pp. 47–66.

Yue Zhuang, 'Hatchings in the Void: Ritual and Order in *Bishu Shanzhuang Shi* and Matteo Ripa's *Views of Jehol*', in Petra ten-Doesschate Chu and Ning Ding, eds, *Qing Encounters: Artistic Exchanges between China and the West*. Los Angeles: Getty Research Institute, 2015, pp. 142–57.

Zatsepine, Victor, *Beyond the Amur: Frontier Encounters between China and Russia, 1850–1930*. Vancouver and Toronto: UBC Press, 2017.

Zhao, Gang, 'Reinventing *China*: Imperial Qing Ideology and the Rise of Modern Chinese National Identity in the Early Twentieth Century', *Modern China*, vol. 32, no. 1 (Jan. 2006), pp. 3–30.

Index

Acheng 11
Aigun (*also* Aihui) 11, 21, 28, 42, 47, 136–7
Aigun, Treaty 42–5, 47–8, 137
Ainu people 13, 92
Alaska 37, 56
Albazin, and Albazinians 26, 28, 31 n.13
Alekseev, Evgenii 49
Aleksei, Tsar 27, 28
Alexander I, tsar 41
Alexander II, tsar 42, 45, 56
Alexander III, tsar 45
Altanbulag 166
Amur Railway 56
Amur River
  as border 47–8, 123–4, 129, 131, 136–40, 158
  geography and nature 144–5, 146
  and indigenous peoples 12–14, 17
  and Manchus 11, 21
  in Russian imperial expansion 3, 5, 15, 26–9, 41–2, 56
An Chung-gun 94
Andong, *see* Dandong
Anna, empress 35, 37
Anshan 65, 128, 158
Argun River 12, 29, 35, 118, 139, 140
Arrow War 42, 177
Arsenyev, Vladimir 13, 118

Baikal, Lake 26, 49, 163
Baikov, Fedor 26–7
Baikov, Nikolai 118
bandits, *see* hong huzi
Baotou 162, 168
Barrow, John 176
Bayer, Gottlieb Siegfried 37
Beidahuang 121–2

Beijing
  Japanese threat to 91, 173
  Mongols and Manchus in 5, 11, 19
  Qing capital and court 47, 154, 175, 177
  railways and communications 48, 57, 154, 167
  in republican-era Chinese politics 78, 80–3, 88, 112
  Russian envoys in 25–8, 33–5, 38
Bell, John 39 n.8
Benxi 154
Bertolucci, Bernardo 100–1
Blagoveshchensk 47–8, 130–1, 136–7, 158
Boduna (Songyuan) 11
Bo Xilai 157
Boer War 48
Bohai kingdom (Korean: Parhae) 147, 154
Bohai Sea 147, 154
Bolshoi Ussuriiskii Island, *see* Heixiazi Island
Boxer uprising 20, 47–8, 69, 77, 136
Buddhism 18, 29, 43, 146, 158, 175
Burlingame, Anson 45
Buryats 163, 165, 170 n.10

Cai Yuanpei 52
Cao Xueqin 117, 158
Catherine I, empress 35
Catherine II, the Great, empress 37–8
Chahar, former province 168, 173
Changbaishan 18, 139, 144–8
Changchun 111, 138, 148–50
  capital of Manchukuo 88, 94, 98, 100–1, 116, 155, 156, 168
  and railways 50, 57, 65
Chekhov, Anton 13
Chengde 175–8

Chi Zijian 117–18
Chiang Ching-kuo 92, 111
Chiang Kai-shek
   in Chinese Civil War 79, 110–11
   Confucian revival 97–8
   and Japan 88, 91, 169, 173
   and Northern Expedition 78–9, 82–3
   and Zhang Xueliang 83, 91–2, 173
Chinese Eastern Railway (CER) 55–60
   in 1929 conflict 83–4
   construction period 47–8, 69–70
   in economy 76
   Soviet policy and sale to Japan 87, 90, 96
   stations 100, 139, 149, 150, 154, 163, 167
Chita 109, 167
Chongqing 110, 112, 136, 157, 169
Churchill, Winston 107
Cixi, empress 88, 177
Coleridge, Samuel Taylor 163, 176
Confucianism 18, 25, 95, 97–8, 177
Cossacks
   Chinese view of 5, 77
   in Qing service 28
   in Russian Civil War 108, 116
   as settlers 29, 42, 84
   in tsarist army 5, 7, 25
Crimean War 42
Cultural Revolution 103, 117, 122–4, 138, 146–7

Dalian (Russian Dal'nii; Japanese Dairen) 156–9
   in economy 66, 76, 154, 157
   in historiography 3, 66
   Japanese period 57, 65–7, 72
   local identity 154
   and railways 55, 129
   Russian tsarist period 47, 49, 55, 57
   Soviets in 108, 110, 121
Damansky Island, *see* Zhenbao
Dandong 65, 121, 158

Daqing 127–9, 138
Dashiqiao 154
Datong 168
De, Prince (De Wang; Demchugdongrub) 167–8
De Xin 37
Deng Xiaoping 121, 130, 145
Deren 13–14
Dongbei, term and identity 3, 6, 127–8, 131, 154
Duan Qirui 80
Duanmu Hongliang 115, 117
Duolun (Mongolian: Dolon Nor) 163

Eitingon, Naum 83

Fangchuan 148
Fedor, Tsar 28
Feng Yuxiang 81, 83, 88
Fengtian, *see* Liaoning; Shenyang
Fengtian-Zhili Wars 80–1
Fleming, Peter 77
Fushun 22, 65, 109, 117, 155, 159
Fuyu County 21
Fuyuan 137–8

Gagarin, Matvei 34
Galdan 29
Gantimur 26–7
Gao E 158
Gao Gang 121
Genghis Khan 5, 139, 163
George III 177
ginseng 12, 19, 144, 147
Gobi Desert 162
Goldblatt, Howard 115
Golovin, Fedor 29
Golovkin, Yuri 41
Gorbachev, Mikhail 124
Gotō Shinpei 64–5, 100
Great Wall
   and Shanhaiguan 70
   symbolism of 71 90
   and Willow Palisade 18–19

Guandong (Kwantung) 52, 63, 70, 92, 156
Gulian 140
Guo Songling 81

Haicheng 158
Hailar 163, 173
Hailong 75
Hankou 57, 88
Harbin 55–61
   Chinese settlement and administration 72, 82, 83
   in historiography 3, 66
   Japanese occupation 88, 94, 96, 101, 103, 108
   literature in 115–18
   PRC period 111–12, 123, 128–31, 136
   Russian legacy 100, 121, 130–1, 136
   Soviets in 108–9
   tsarist administration and Russian emigration 47, 94, 96
   see also Chinese Eastern Railway
Harris, Sheldon 101–2
Hawaii 92, 98
Hebei province
   and Chengde 3, 175, 178
   migrants to Manchuria from 58, 70, 136
   Qing tombs in 88
Heihe 21, 42, 130, 131, 136–7, 158, 167
Heilongjiang province 135–40
   Chinese migration to 69, 75
   in economy 150, 154
   indigenous peoples in 11–12
   Manchus in 11, 21–2
   name 136, 149–50
   PRC period 121–3, 127–8
   rivers in 13, 144
   in Russo-Japanese war 48
   see also Amur River; Songhuajiang; Harbin
Heixiazi Island 124
Henan province 127, 136

Hetu Ala 155
Hirohito, emperor 83, 98, 107
Hitler, Adolf 91
Hohhot (Chinese: Huhehaote) 162, 166, 168
Hong Hu 129
hong huzi 51, 77–9, 94
Hong Taiji 17–18, 154–5
Hongwu emperor 20
Hoover, Herbert 87
Hosie, Alexander 4
Hsü, Immanuel C. Y. 37
Hu Jintao 128
Hu Shi 91
Hui people 24 n.16, 96, 136, 143, 154, 162
Huizong emperor 5
Hulan 75, 115–16
Hulunbuir 11–12, 163, 164, 168
Huma River 13
Hunchun 11, 148

Ides, Isbrand 33
Ignat'ev, Nikolai 42
indigenous peoples of Manchuria 11–15, 118, 136, 137
Inner Mongolia 161–9
   Cultural Revolution in 123
   former provinces 173
   indigenous peoples in 11, 12, 118
   in literature 117–18
   Russians in 84
   see also Mongol people; Mongolia
Irkutsk 34
Ishii Shiro 101–2
Ishiwara Kanji 87
Ito Hirobumi 94
Ivan the Terrible, Tsar 25
Izmailov, Lev 34

James, Henry E. M. (Evan) 145
Japan, *see esp. under* Manchukuo; migration and settlement; Russo-Japanese War; Sino-Japanese Wars

Jesuits 6, 28–9, 176
Jewish Autonomous Region 138
Jews 96, 107–9, 118, 138, 144
Jiamusi 138
Ji'an 148
Jiandao 146
Jiang Zemin 128
Jiaodong peninsula 154
Jiaozhou Bay 47
Jiaqing emperor 41, 177–8
Jilin province 143–50
    bandits in 78
    Chinese migration to 19–20, 136
    in economy 75, 154
    Japanese occupation 94–5, 101
    Manchus in 11, 22
    PRC period 121, 128, 129
    in Russo-Japanese war 48
    see also Changchun
Jilin, town 19, 21, 88, 149–50
Jin dynasty 5, 17, 154, 158
Jinan 82
Jingbo Lake 138
Jinzhou 81, 91, 115, 149
Johnston, Reginald 88
Jue Qing 117
Jungharia 29, 34–5, 36–7, 163–4
Jurchen people 5, 17, 43–4
    see also Jin dynasty

Kaiyuan 19, 53 n.16
Kalgan, see Zhangjiakou
Kalmyk people 37
Kamchatka 41, 50
kang 73
Kangxi emperor
    and Changbaishan 18, 145–6
    and Chengde 175–6, 178
    and Junghar campaign 29, 34, 163
    and Russia 8 n.12, 27, 29–30, 33, 34
Kashgar 42, 164
Kaspe, Semen 96
Kaufman, Abram 108–9
Kaufman, Konstantin von 45

Kaufman, Teddy 109
Kawashima Yoshiko 173
Kazan 25
Khabarov, Erofei 26
Khabarovsk
    and 1929 conflict 84
    as border city 124, 129, 138
    and indigenous peoples 13–4
    Japanese war tribunal 102–3
    name 26, 43
    Puyi in 109
    and railway 56
Khalkhin-Gol (Nomonhan), battle 168
Khanka (Xingkai) Lake 13, 138
Khasan, Lake 168
Khutuktu 37, 165
Kiakhta 34–8, 41, 165, 166, 167
Kiakhta, Treaty 33–8, 41, 166
Kim Il Sung 94
Kim Jong Il 94, 148
Kipling, Rudyard 55
Kitai, and Cathay, terms 5
Koguryo 147
Kōmoto Daisaku 82–3
Korea
    border with China 65, 145–6
    at the end of Second World War 107, 110
    and imperial China 17, 19, 176
    Japanese occupation and resistance 46, 78, 93, 94
    North Korea 121, 129, 147–8, 158
    in Russo-Japanese war 48–50
    South Korea 146, 148
Korean people 78, 92, 96, 136, 143, 146–8, 154
    see also Yanbian
Korean War 102, 111, 121, 158
kowtow 26–7, 34, 41, 145
Krusenstern, Iva 41
Kubilai Khan 163, 164
Kuril Islands 50
Kuropatkin, Aleksei 49

Kurosawa, Akira 13
Kwantung Army 65–70, 82–3, 87–8, 95

Lalin River 144
Lamaism 18, 37, 164–5, 176–7
Lange, Lorenz 34–5
Lattimore, Owen 4, 6, 13, 169
League of Nations 88–91
Li Dazhao 82
Li Hongzhang 46–7
Li Hongzhi 150
Li Zhensheng 123
Liao River 153–4
Liao state 5, 153, 158
Liaodong Bay 147
Liaodong peninsula 46–7, 49, 52, 63, 69, 70
Liaoning province 153–9
    Chinese migration to 20, 69, 71, 136
    during Cultural revolution 123
    economy and railways 75, 121, 138
    indigenous peoples in 135
    Manchus in 22
    name 19, 150
    in Russo-Japanese war 48
    see also Dalian
Liaoyang 17, 49, 53 n.16, 128, 155, 158
Lifanyuan 25–6
Lin Biao 112
Lisianskii, Yuri 41
Livadia, Treaty 45
Lu Xun 51, 115–16
Lüshunkou 46–7, 157

Ma Xiangdong 127
Ma Yansong 130
Ma Zhanshan 93–4
Macartney, George 177
Mairanovskii, Grigorii 102
Makarov, Stepan 49
Mamiya Rinzō 14

Man Tai 36
Manchu language 7, 17
    disappearance 21–2
    learned by foreign scholars 38, 175
    traces in place names 58, 136, 138, 143
    Tulišen report in 34
Manchu people 5, 17–24
    and Albazinians 28
    and Manchukuo 96–7, 173
    in Manchuria garrison towns 5, 11, 47, 139, 148, 162
    name 6
    in the Northeast today 136, 143, 154
    in Qing administration 26
    see also Qing dynasty
Manchukuo 87–103, 107
    and China 76, 173
    collaboration issue 109
    industrialization 138, 155
    literature in 116–17
    and SMR 63
    and Soviet Union 60, 168
    territory 6
    see also Changchun; Dalian; Puyi
Manchuria, term and territory 3, 5–6
Manzhouli 59, 163, 167
Mao Yuanxin 123
Mao Zedong 79
    in Civil War 110, 112
    death of 150
    and the Northeast 127–8, 138, 166
    and relations with Soviet Union and USA 124
Marshall, George C. 111
Martini, Martino 28
Meiji emperor 46, 49
Mengele, Josef 101
Mergen, *see* Nenjiang
migration and settlement, Chinese 19–20, 69–73, 75–7, 82, 90, 92–3
    confrontation with Mongols 161–4, 169

effect on indigenous peoples 12
in Dalian 66
in Harbin 58–9
in Heilongjiang 136
in Liaoning 154, 156, 158
PRC period 121–2
in Russian Far East 56, 130–1
migration and settlement, Japanese 65, 92–3, 98, 100, 138
and war orphans 107–8
migration and settlement, Korean 136, 146–7
migration and settlement, Mongol 37, 163
migration and settlement, Russian
in Dalian 67
departure from Manchuria 96, 109, 121
émigré literature 118–19
in Harbin 57–60
in Inner Mongolia 84
Milescu, Nicolae (Spafarii) 27–8
Ming dynasty
defeat by the Qing 5, 17–8, 70
and Japan 46
presence north of the Amur 43–4
settlement of Liaoning 20–1, 154–5, 157–8
Mo Dehui 82
Mohe 117, 139–40
Mongol people 139, 162–9
Khalkha 35, 37, 39 n.11
and Manchukuo 97
in the Northeast today 136, 143, 154
and the Qing 19, 26, 177
in Russia 33
see also Inner Mongolia; Mongolia; Yuan dynasty
Mongolia
post-1990 148
and the Qing 25, 29, 46, 163–4, 176
and Russia 45, 56, 164–6
Mongolian language 17, 38, 163, 164, 168–9

Moscow
connected by railway to Manchuria 55
Red Square 163
as tsarist capital 19, 27–8, 30, 36
Mu Suixin 127
Mudanjiang 11, 138–9
Mukden, see Shenyang
Mukden incident 63, 65, 87, 91, 103, 169
Mulan 178
Murav'ev (Amurskii), Nikolai 41–2, 47
Mussolini, Benito 91

Nanjing (*also* Nanking)
and Cao Xueqin 160 n.10
as capital 78, 83
Manchus in 21
taken by the Communists 112
under Japanese occupation 97 103
Nenjiang 11, 27, 93, 136, 139, 140
Nerchinsk 27, 29, 33, 35
Nerchinsk, Treaty 29–30, 33, 44
Newchwang (Niuzhuang), see Yingkou
New Delhi 57
Nevel'skoi, Gennadii 41–2
Nicholas I, tsar 41–2
Nikolaevsk-on-Amur 42, 43
Ning'an 11, 21, 138
Ninguta, see Ning'an
Nixon, Richard 124
Nogi Maresuke 49
Nurgan 43
Nurhaci 17
honoured by Kangxi 146
legends about 139, 147
mausoleum 154–5

Opium War 41
Ordos 162

Park Chung Hee 94
Paul I, tsar 41

Pearl Harbor 49, 92
Peking, *see* Beijing
Peking, Treaty 42–4, 123–4, 177
Pereleshin, Valerii 118
Peter I, the Great, tsar 27, 28, 30, 33–5, 177
Peter II, tsar 35, 36
Peter III, tsar 37
Petlin, Ivan 25, 28
Pogranichnyi 139
Poiarkov, Vasilii 26
Polo, Marco 163
Port Arthur 46–7, 49–51, 63, 88, 94
  see also Lüshunkou
Pujie 109
Pusan 65
Putin, Vladimir 130, 131
Puyi 88, 95, 98–101, 168, 173
  after abdication 108–9

Qianlong emperor
  ban on Han settlement in Manchuria 19
  and Chengde 175–8
  conquest of Xinjiang 163–4
  and Manchu identity 7, 18
  Russia policy 38
  tomb desecrated 88
Qianshan range 158
Qidan people 5
  see also Liao state
Qing banners 7
  Cossacks in 28
  disbanded 88
  Han Chinese in 21–2
  indigenous peoples in 11–12
  land ownership in Manchuria 69
  in literature 117
  training 178
Qing dynasty, *see esp.* Introduction, chapters 1–6, 19–2
  emperors' tombs 154–5
  see also Manchu people
Qingdao 47, 57, 72, 115
Qiqihar 11, 21, 101, 129, 139, 149

Rehe, former province 173
Ripa, Matteo 176
Roosevelt, Franklin D. 107
Roosevelt, Theodore 50
Rozhestvensky, Zinovii 50
Russia, *see esp.* Introduction, chapters 3–7, 12
Russian-Chinese pidgin 58
Russian Orthodox Mission 33, 38
Russo-Japanese War 48–52
  and banditry 78–9
  consequences 67, 76, 148–9, 156–7, 164, 168
  postwar rapprochement 63
  and Soviet revanchism 107
Russo-Turkish War 46

Saihanba, National Park 178
St Petersburg 33, 35, 37, 45, 50
St Petersburg, Treaty 45, 166
Sakhalin Island
  exploration 41
  indigenous peoples of 13–4
  Japanese migration to 92
  name 136
  as part of Outer Manchuria 3, 90
  Russian and Japanese control of 50, 107
Sanxing, *see* Yilan
secret societies 78, 95
Selenginsk 29, 33, 34
Semenov, Grigorii 108, 165
Shaanxi province 21, 112
Shahe 49
shamanism 12–13
Shandong province 47, 81–2, 154
  as origin of migrants to Manchuria 58, 66, 69–74, 76–7, 136, 156
Shanghai 52, 60, 81, 82, 87, 121
  compared with Harbin and Dalian 4, 59, 66, 118, 136
  as literary centre 115–16
Shangzhi 130

Shanhaiguan 19–20, 70–2, 90, 149,
    154, 173
Shanxi province 70, 82, 162, 166,
    168
Shenyang 150, 154–5
    capital of Zhang Zuolin 79–83
    in the civil war 149
    Japanese in 100
    literature in 116
    in PRC period 127
    and the Qing 17, 18, 21, 158
    and railways 65, 75, 82
    in Russo-Japanese war 49, 53 n.16
    see also Mukden incident
Shijiazhuang 57
Shimonoseki, Treaty 46
Shinto 98
Shuangcheng 136
Shunzhi emperor 18
Siebold, Philipp Franz von 6
Sino-Japanese War (First, 1894–95)
    46–7, 50
Sino-Japanese War (Second,
    1937–45) 92–3, 101–3, 107–8
    background 63, 83, 87
    in literature 116
Sinuiju 158
Siping 111, 150
Songhuajiang (Songhua River) 11,
    136–9, 143–5, 149–50, 154
    and indigenous peoples 13
    and Manchu lore 139
    pollution 129
Song Meiling 91
Sophia Alekseevna, regent of Russia
    28, 30
South Manchuria Railway (SMR) 50,
    57, 63–7, 82, 87
    and Changchun 149
    and Dalian 156–7
    in economy, 159
    and Kwantung Army 100
    and SMR zone 92, 95
soybean trade 66–7, 76–7, 154
Sretensk 56

Stalin, Joseph 83, 91, 96, 107, 109–11,
    168
Stanovoi range 3, 29
Stimson, Henry 87
Suez Canal 49, 166
Suifenhe 59, 139
Suiyuan, former province 162
Sun Chuanfang 81–2
Sun Dianying 88
Sun Jiagu 45
Sun Yat-sen 78, 97
Sungari River, see Songhuajiang

Taiping rebellion 19, 42
Taiwan 46, 64, 92, 103, 112
Tanaka Giichi 82–3
Tanggu Truce 91, 173
Tangun 147–8
Tarabarov Island, see ???
Tartary, Strait 3, 13, 41
Tartary, term 6
Tian Fengshan 127
Tianjin 69, 72, 88, 112, 136, 169
Tianshan mountains 34, 37, 45
Tibet 25, 38, 96, 162, 165, 176–7
    see also Lamaism
Tieling 158
Tobolsk 25, 34
Tōgō Heihachirō (admiral Togo)
    49–50
Tokyo
    Japanese government in 87–8
    Puyi's visit to 98–9
    and SMR 63, 65
    war tribunal in 109
Tonghua 128
Tongjiang (Lahasusu) 137–8, 145
Torghuts 34, 37
Trans-Siberian Railway 49, 55–6
tribute relations
    and Chengde 177
    and indigenous peoples 12–13, 17,
        139, 144
    and Russia 25–7, 36, 46
Tsurukhaitui 35

Tsushima Straits 49–50
Tulišen 34
Tumen River 11, 145, 147–8
Tungus people 12, 27, 33
Tuo Shi 36
Turkestan 45, 162, 168
Turner, Frederick Jackson 55
Tyr 43

Udinsk (Ulan-Ude) 34, 163
Ulan Bator (Ulaanbaatar) 41, 42, 165, 166
Ulanhu 166
UNESCO
  on endangered languages 14, 21
  and heritage sites 132 n.9, 146, 155, 163, 175
Ungern-Sternberg, Roman von 165
Unit 731 101–3
Urga, see Ulan Bator
Ussuri River
  as border 137–8
  conflict in 1969 123–4
  and indigenous peoples 13
  railway 56
  in Russian imperial expansion 3, 42

Verbiest, Ferdinand 28
Victoria, Queen 177
Vladislavich (Raguzinskii), Savva 35
Vladivostok 43, 148
  port of 46, 69, 76

Wang Delin 94–5
Wang Jingwei 97
Wang Yongjiang 75–6, 80–1
Wanli emperor 25
warlords, term 78–9
Weichang County 178
Weihai 47
Willow Palisade 18–19
Wilson, Woodrow 97
Witte, Sergei 50, 56, 64
Wordsworth, William 176

Wu Peifu 80–1
Wu Sangui 70
Wudalianchi 139

Xanadu (Shangdu) 163
Xi'an 21, 91
Xianfeng emperor 177
Xiao Hong 115–17
Xiao Jun 115–17
Xinbin 22, 154
Xibo people 22
Xilinji 140
Xing'an range 12, 144
Xing'an (Hsingan), former province 173
Xinjiang
  as border 4, 36
  Daurs in 11
  exile to 21
  Torghuts in 37
  Xibo in 22
  Qing conquest of 45–6
  East Turkestan Republic 168
  Han Chinese settlement in 161
  see also Jungharia
Xu Ming 157–8
Xu Shuzheng 165

Yabuli 130
Yakub Beg 45
Yalta Conference 107, 157
Yalu River 145
  as border 158
  in economy 154
  in First Sino-Japanese War 46
  and railways 19, 65
  in Russo-Japanese war 48–9
Yamato hotels 65, 149, 156
Yan Xishan 82
Yan'an 112, 115–16
Yanbian 146–8
Yangtze River 57
Yanji 94, 148
Yantai 69
Yilan 11, 139

Yili valley 34, 37, 45
Yingkou 53 n.15, 154, 158
Yining 45
Yinlong Island 124
Yitong River 149
Yongzheng emperor 36, 175
Yuan dynasty 5, 158, 163
Yuan Shikai 78, 164, 173

Zabaikal'sk 167
Zeng Jize 45
Zhalainor 163
Zhalong Nature Reserve 139
Zhangjiakou 33, 166, 168

Zhang Xueliang 81, 83–4, 88, 98, 173
  and Xi'an incident 91–2
Zhang Yinhuan 47
Zhang Zongchang 82
Zhang Zuolin 78–84, 158
  capture of Beijing 88
  development policies of 71, 75
Zheltuga 140
Zhenbao Island 123–4
Zhifu (Chefoo) 69
Zhigang 45
Zhou Enlai 91, 169
Zhu Shengwen 129
Zuo Zongtang 45

www.ingramcontent.com/pod-product-compliance
Lightning Source LLC
Chambersburg PA
CBHW052041300426
44117CB00012B/1927